ENCORE TRAVELLERS' FRANCE

Arthur Eperon is one of the most experienced and best known travel writers in Europe. Since leaving the RAF in 1945 he has worked as a journalist in various capacities often involving travel. He has concentrated on travel writing for the past ten years and contributed to many publications including *The Times, Daily Telegraph, Sun, Woman's Own, Popular Motoring* and the *TV Times*. He has appeared on radio and television and for five years was closely involved in Thames Television's programme *Wish you were here*. He has written three previous books in the *Travellers'* series: *Travellers' France, Travellers Italy* and *Travellers' Britain*, all of which have been featured in BBC TV's *Holiday* programme.

ENCORE TRAVELLERS'

Arthur Eperon

FRANCE

Maps and drawings by Ken Smith

Pan Original
Pan Books London and Sydney

Also by Arthur Eperon in Pan Books

Travellers' France (new edition for 1983)
Travellers' Italy
Travellers' Britain

How to use this book

Each page is divided into three columns.

The left-hand column gives you the road numbers to follow along the route, the places you will go through and towns or villages which are worth stopping at. The distances are given in parentheses.

The middle column recommends places to eat and stay at.

The right-hand column mentions points of historic, architectural or scenic interest about the area.

First published 1982 by Pan Books Ltd,
Cavaye Place, London SW10 9PG
© Arthur Eperson 1982
Maps and drawings by Ken Smith
ISBN 0 330 26861 9
Printed in Britain by Collins, Glasgow

Acknowledgements

My heartfelt thanks to many people who have helped me with this book, especially travel writer Barbara Clegg, my wife, who gave up her own job to work full-time on it and suffered agonies getting her figure back after seven months of doing the final checking on four routes; to my friends at Townsend Thoresen Ferries (especially Bob Bevan, a model of friendly efficiency), Brittany Ferries, Sealink, and the great enthusiasts of the new Hoverspeed hovercraft service, all of whom have not only carried me but given me helpful suggestions about France; to my old friends at the French Government Tourist Office in London – René Bardy, Director, Pauline Hallam and Martine Williams; to many French friends who have given freely their expert advice on various regions, such as Michel Place of French Travel Service, expert on all France but especially the Auvergne; and to my old friend Humphrey Downes, for long with British European Airways, now living in the Dordogne, with his nose for good value in menus.

Contents

9 Author's preface

20 **Route 1**
St Malo to Biarritz or through the
Pyrenees to Perpignan

52 **Route 2**
Cherbourg/Le Havre through Dordogne,
Auvergne to Montpellier (for Cap d'Agde)

79 **Route 3**
La Havre/Dieppe to Dourdan, through
Burgundy, Savoie to Nice

110 **Route 4**
Calais/Boulogne through Champagne,
Jura, Annecy to Mont Blanc

135 **Route 5**
Round Brittany

167 **Route 6**
Round the Loire valley, Loir and Cher

195 **Route 7**
Round north Dordogne, Lot and Quercy

216 **Index**

Preface

A Friday queue in the bank at Souillac, a business friend late for an appointment, and we were very late to meet our daughters in the village inn at Larche on the Périgueux road. So Barbara took one of her famous 'short cuts' across the Périgord countryside.

It was a lovely trip – round hills and through valleys, past poplar-lined streams, walnut plantations, woods and pastures, farmhouses and hamlets, a few people in fields, one tractor, no cars. Then came a hamlet with one inhabitant visible – a beagle, standing in the road centre barking; we ran out of road in a farmyard.

Barbara's short cuts may cost time but they bring us some of our most delightful discoveries. Anyway, we were only two hours late and the girls had wisely picked one of the few little village inns in France with a swimming pool in its back garden.

People tell me that 'the Dordogne', meaning Périgord and much of Quercy, is 'spoiled – knee-deep in Germans and all the houses taken over by refugees from Britain and Paris'.

Well, I have been travelling this superb area called by Henry Miller 'the nearest thing to Paradise this side of Greece' for over thirty years and I can still make new discoveries and even get lost. Just look at the yellow Michelin maps for Périgord or especially for Quercy all around Cahors, and see all those little white roads with their hamlets and superb scenery awaiting discovery. Nearly forgotten castles, too, where Richard Lionheart or his enemies once stumped the courtyard, and village inns with four-course meals, often with wine included, for under £3 – all fresh local ingredients, freshly cooked. Drive a kilometre or two off the main Périgord-Brive road, southward or especially north, and you are in a world of farming where tourists play no part.

Not just in remoter areas like Dordogne, either. Just behind Calais and Boulogne, among wooded hills, streams jumping with trout, and lush meadows with cows producing lovely cream and cheeses, are small roads and hamlets which motorists hurrying through the Channel ports do not dream exist.

I used to say that motorists were divided basically between dedicated sun-worshippers, who belt straight down the motorways, living on bread, pâté and their nerves, and travellers, who enjoy France, explore a little and eat better and cheaper than in Mediterranean France and much better than in Spain – people who make the journey an enjoyable part of their holiday rather than a chore to be disposed of with determined and sometimes dangerous haste.

My book 'Travellers France', now updated, with six routes across France missing motorways and big cities, was written for those of you who are going somewhere eventually but would like to take longer getting there in order to see interesting new things and places, enjoy beautiful scenery and unusual scenes, to try new dishes and eat good meals cooked with expert care.

Four routes in this book are designed along the same principle; but these routes go through other parts of France, wander much more often into remoter areas and on to the little 'white' local roads, and may sometimes seem downright eccentric. For I also want to cater for a growing third group whom I shall call wanderers – those of you who put exploring France ahead of any other part of their holiday. We British have re-discovered France. Despite economic problems, there has been a big boom over four years in Britons motoring around or through France, and many who once travelled through to the South are taking their whole holiday wandering around other areas. So, I have included three tours – of Brittany, the Loire and the Dordogne and Quercy area. In all three I have tried to keep away from the main tourist routes without missing the best sites and places. The château of Chenonceau in the Loire, for instance, can be packed with tourists, but anyone who has not seen it will not want to pass a few miles away and miss one of the most beautiful houses in the world. The same can be said of Orléans, Blois and Angers, if you haven't seen them before.

Since I first wrote *Travellers' France*, a new factor has come into motoring round the country. At that time, Brittany Ferries, with routes to St Malo and Roscoff, were just starting and there was no guarantee that they would continue. Now they are established and the St Malo route not only helps us to explore Brittany but is most useful for anyone heading for south-west France – Bordeaux and beyond.

As in *Travellers' France*, most of the hotels, auberges, Logis and Relais mentioned are family-run. Prices are nearly all for a double room without breakfast. There is a great shortage of single rooms on the Continent. Inflation has hit France as hard as it has hit us and hotel room prices have gone up in five years by about 50 per cent. But they are still some of the cheapest, cleanest, most presentable rooms in Europe. 60–80F (£5.50–£7.25 approximately) is cheap for a room *for two people*. Similar British hotels may charge about double. Continental-type breakfast costs 8–20F according to the type of establishment. The prices were correct as far as possible at late autumn 1982, but with inflation still rife throughout Europe and climbing in France, it is essential to check them before taking the room. Check also if they include taxes and service.

Always ask to see your room before taking it. This is normal in France, especially in smaller hotels, and wise in some because rooms can vary greatly in the same hotel. There may be twenty pretty, well-furnished bedrooms and a couple in the attic with junk furniture – let to latecomers when the others are full.

Some readers new to touring in France have complained about hotel bedrooms, comparing them unfavourably with modern bedrooms of the Spanish resort 'filing-cabinet' hotels. True, you are more likely to get a *cabinet de toilette* (usually like a cupboard with washbasin and bidet) than a fully equipped bathroom, and you may have to pay more for a bathroom. But most people going to France plump for individuality, ambience and character above private plumbing and accept that in most French hotels under 3-star, kitchen and dining room take priority over bedrooms. Anyway, tour Spain away from the cities and resorts and you will get quite a nasty shock with hotels unless you pay heavily.

Many French hotels do not hold rooms after 6 pm even if you have booked. Times are hard and they will not take the risk of someone not turning up if there is a cash customer waiting at the desk. If you are going to arrive after 6 pm, telephone ahead.

On the whole, French restaurants are still the best in the world and some family-run establishments are quite the best value, especially when the *patron* does the cooking and, just as important, the buying at market.

As in every country, meals have shot up in price – by about a third in four years. Usually, the old 30F meal costs 42–45F; the 45F meal costs about 60F. You won't find a better £5.50 meal in any other country. There are little inns still offering 22–26F menus, and those are often the places where they put a huge tureen of soup or terrine of pâté on the table to help yourself.

Restaurants are legally bound to display their menus outside, including a *menu touristique*. A few restaurants who resent this cheap tourist menu offer a thin choice and small portions, but mainly the meals are basic but good. Please don't expect full gastronomic meals at tourist-menu prices. Often, the second-priced menu is very good value – worth paying the extra 10F or so above the cheapest.

I have had a number of complaints about sauces and vegetables: 'a piece of chicken with lemon juice on it and two tiny carrots almost raw and a couple of tiny boiled potatoes', as one reader put it. That is 'Nouvelle Cuisine', the new cooking, as interpreted by a lazy chef.

Nouvelle Cuisine came in a few years back with the fanatical French campaign for slimming and I am glad to report that among leading chefs it is already going out of fashion. It contradicts all classic French cooking which most of us love so much, and owes its temporary success to three factors – the French obsession with getting fit even when fit already, the approval of the French food guide of Gault Millau, a most enthusiastic supporter, and the support of lazy chefs who saw a way of saving time, trouble, and money. It was intended to cut down calories by avoiding cream, flour and butter; if sauces are thickened at all, it is by reducing, and cottage cheese is used instead of cream. One good thing is that vegetables are cooked very lightly to retain flavour and crispness, but good French chefs did that already. Well done, the new cooking can be delicious (but can still get boring); in sloppy kitchens it deteriorates into apricots or raspberry vinegar with everything and Pernod or lemon juice dressing. 'Minceur' menus are for the genuine slimmer.

I am happy to say that most of my readers so far have been called '*très gentils*' and even '*très correct*' (a great accolade in France!) by French hotel-keepers, despite the French press and TV telling them that we are all football louts, hell-bent on bankrupting poor French farmers and fishermen. French manners are rigid. You must say 'good-day' regularly, including to the waiter and chambermaid, shake hands with everyone, call the waiter *monsieur* (not garçon), and assume that it is a compliment if he leaves you with the menu for ten minutes to show that you are a serious eater (that's another accolade – to be *très sérieux*!).

And please do not expect the slick, faceless service of a heavily staffed, expensive group hotel when you go to a small family-run logis. Be happy to be treated as a family guest.

In a bar-restaurant in Normandy recently I was received by everyone from the *patron* to the most regular customer, a garage owner, like a long-lost uncle. An Englishman with what the French call the reserved 'English M'Lord manner' said: 'I suppose you're an old friend?' 'Oh, yes,' I said, 'since yesterday!' A couple of drinks at the bar talking to people before you dine can work wonders in France. And *someone* will speak English.

Reminders

Many restaurants have a special Sunday meal with a different price from weekdays. French families still take an almost ceremonial restaurant lunch on Sundays when they can afford it, and are ready to pay a little extra for good value.

Check the menu card outside to see if prices are 'Service, Taxe Compris' (STC) – service and VAT included. Some offer cheap menus 'compris' but do not include service and VAT in advertised price of dearer meals.

In the week, the French now eat between 12 noon and 2 pm, and in some restaurants you cannot order lunch after 1.45 pm

French police now apply road laws strictly, are much tougher about speeding than our police. Speed traps abound, fines are heavy for any breach of the law, rise with increased speed, and are collected on the spot. So French drivers are more careful than they were and resent foreigners who are not (especially Belgians!). But they do not always keep to the 130 kph (81 mph) on the toll motorways unless they suspect that the police are about. Speed limits are 60 kph (38 mph) in town, 90 kph (56 mph) outside town, 130 kph (81 mph) on dual carriageways.

You must have headlamps altered to dip left. French motorists also object if your beams are not yellow. Do both jobs by using yellow plastic lens converters or plastic stick-ons with yellow paint provided.

The AA reminds us regularly that few Britons are used to driving more than 250 miles a day during the working year; 100 miles is enough for one stretch without a rest or walk. That applies to passengers as well as drivers, so switching drivers and pressing on does little to help you or your car. The French have 'fatigue' zones. They reckon that Beaune, 200 miles from Paris on the motorway, becomes a driver 'fatigue' zone. That is where those coaches packed with children crashed in summer 1982.

Every year many Britons get into trouble abroad and lose a lot of money by not checking their insurance sufficiently. Legally you no longer need 'green card' insurance to drive in Common Market countries, nor a host of others. Exceptions include Spain, Morocco and Turkey. But your own insurance policy will almost certainly give only third-party cover abroad and you may not be covered, for instance, against theft, damage or injury to passengers.

There are still such problems as getting help if the car breaks down or if a member of the party gets ill or is injured and such unexpected items as freighting spares from Britain (Continental garages do not usually carry spares for right-hand-drive cars, even of their own makes), a hire car to continue a journey, hotel costs while awaiting repairs.

The nearest thing to comprehensive insurance is offered by the AA and RAC to members and by specialist brokers like Europ Assistance and Perry.

In EEC countries such as France you are entitled to the same medical treatment as insured nationals of the country. But do get form E 111 before you go (you need booklet SA 30 from your local Social Security Office to tell you how to apply). I broke four bones in my back in France and ended up in Fréjus hospital. Hospital fees were £70 a day, plus consultant and X-ray charges. I had to pay a fifth of the hospital fees before I left. If I had not had the form, I should have had to pay the whole bill and waited to get the money back when I returned to Britain, after several weeks.

This also shows that it is worth taking out a personal medical insurance. A fifth of £70 a day, plus the other fees, is a considerable sum of money.

Ferries

Dover/Folkestone – Boulogne
(1 hr 50 mins – Sealink, P & O)

Dover/Folkestone – Calais
(1¼ hrs and 1 hr 40 mins – Sealink, Townsend)

Newhaven – Dieppe (4 hrs – Sealink)

Portsmouth – Le Havre/Cherbourg
(5½ and 4 hrs – Townsend)

Southampton – Le Havre
(6½, 8 hrs – Townsend, P & O)

Southampton – Cherbourg (5 hrs – Townsend)

Weymouth – Cherbourg (4 hrs – Sealink)

Portsmouth – St Malo (8½ hrs – Brittany Ferries)

Plymouth – Roscoff (6 hrs – Brittany Ferries)

Ramsgate – Dunkirk (2½ hrs – Sally Line)

Hovercraft – Dover – Boulogne/Calais (35 mins)

(Hoverspeed – also from Ramsgate in summer – 40
mins)

Basically, for the first four routes, you can follow
routes on the red Michelin maps (1 cm to 10 km).
Some local road diversions are not on these maps, and
although the signposts in France have improved
enormously in the last few years, the local yellow
Michelin sectional maps are not only useful for these
few stretches but are also interesting. I find them well
worth buying. For the tours of Brittany, Loire and
Dordogne you will need yellow Michelin maps.

An important warning about road numbers: the French
Government, responsible for national roads, has
handed over responsibility for many to the
départéments, leading to renumbering. The numbers
on your maps may well be out of date. For instance, a
road marked N99 on your map may now be the D999.
It is not difficult to spot them, for usually they have a
'9', '6' or '3' added to the front or substituted for the
first of the three numbers.

Alas, some local authorities have not altered their
signposts, so signposts along a road can read 'N23' in
one village, 'D923' in the next.

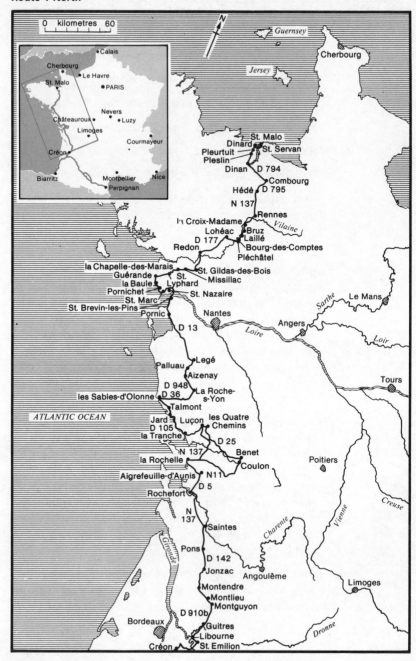

Route 1 South

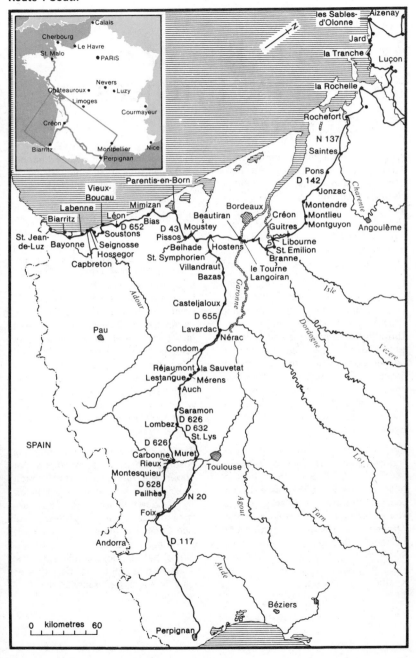

Route 1
St Malo to Biarritz or through the Pyrenees to Perpignan

A most unusual route south. Great variety of scenery, peoples and food. It misses main tourist roads almost entirely, finishing by crossing the great Landes forests on smaller roads away from the dreaded N10 or crossing the Pyrenees by quite rugged but truly beautiful and spectacular roads to Perpignan.

A nice run through east Brittany, on smaller roads, charming small towns, rich countryside, and pleasant streams to the big resort of La Baule. Through Vendée to small Atlantic resorts with fine beaches and on to La Rochelle, a delightful old port with big fishing fleet. Through the Charentes and lovely, little known places like Condom and the Armagnac country to the Bordeaux wine country at St Emilion.

Over the Dordogne and Garonne rivers, where the route divides. One way goes through Landes Forests to the Atlantic coast, with huge sand beaches and massive Atlantic rollers. The other goes diagonally over the Pyrenees through magnificent scenery, with little mountain towns. Some roads are rugged, but rewarding. Alternatives given for bad weather or tired cars.

Few Britons will have gone south this way.

Motorists using Le Havre or Channel ports can join at St Malo, seeing D-Day landing beaches on way, or at Rennes.

In Brittany you find oysters, mussels, crabs, pré-salé lamb (from sea-marsh pastures), duckling from Nantes, splendid fruit, vegetables, cream, cider and those crêpes (pancakes) filled with anything from jam to ham in cream. Try mouclade (mussels in cream), cotriade (mixed fish stew), St Paulin cheese. Only wines – Muscadet (dry fruity white), Gros Plant (young, acidic). Charentes has some of France's most fertile, productive land. Dishes, as around Bordeaux, cooked in butter, enriched with cream and wine; beef and super lamb; superb vegetables; Charentais melons; meals for hearty appetites.

Basque country around Bayonne has unsurpassed cured ham; salmon of Adour and mountain crayfish often cooked in red wine (delicious). Catalan and Basque traditions add a 'Spanish' taste to many Pyrenean dishes. Some nice Catalan garlic sauces. Bitter oranges used, too. Cassoulet – superb dish of beans, goose confit and other meats and sausages simmered for at least 24 hours, preferably 24 days!

St Malo

Hotel Porte St Pierre, pl du Guet, (99)40.91.27: one of my favourites; little old-style hotel right under sea walls. Brightly coloured old dining room; simple, clean, little bedrooms. Excellent sea food platter and white fish – fresh from St Malo quay; fish rillettes; Breton lamb. Terrace with sea view; menu 40–100F; wines 15–100F; rooms 80–150F. Shut Tuesday.

Chiens du Guet, pl du Guet, (99)40.87.29: next door to Porte St Pierre; named after mastiff guard dogs (English!) which for centuries guarded St Malo approaches at night – recalled by trumpet at dawn; pleasant solid comfort once more, good seafood and white fish, good value; menu 40–70F; rooms 60–100F. Shut Monday

Central, Grande rue, (99)40.87.70: large; popular for excellent local fish and cancale oysters; menu 75–120F; rooms (varying standard) 140–290F. Restaurant shut January.

At Paramé, outside walls – Rochebonne, bd Chateaubriand; (99)56.01.72: white, comfortable, end-of-century hotel; rooms good value; menus include Alsatian meal with full sauerkraut for 60F; other menu 42F (weekday);52–100F. Restaurant shut Wednesday in winter.

A delight – superb old port to arouse a sense of drama in coldest hearts. As the ferry weaves through rocks and reefs, the City of Corsairs (French title) or Pirates' Nest (English version) looks menacing and indestructable; behind its walls in narrow streets with old stone buildings, it is snug and friendly. St Malo corsairs were a curse to British shipping from 16th-century reign of René Duguay Trouin – dandy, womanizer, witty, polite hero – to Robert Surcouf, bloodthirsty Napoleonic privateer who captured British merchantmen as far away as the Bay of Bengal. Corsairs had Royal permission to take foreign ships; pirates were freelances – a difference academic to victims. Old St Malo was destroyed, except its walls, in a 1944 battle between Germans and Americans; magnificently restored in detail, blessedly with new drains: style medieval to 18th century, with good shops. Walk round ramparts – sea, river, island views – starts at stairs by St Vincent Gate; aquariums built into sea wall by Porte St Thomas; you can enter courtyard of 14th-century castle (now town hall) and from Easter to 20 September go into Quic-en-Groigne tower alongside; built by last Duchess of a free Brittany, Anne (King Charles VIII married her to get hold of

St Malo
continued

Brittany). Historic waxworks museum in tower; more scholarly historic museum in town hall. Jacques Cartier, French discoverer of Canada, born here; also writer Chateaubriand, whose themes of sadness and loneliness still affect French literature. He was buried in 1848 on deserted, tiny islet of Grand Bé, which you can walk to at low tide (¾ hour return). Chateaubriand steak invented by his chef Montmireil – middle fillet grilled in butter with sauce of wine, shallot, tarragon, lemon.

D301 St Servan
(5 km)

Le Valmarin, rue Jean XXIII, (99)81.94.76: pricey but restful; charming bed and breakfast hotel in 18th-century house which probably belonged to a retired corsair! Peaceful garden; all rooms with bath, WC; 160–260F.

Resort at mouth of river Rance; beaches to sea and river; quiet; big swimming pool made in Anse des Sablons; walk round Cornich d'Aleth gives lovely views of Dinard, Rance estuary and St Malo. Tour Solidor built 1382, has model of first round-world ship (1519 – 1084 days).

D168 across
Rance dam,
right on D266
Dinard (9 km)

Altair, bd Féart, (99)46.13.58: Patrick Léménager's good cooking and generous portions well-known to Britons; 45F menu a bargain; 90F fish meal formidable and excellent: menu 45–155F; rooms 58–160F. Shut Wednesday (except July, Aug); 15 Dec.–15 Jan.

Des Dunes rue Clemenceau, (99)46.12.72: old favourite of mine; opposite casino and

Bright, happy beach resort in superb setting on Rance estuary; beaches facing three ways, useful for wind-evasion – huge sand Grande Plage with casino alongside; St Enogat beach under attractive cliffs; Prieuré beach with rocks and pools. Dinard was fishing village discovered in 1850 by British; many lived there until 1939. Gardens, parks, nice villas. Rance estuary brings warm

beach; friendly; charming welcome from Phillipe Foucart, yachtsman well known in Britain. Most comfortable; two gardens; wood-fired grill; menu 59–92F; good seafood; rooms 75–230F (family). Shut Monday low season, Nov.–end Jan. but open over Christmas.

Hotel Roche – Corneille, Restaurant La Coquille, rue Clemenceau, (99)46.14.47: very nice hotel by beach; pretty flower garden; comfortable rooms; excellent cooking; imaginative à la carte dishes – John Dory in fresh mint; sole à l'orange; duck breasts in peach sauce; menu 70–90F; rooms 100–265F; restaurant shut Wednesday low season; hotel 15 Oct.–1 April.

De la Paix, pl République, (99)46.10.38: typical little restaurant which locals choose for good value and cooking; in main square. Rooms.

currents, so winter much warmer than inland. Has been compared with Torquay. Many secret coves and bays near by. Heated indoor pool. Rance Tidal Power Station uses tide for hydro-electric power; the estuary is closed by a dam 750 m (800 yd) long with the road over it, bringing St Malo and Dinard about 60 km nearer each other; reservoir is 22 sq km (8 sq miles); boats pass through a 65 m (72 yd) lock; power station in a huge tunnel, 390 m (400 yd) long, in centre of dam; visits 8.30 am – 8 pm (luminous panels explain the works); generators of 240,000 kw, produce 550 million kw a year. Good view from dam platform over estuary.

Dinard
continued

Hôtel Marguerite, pl
Duguesclin, (96)39.47.65;
popular, comfortable;
interesting fish dishes
(escalope of turbot
Bordelaise); try langoustines
cocktail; local chitterling
sausage Andouille; menu 45F
with ¼ litre wine; 60–90F;
house wine 20F; rooms 65–
150F. Shut January.

D266 Pleurtuit,
D766 Plêslin,
Dinan (22 km)

Hôtel d'Avaugour, pl du
Champ Clos, (96)39.07.49:
take an aperitif at a table
outside this fine old house,
looking across to place du
Guescelin; behind is a flower
garden above the ramparts
and castle lawns. Georges
Quinton offers 'cuisine du
marché du jour' and that
often means fresh crayfish,
duck, and lobster as well as
white fish, fresh local
vegetables and fruit –
sometimes incorporated into
meat and fish dishes (duck
breasts with orange salad
and turnips); menu 70–120F;
rooms pricey: 220F.

Pelican, rue Haute Vole, (96)
39.42.05: packed with locals
when I found it 20 years ago.
Still is, but many Britons too.
Perhaps I should not have
written so much about it!
Family cooking in Breton
butter; fresh cooking of local
ingredients; generous
portions; huge bowls of soup
on table to help yourself;
exceptional value; menu 30–
60F. Shut Tuesday and
Sunday evenings.

Dinard airport is at Pleurtuit.
Dinan – beautiful, interesting
medieval town on Rance,
inevitably popular, so nicer in
spring or autumn. Its old
houses and narrow streets
almost entirely enclosed in
its old walls, 200 foot above
river Rance, now crossed by
a viaduct. Window boxes of
old houses often bright with
flowers especially in rue
Jerzual, where painters,
sculptors, weavers and
potters live. From Jardin
Anglais are views over the
Rance. In church alongside
(St Sauveur) is buried the
heart of Bertrand du
Guesclin, local lad who died
in 1380 after 20 years
fighting for the King of
France. He and his brother
Oliver were defending Dinan
in 1359 against the Duke of
Lancaster when Oliver was
taken prisoner by an English
knight, Sir Thomas of
Canterbury, during a truce –
against rules of chivalry.
Bertrand challenged
Canterbury to single combat,
with Lancaster presiding.
Guesclin won, Canterbury
was discharged from English

Restaurant des Terrasses, le Port, (96)39.09.60: delightful; alongside river, tables under umbrellas on quay; glass terrace, shut and heated in winter; good cooking; try fish terrine; barbue (brill) in champagne; best end of lamb in orange sauce; menu 38–150F. Shut Tuesday; November.

army, which withdrew. Guesclin was captured three times by the English, who liked him. He lived freely at court. He had personal friends among the knights he fought. The castle is still there, with an enormous 14th-century tower, 34 m (100 ft) high. Grand-Fossés Promendade is a fine avenue with garden alongside rampart walls. From rue Jerzual rue du Petit Fort leads down to old bridge across the Rance; from the Port take a boat to St Malo (2 hours) – best way to see the Rance; you may have to return by bus; parking difficult in season.

**D794
Combourg
(13 km)**

Du Château, (99)73.00.38: comfortable, excellent hotel with attractive terrace and garden; friendly; good service; Breton influence in cooking not total; try mussels in cream sauce with sweet peppers; Chateaubriand fillet of steak; lamb ragoût in cider; excellent dessert choice; menu 47F (weekdays), 70–120F; rooms (pleasantly furnished) 57–200F. Boules pitch, children's playground. Shut 15 Dec.–15 Jan.

La Charrette, pl l'Eglise, (99)73.00.60: good value, especially fish; also sometimes couscous, paella; cassoulet; menu 38–72F; rooms being reconstructed. Shut Wednesday evenings.

I like this simple old town; on shore of little lake; dominated by 11th-century feudal castle; it belonged first to du Guesclin family, then in 18th century to the Count of Chateaubriand, father of the great writer, who lived there unhappily in his youth. His father was almost a recluse whose room was in Tour de Chat (Cat Tower), haunted by a former owner who had a wooden leg and a faithful cat; sometimes only the leg and cat appeared! The cat's skeleton was found under the stairs later and some swear that the wooden leg walks around looking for it. Fine view from tower top; castle open Easter–September.

Combourg
continued

De France, rue Princes
(99)73.00.01: much better
than it looks; very good
value; good grills; fine
shellfish; gastronomic menu
at 120F, includes foie gras
and lobster. Other menus 45,
70F; wines from 20F; rooms
60–80F. Shut February.

Du Lac, (99)73.05.65: beside
lake; views from dining
room; nice bar; cosy
bedrooms; specializes in
seafood, fish; menu 46–150F;
house wine 25F; rooms 60–
150F. Shut November.

**D795 Hédé
(14 km)**

Hostellerie du Vieux Moulin,
(99)45.45.70: on N137,
delightful old inn; pretty
dining room; we had
langoustines, guinea fowl in
55F menu; also try stuffed
oysters; brochette from
wood-fired grill (scallops with
béarnaise sauce); excellent
quality, quantity; menu 55–
80F; rooms 80–140F;
restaurant shut Sunday
evening, Monday.

'Valley of Windmills' –
peaceful valley of flowers
woods, small lakes – very
attractive. Village is on a hill
between canal and a pool;
photogenic, with hanging
gardens, to houses, castle
ruins topping a rock. Les Iffs
village (6 km W.) has 15th-
century church with stained
glass and remains of
Montmuran castle.

**D795, N137
Rennes (20 km)**

At Betton (9 km N. on N776)
– Hôtel de la Levée, rue
Amérique (99)55.81.18:
lovely old house close to
canal and Rance river; open
fireplace; fresh and seawater
fish; good cheap meals and
carte. Menu 32–49F; house
wine 17F; Gros Plant 21F;
Muscadet 24F. Rooms 54F.
Shut Sunday evening,
Mónday.

Rennes has grown in all
directions – population,
suburbs, industry and
university; old town
appalling for traffic but good
for pedestrians; oddly, centre
is 18th century; narrow,
medieval streets with half-
timbered houses surround it.
Old centre burned down in
1720 by drunk; soldiers
brought in to quell flames
merely looted. Cathedral

Rennes – Lecoq-Gadby, rue d'Antrain, (99)38.05.05: several dining rooms in styles of different periods – Belle Epoque to 1930s; classic dishes; menu 60F (weekdays), 88F, 120F, (Sundays). Shut Monday; 1–19 August.

Le Baron, rue St Georges, (99)30.45.36: slightly Nouvelle Cuisine but not afraid of cream or classic dishes; very well chosen, reasonable wine list, up to 1st cru wines; menu 50F. Shut Saturday lunch; Sunday; 3 weeks in August.

Corsaire, rue d'Antrain, (99)36.33.69: splendid cooking of fish; excellent value menu at 72F, often includes 6 oysters; carte reasonable for such good cooking; try terrine of langoustines; brill soufflé in Calvados; shut Sunday evening off-season; all Sunday mid-summer.

disappointing. Excellent Museum of Brittany, includes fine historic costumes and first-class audio-visual rooms – but you must understand French. Not a lively city but friendly and bright with flowers. The siege of Rennes in 1491 effectively ended Brittany's independence of France. Charles VIII of France besieged it because Anne, Duchess of Brittany, had refused to marry him. He was morose and slow witted; she was happy, charming and highly educated. The starving citizens of Rennes pleaded with her to marry him. She met Charles, liked him and married him. Breton car museum of old vehicles 2 km along N12 Fougères road.

D177 La Croix-Madame (3 km) left through Bruz, on to D77 through Laillé, Bourg-des-Comptes, Pléchâtel, until it crosses river Vilaine at St Malo-de-Phily, D49 to Lohéac (about 30 km)		Bruz: well planned country town with beautiful church of rose-veined rock. A route of little local roads used only by farmers and villagers, past hamlets and through part of Brittany few travellers discover. Lovely glimpses of Vilaine valley at Bourg-des-Comptes, Pléchâtel.
D177 Redon (32 km)		River Vilaine and Nantes-Brest canal cross at Redon. Quaint old houses in Grande-rue; Monday farm market; some industry. St Saveur Church, with Romanesque tower, was part of great old abbey.
D164, D773 St Gildas-des-Bois D2 Missillac (28 km)	Hôtel Golf de la Bretesche, Missillac, (40)88.30.05: comfortably converted from the Bretesche castle stables and farm, with its own tower; delightful country-house hotel with golf course laid out originally for a French woman champion and described by Cliff Michelmore on BBC *Holiday* programme as 'one of Europe's most pleasant golf courses'. Good riding centre. Menu 70–120F; rooms 190–280F. Independent Chateaux Hotel.	At St Gildas-des-Bois: 13th-century church of Benedictine monastery. 14th-century Bretesche Castle, beside a little lake, is delightful – fairy-tale turrets, ramparts shielding lawns; beautiful background of water, woods and the greens, fairways and bunkers of golf course of nearby hotel. Castle built by de Montfort family; Kings of France stayed to hunt in the Bretesche forest alongside. Damaged in Revolution; sold with big estate for £400. Visits except Mondays and also Thursday morning in season.

D2, D50 La
Chapelle-des-
Marais, D51 St
Lyphard,
Guérande
(24 km)

Brière Regional Nature Park; strange marsh and peat bog of 99,000 acres, caused when sea flooded forests 5000 years ago; drained by pumps and canals since, but areas still flooded. Rich in wildfowl and fish; grazing in summer; small channels ablaze with yellow iris mid-May/June/late July. Boat trips from villages. La Chappelle-des-Marais has in its town hall a fossilized tree trunk 7 m (23 ft) long. Guérande, between drained marshes and Marais Solents, once a bay where Julius Caesar's galleys under Brutus defeated sailing ships of the Veneti; now salt marshes because sea retreated. Town's medieval walls are intact; 15th-century, flanked by eight towers, four fortified gateways; moats, filled in to make boulevard.

D92 La Baule
(8 km)

Wide choice of hotels and restaurants of all sizes, types and prices; some take only 'pensioners' – half-board for whole week in season. But ask; there are more vacancies these days.

L'Espadon, residence du Golfe, ave de la Plage (40)60.05.63: on 5th floor of modern apartment block with glass walls, fine panorama over whole bay. Excellent cooking by the patron's son; interesting cassolotte of scallops; little red mullet in basil served cold as a starter; poached John Dory; best

Elegant resort, rarely fully closed; lively spring/autumn; crowded mid-summer; but splendid 5 km (3 miles) of fine sand, is never crammed. Protected by 1000 acres of maritime pines. Nice promenade; smart villas and gardens; night life; casino; yacht harbour; international show-jumping; good riding stables; many festivals. *Chic* atmosphere; colourful scene. I like it very much; some call beach 'most beautiful in Europe'.

La Baule
continued

ingredients from local markets, cooked fresh; splendid patisserie; menu 65–190F; pricey apartments 230–650F. Shut 1 Oct.–10 Nov. 3–31 Jan.

Hôtel la Palmeraie, allée des Cormorans, (40)60.24.41: under pines very near sands; pretty garden; covered terrace; neat, unexciting furnishing; pleasant cooking; menu 64–72F; wines from 28F; rooms 120–190F. Open 1 April–1 Oct.

Chalet-Suisse, ave de Gaulle, (40)60.23.41: restaurant popular with regular visitors; good fish; menu 40–140F; Shut Tuesday evening; Wednesday.

Office de Tourisme, 8 pl Victoire, (40)24.34.44: For information on hotel vacancies etc.

Le Croisic (10 km on N171) – photogenic little fishing town surrounding harbour, divided into docks; 17th-century houses; crowded high season; two beaches.

D92 Pornichet (6 km)

Originally salt-marsh workers' village; now resort on sands which, with La Baule beach, form 8 km (5 mile) stretch; jetty, yacht harbour; racecourse.

D292 Pointe de Chemoulin, St Marc, small left over D92 to D492, D99 skirting St Nazaire over toll-bridge to St Brévin-les-Pins (23 km)

St Brévin – Normandy, ave Président-Roosevelt, (40)27.20.65:good seafood platter; duckling in Muscadet; reliable cooking; menu 50–70F; rooms 70–120F. Open 1 June–20 Sept.

Le Débarcadère, pl Marine: Logis; cheap menus, good value; menu 35–90F; rooms 60–115F. Shut 15 Oct.–15 Jan; Sunday, out of season.

St Marc: village backed by cliffs with views of Chemoulin point; good fishing. M. Hulot holidayed here – in the film. St Brévin-les-Pins in middle of forest of pines, acacia, oak, miles of sand beneath wooded dunes.

D213 Pornic
(18 km)

Relais St Gilles, (40)82.02.25: super old relais with tall, arched gate for coaches, and courtyard. Very good value; seafood specialities; menu 36–45F; house wine 18F; rooms 50–165F. Shut Oct.-April.

Hostellerie Ourida, rue de Verdun (40)82.00.83; attractive, cosy; glass ceiling to dining room; meals good value; excellent fish, mussels, other shellfish; good service; menu 30F (weekday); 41–83F; meals on terrace in garden; rooms 55–130F. Shut 1–15 March.

Delightful little resort, forming amphitheatre around inlet with natural harbour from which boats sail into Bay of Bourgneuf and to Isle of Noirmoutier in season – though that can be reached by road! Pinewoods; 17th-century cross to 200 Huguenots, murdered here. A few fishing boats, yachts in new port; small beach below 13th-century castle which once belonged to Gilles de Rais. Gilles – hero of the siege of Orleans when fighting with Joan of Arc; Marshal of France at 25; retired to his estates, terrorized the area, kidnapping children and women for his lusts and orgies. Prototype of Blue Beard (Barbe Bleue).

D13, left on
D753 Legé,
right on D978
Palluau
Alzenay; left on
D948 La Roche-
sur-Yon
(75 km)

La Roche-sur-Yon-Gallet, bd Mar. Leclerc, (51)37.02.31: handsome creeper-clad hotel with pavement tables; excellent furnishing; Louis XIII-style dining room; open fire; comfortable bedrooms; patron-chef cooks with great care; try ragout of shellfish; terrine of red mullet; duck in cassis; menu 70–120F. Also Grousse d'Ail restaurant with good-value 42F menu; rooms 95–250F. Shut Sunday in winter; 2 weeks December.

Route skirts Le Marais Breton –Vendéen, waterways made to drain marshland and used for centuries for transport; dairy herds and sheep graze in fields; some canals used for fish farming (mullet, eels) duck plentiful.

La Roche-sur-Yon: Napoleon ordered the building of the town on a hill to dominate the Yon valley; built in clay (only material available), named 'Napoléon-Vendée', nicknamed 'City of Dirt'. On return of royalty, renamed Bourbon-Vendée. Called La Roche after the Revolution.

D747, D36 Les
Sables-
d'Olonne
(37 km)

Hôtel le Théátre, bd
Roosevelt, (51)32.01.70: good
value; with low price menus;
known for fish and fish soup
but good meat too; menu 28,
35, 45, 85F; rooms 60–80F.
Shut Tuesday evening,
Wednesday except July,
August.

Les Navigateurs, quai Guiné,
(51)32.01.70: cheapish; very
good for fish; seafood
platter; good moules
marinières; menu 35, 55,
70F. Shut Thursday.

L'Etoile, cours Blossac,
(51)32.02.05: good
straightforward French family
cooking; menu 42, 80F
(Sundays); house wines 17F;
restaurant, open 1 June–15
Sept., hotel to 30 Sept.
Family atmosphere; rooms
67–125F. Good place to meet
the French.

This area, La Vendeé, stayed
loyal to Royal Bourbons after
the Revolution and fought
against Republican armies
for two years. Haras (stud) is
one of most important in
France; includes trotters.
Visits 1 July–15 Sept.

Growing resort; clean water,
fine sandy beach; big fishing
port, catch mostly cod for
morue (salt cod); also
sardine and tunny boats; salt
marshes to north, once used
for panning sea-salt, now an
oyster, mullet, eel and frog
farms. Superb promenade
built as protecting sea wall in
18th century, now lined with
luxury holiday flats,
boutiques. Cafés (called le
Remblai); pool, casino; La
Chaume, across harbour
channel, is true fishermen's
quarter, around restored
17th-century fort for guarding

Beau Rivage, prom G. Clemenceau, (51)32.03.01: expensive – worth the price; fine terrace with view. Superb seafood platter; outstanding mouclade (mussels in creamy wine sauce – called 'mytiliade' here); cotriade (four types of white fish, stewed with mussels, herbs, cream); 150F menu includes wine; 72F menu good but simple, out of season only. Good cheeseboard with nut and rye bread made by chef. Rooms 100–200F.

harbour entrance. Forest (take D87a) of oaks covering dunes, 5 km. Moors settled this coast after being banished from Spain; some Moorish survivals in peasant costume. Good museum in 17th-century Benedictine abbey; prehistoric finds, local costumes; old household items; contemporary art; interesting. Open 15 June–30 Sept.

D949 Talmont, D21 Jard-Sur-Mer, D105 La Tranche (38 km)

Jard – Hôtel du Parc de la Grande, (51)33.44.88: delightful Logis and France Accueil hotel; bright, sunny décor; glass-walled summer dining room, plus pine room with open fire for colder days; terrace; charming garden surrounding swimming pool; tennis, snooker, table tennis; sauna; friendly place; restaurant open to public; hotel is demi-pension only – prices most reasonable: menu 48, 65F; good sole, steak, daily change of dishes. Half board 130–198F. Open 2 Apr.–1 Oct.

La Tranche – Les Pins, La Grière, (51)30.34.24: modern; shady garden; clean, pleasant – good value; inevitably, good fish; menu 35–50F; rooms 120–160F. Open March–September.

Château de Talmont: substantial ruins of 11th-century castle, improved by Richard Lionheart; chapel; tower with good coast views.

Jard: Richard Lionheart built abbey; few well-preserved halls remain. Small beach resort, just being discovered by pioneer Britons.

La Tranche has the blue ribbon of unpolluted beaches in France. Big beach below dunes and pines; after centuries of growing garlic and onions, many locals have switched successfully to tulips and gladioli; flower festivals at end March and beginning April.

D46
L'Aiguillon,
D746 Luçon
(31 km)

L'Aiguillon – Du Port, rue Belle Vue, (51)56.40.08: modern, balconies to bedrooms; heated pool; menu 36–80F. Try hot oysters in champagne; pleasant rooms 71–150F. Open 1 April–30 Sept.

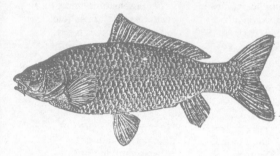

L'Aiguillon-sur-Mer – on estuary of Lay river – bar of sand dunes (Pointe d'Arcay) which is seabird sanctuary. Beginning of Marais Poitevin – an almost secretive area of waterways, lush meadows, willows, reeds, little villages; marshes drained from the 11th century. People live as much by fishing for carp, perch, crayfish and tiny eels (anguilles) as dairy farming with cows and goats. Flat-bottomed boats (plattes) propelled by poles still used for moving stock and taking people shopping, to church and school.

Luçon – Richelieu became bishop here, aged 23, in 1608 when it was ruined by Wars of Religion; he restored cathedral and bishop's palace. Oddly, the Gothic cathedral front was 'restored' in 1700 in Greek-Roman style. Pleasant town.

D50, D25
Benet, Coulon

Au Marais, quai Louis Tardy, (49)25.90.43: place to try local dishes: mouclade Maraichine (local mussels in cream and wine), bouilliture d'anguilles (small eels stewed in white wine, with onions and eggs); crayfish; fish terrine; nice local gâteau; great wild game; menu 48–87F; rooms 132F. Try also Pineau, Charente's mixture of brandy and grape juice which can be drunk with shellfish, as an aperitif, or, says the publicity, 'at tea time'. Restaurant (not hotel) shut mid-Dec. to mid-Jan.

Coulon: capital of Marais; church in main square dated back to Charlemagne; take a 'platte' from here for peaceful water trip, under arches of trees, to see other villages. Abbey of Maillezaise, 10th century, has ruined church, 14th-century abbey buildings and parish church with a superb Romanesque façade. From here you can take a 'platte' trip of ¾ hour.

D1, N11 right
to La Rochelle
(57 km) –
alternative
D949 Les
Quatre
Chemins, N137,
N11 to La
Rochelle
(50 km)

Restaurant Le Vieux Port and Hôtel St Jean d'Arc, pl de la Chaine, (46)41.73.33: tables on pavement opposite the towers in old port; small hotel above with modern décor; fish specialities – langoustines, sole, lobster; outstanding seafood platter; menu 55–80F; rooms, sound-proofed, all new, WC, bath or shower 140–180F.

La Cagouille, bd Joffre, (46)41.46.08: cagouilles are snails, and here they are served stuffed; modern restaurant in park, with lots of glass; pleasant meals; menu 50–90F. Shut Monday.

Trianon et Plage, rue Monnaie, (46)41.21.35: charming hotel; very near port, beach, town, parks; attractively furnished; known for mouclade and for fish; also a fine old-fashioned blanquette de veau. Menu 50–86F; rooms 84–152F.

De France et d'Angleterre, and Restaurant Le Richelieu, rue Gargoulleau (46)41.34.66: very comfortable rooms, tastefully furnished; small garden; restaurant with deserved Michelin Star; fish carefully chosen from market each morning by patron's wife; choice of classic and Nouvelle Cuisine dishes; menu 100F; rooms 106–223F. Restaurant shut Sunday.

La Taverne, rue de la Chaine, (46)41.07.26: overlooking port; good value 85F menu, with oysters; good mouclade; menu 60F (weekdays), 85, 100, 140F.

Despite wars, sieges and one of world's biggest naval and submarine bases alongside, La Rochelle is one of the most picturesque cities in France. Old port, surrounded by lovely buildings and cafés and fish restaurants, is a delight. Still protected by towers, St Nicolas and La Chaine, from which a chain could be lowered to stop ships entering or leaving. Port dates from Middle Ages; is still a very important fishing port. Both towers can be visited – St Nicolas all year, except Tuesday; La Chaine – times and days vary through year, so check. Fine views from St Nicolas. Third tower, Lanterne, once a lighthouse (15th century), has views from balcony half-way up. Town hall, founded in 12th century but mostly an ornate Renaissance building, is grand and interesting; leading to it is Grande Rue des Merciers, street of fine old houses and arcaded pavements. A multitude of treasures around the city, including splendid Café de la Paix in pl Verdun, left over from last century, with ornate décor. Rochelle belonged twice to England; was stronghold of Protestants in Wars of Religion, withstood a long siege by the King, but was besieged again by Richelieu who had a dam built to cut off the city from the sea and its supplies. Only 5000 people of 28,000 survived. Rochelle's modern port is La Pallice whose indestructible submarine

bunkers were used to appalling affect by Nazi submarines preying on Atlantic shipping in World War II. (Incidentally, I was shot down here in 1941 helping to stop the *Scharnhorst* battle-cruiser going raiding in the Atlantic, spent 4 years as guest of the German Government – food appalling and service non-existent.) La Rochelle's town beach not good, but 12 km south in Châtelaillon-Plage, and boats go from La Pallice to Ile de Ré (15 minutes) with magnificent sand beaches, dunes, pine woods, and oyster beds. Once a staging post for criminals on route for dreaded Devils' Island.

D939
Aigrefuille-d'Aunis, D5
Rochefort
(42 km)

Des Remparts, ave Camille-Pelleton, (46)87.12.44: modern hotel with its own thermal treatment and lifts designed to assist handicapped; all rooms bath or shower, WC; good duck, fish dishes; specializes in Poitou wines; reasonable prices; menu 48–90F; rooms 130–200F. Shut 15 Dec.–15 Jan.

La Tourne-Broche, ave Charles de Gaulle, (46)99.20.19: very good value; try moules marinière; home-made rillettes of goose liver; Boutargue (caviar blanc of tunny roe); grills over wood fire; menu 39, 69F.

Rochefort: home of Pierre Loti, author of *Icelandic Fisherman* (1850–1923), navy officer who wrote so superbly about sea life that he was elected to l'Académie Française. His birthplace and his later home were next door; both now a museum; contain Renaissance dining room with five Gobelin tapestries. Also naval museum in 17th-century Hôtel de Cheusses; includes good ships models (shut Tuesday). Port founded by Colbert, French Minister in 17th century, as a fort against English navy, well protected by isles of Ré and Oléron. Vauban's ramparts

Shut Sunday, Monday 26 June–10 July.

mostly replaced by promenades. Hôtel du Marine, now naval HQ where Napoleon spent his last night on mainland on route for exile in St Helena.

N137 Saintes (45 km)

La Vieille Forge, (46)93.33.30: delightful converted forge in village St Georges des Coleaux (6 km back on N137 towards Rochefort – just off road); large garden. Lobster from tank; sole with cèpes (delicate mushroom); mouclade (mussels in cream); steak; menu 58F (weekdays), 120F. Shut 7–29 June; also Tuesday.

Brasserie Louis, Hôtel Avenue, ave Gambetta, (46)74.16.85: modern; good value; rather dull décor, speciality seafood platter; anguilles (eel) offered as choice on all menus (pity I don't like eels!); menu 48–68F; rooms 70–105F. Shut Monday; October.

Hôtel France, Rest le Chalet, pl Gare, (46)93.01.16: good value; traditional dishes, prepared excellently; trout ponds; lobster tank; try stuffed snails (escargots), mussels in Pineau (brandy and grape juice), trout in cream; coq au vin; rib of beef in marrow sauce; menu 36–85F. Solid comfort – panelled rooms, leather chairs, neat bedrooms; rooms, with bath, WC, 92–135F. Pleasant garden, terrace. Shut November.

At St Porchaire, 16 km before Saintes, take small left for 2 km – Château de la Roche Courbon, called by Pierre Loti 'Le Château de la Belle au bois dormant' (castle of the Sleeping Beauty). Built in 17th century, neglected from 1817, absentee landlord from 1856 never visited it but had guard to prevent anyone entering; Loti's childhood imagination was fired by it; when it was for sale in 1908 he appealed for it to be saved; in 1920 a friend bought it, restored castle grounds and forest. Many ornately painted ceilings and walls, especially in remarkable bathroom at base of tower; 18th-century clockwork spit in working order, lovely gardens, lake; looks like fairy-tale illustration.

Saintes: capital of Gaulish tribe, then Roman capital; strides river Charente with pleasure craft, summer trips to La Rochelle. Roman Arch of Germanicus once stood on bridge, saved and moved to bank in 1842 by Prosper Merimée, author of *Carmen*; lovely old houses and quays on opposite bank.

At Haras is a horse stud (purebred English, Anglo-Arab, Norman, trotters); open 15 July–28 Feb.

N137 Pons
(21 km)

Auberge Pontoise, ave Gambetta, (46)94.00.99: pleasant, warmly furnished auberge, with classical dishes; try pintadeau (guinea-fowl) in a Pineau sauce (Pineau makes excellent sauces!); rooms 110–180F, all with bath or shower, WC.

Castle (now ruined) owned by very powerful lords until Religious Wars; still some old walls beside river Seugne; on bank opposite is Château d'Usson, dismantled on its old site near Lonzac, moved here in 1890s. Beautiful Renaissance castle; visits to outside 1 July – 15 Sept; inside only with written permission; a pity – magnificent white and gilt woodwork of Louis XV period; also medallions of 12 Caesars. Pons produces Pineau, butter, brandy.

D142 Jonzac,
D19
Montendre,
D730 Montlieu,
Montguyon
(77 km)

Montguyon – Le Saintongeais (46)04.11.66: pleasant local hotel-restaurant; good confit of duck; veal; charentaise snails; menu 35–75F; rooms 65–105F. Shut Mon.; Oct.

Post, (46)04.19.39: modern, garden, pool; good value; menu 32.50, 42.50, 57.50F, all include wine 'ordinaire'; tidy modern rooms 70–90F.

Jonzac: church bell-tower 36m (120 ft) designed as burial memorial for Katherine, wife of Jacques de Genouillac, master of artillery under Francis I; encircling motifs say, 'I love one dearly.' 15th-century castle with pointed towers in fairy-tale style.

D910b Guîtres,
Libourne
(35 km)

Libourne – Hôtel Loubat, rue Chanzy, (56)51.17.58: charming house, beautifully kept; restaurant called Les Trois Toques; regional dishes; try duck, salmon; menu 75–180F; 250 wines.

Attached restaurant, Le Landais, rue des Treilles, has pleasant garden; very good value; try coq au vin, confit of duck; menu 25–64F; wine 20F a litre; also merchants of Bordeaux wines; rooms 90–222F.

Guîtres; nice old town with 12th-century church on river Isle; old alleys climb from river to tree-shaded square.

Libourne: at meeting of rivers Isle and Dordogne. Since English were here in 100 Years' War, has been big port for wine export; wines poled down river on gabares (flat-bottomed boats), which were broken up at Libourne to make wine casks; still market centre for its own area – St Emilion, Pomerol,

Fronsac. Good view of Dordogne from Fronsac – 3 km W. Libourne was founded by a Kentish knight, Roger of Leybourne.

D17E St Emilion (8 km)

Hostellerie de Plaisance, pl du Clocher, (56)24.72.32: I could end my days at this little hostelry looking towards Dordogne valley, eating great food and drinking the wine; I used to eat here when a huge meal cost 20F. Alas the price is now nearer 130F. A new patron-chef has arrived and I have not tried his cooking yet, but shall soon. First reports are good, especially fricassé of farmyard chicken in St Emilion wine; mussel soup; duck; menu 78, 130, 170F. Rooms rather pricey 200–270F.

Logis de la Cadene, pl Marché au Bois, (56)24.71.40: lunch only; excellent value; delightful 18th-century house; chef-patron Françoise Moulierac here since 1953, still keeps prices down for pleasant meals; try confit of duck; river lampreys; chicken 'crapaudine' (split down middle and grilled); menu 30, 40, 55, 70F. Remarkably cheap St Emilion wines; family owns Château La Clotte (grand-cru classe) sells at table at cellar prices – 45–60F a bottle. Shut 15–30 June, 1–15 Sept.

One of the most delightful little towns in France. Built on two hills with views across rooftops to valley of the Dordogne; little houses crammed into steep streets – mostly old, with their own wine cellars, and of yellowy stone which shines gold in sunshine. The market place with an old acacia tree, called Tree of Liberty, is calm, almost deserted until market days, when it is crowded and fun. Once fortified. St Emilion still has ramparts and an old tower from days of Henry III, Plantagenet King of England, who founded the castle, St Emilion's own 7th-century hermitage is hewn from rock, complete with bed, table and fountain to make a bathtub. A huge underground shrine near by, like a ballroom, was hacked out of rock by monks. The atmosphere of the place holds you – helped by splendid wine. Cheval Blanc, which is red, rates almost with Lafite and Latour in some years; it is strong and robust.

D122 over Dordogne river to Branne (6 km)	De France, pl Marché, (56)84.50.06: redecorated; very fair value; specialities of Dordogne and Bordeaux; among Bordeaux wines, a Pomerol from hotel's own property; menu 35–90F; rooms 95–150F. Shut Tuesday in winter; October.	Pleasant little town on Dordogne river, edge of Entre-Deux-Mers wine district. Branne wine mostly dry white but also some sparkling mousseux, red and rosé. Also sweet white, much prized locally.
D936, D20 left to Créon, D20, D13 to cross river Garonne at Le Tourne; D115 Portets, Beautiran D1E, D651 Hostens (65 km)		Créon: agricultural market and centre for Entre-Deux-Mers wines. La Sauve (6 km N67) has 11th century abbey; also 12th-century church. Hostens is holiday village between shallow lakes; in Val de l'Eyre regional park – a nature protection area.
(route Hostens-Perpignon follows after this route to Bayonne – see p. 44 D651 Belhade, D120 Moustey, N134 Pissos, D43 Parentis, D46, D626 Mimizan (68 km) 	Mimizan – Bellevue, (58)09.05.23: attractive modern hotel with period furnishing; reasonable prices; local dishes, especially duck; menu 45–90F; wines from 17F; rooms 53–117F. Shut November – beginning March. Du Parc, (58)09.13.88: another modern hotel with competitive prices; garden with children's swings; all bedrooms with balcony, bath or shower, WC; 45F menu includes steak or chicken; menu 45–80F; rooms 110–150F. Shut 20 Dec.–31 Jan.	An oil field at Parentis; beside a nice lake. But this is the regional park of Les Landes de Gascogne – created in 1970 to preserve naturally this area so little known. For centuries it flooded and the shepherds tended their sheep by walking on stilts, as they did in the Fens of England. Folklorique groups still dance on high stilts. The bog was unhealthy, mosquito ridden. In 1788 shifting dunes were stopped by huge pine and cork oak plantations; land drained; now forests cover nearly 1,000,000 hectares; perfume of Les Landes is pine resin; the dunes are being turned into small holiday beach resorts for campers and self-catering hamlets; huge Atlantic rollers make beaches better for expert surfers than paddlers

or swimmers. The ancient town of Mimizan was covered by shifting sand dunes in 18th century. A market town here now. Magnificent beach at Mimizan Plage, where holiday and retirement houses being built; attractive Aurelihan Lake to north; windy winters.

D652 Bias, Léon (41 km)

Léon – Central, on the square: the local 'pub' serving meals of remarkable value; good choice, under 30F including wine. High season, pop in early and book a table.

Hôtel du Lac, by the Etang, (58)48.73.11: delightful, fairly simple hotel in nice position; colourful views of sunset over the Etang; menu 39, 49, 70F; house wine 18F; rooms 66–100F. Shut 1 Oct.–1 April.

Léon, typical, pretty, small Landes town around main square, with market – and even tiny cinema – becomes the 'mighty metropolis' for campers in July, August. You must book in two restaurants. Canoes, rowing boats and pedalos for hire on the big shallow 'étang' (lake) where wild fowl normally live in tranquillity; no good if you dislike crowds, but fun. These étangs are old estuaries, blocked by sand.

D952 Vieux-Boucau, Soustons (22 km)

Vieux-Boucau – Côte d'Argent, (59)48.13.17: well run, charming service; local dishes – real piperade (fluffy scrambled egg with tomatoes, peppers, onions, ham); salmis of wild pigeon (half-cooked by roasting, finished in red wine sauce with onions, ham, mushrooms). Menu 45–70F; 90–120F on Sundays; rooms 55–120F. Shut Monday out of season; 1 Oct.–1 Nov.

Soustons – Du Lac, ave Galleben, (58)48.08.80: not quite in same class for food as 'Pavillon Landais' (Michelin starred) but good value and half the price; many rooms

Vieux-Boucau: for 250 years called Port d'Albret, at mouth of river Adour; the eccentric river changed course many times, meeting the sea at Capbreton, Port d'Albret then Bayonne. Plantagenet kings fortified Bayonne, but river returned to d'Albret. In the 16th century a canal dug to return it to Bayonne, leaving Vieux-Boucau unimportant. Now the magnificent 'Courant' (stream) running from the pretty L'Etang de Soustons, and the sands, make Vieux-Boucau a pleasant tiny resort.

Soustons
continued

overlook L'Etang; change of menu daily according to market; fish specialities; moules, salmon; duck; menu 55–100F; half-board 145F per person.

D652
Seignosse,
D89, D79
Hossegor,
small road on
landward side
of lake, on to
D152
Capbreton
(25 km)

Hossegor – La Bon Bonnière, ave du TCF, (58)43.50.21: super, fairly simple hotel alongside lake; garden; lake views from dining room; try piperade; stuffed goose neck; duck confit; all Basque dishes; menu 39–94F; house wine 16F; rooms 72–112F. Shut 1 Oct.–15 May.

Capebreton – Du Centre, ave Pompidou, (58)72.01.13 good moules marinière; chipirons in Armoricaine sauce (local Basque squid); tripes à la Landaise; menu 50–85F; rooms 60–100F. Shut in winter.

Hôtel le Béarnais, (58)72.13.33: chef-patron Guy Fontain offers good choice of fish and meat dishes; also, if ordered, paella or couscous for six people; try chicken in crayfish sauce; fish of the day in saffron bisque (lobster-based) sauce; cream fish soup. Good 42F menu, with fish or meat choice; carte dishes reasonable; rooms 50–60F. Shut 20 Sept.–1 June.

Hossegor lake formed when sands stopped flow of river Adour; now good boating centre; lake still joined to sea by a stream, so affected by tides; many seabirds; resort is between lake and sea and dunes – superb for families; sea for surfing; lake for sailing, swimming; background of pines.

Capbreton: important port when Adour flowed here; now family resort, fine sands; small port, some fishing boats, mostly pleasure boats.

D652 Labenne
N10 Bayonne
(30 km)

Bayonne – Restaurant Euzkalduna, rue Pannecau, (59)59.28.02: genuine Basque cooking; fish specialities; dishes such as chipirons in dark spicey sauce; tripotch (veal sausage); piperade;

Bayonne: capital of the French Basques, it became English when Eleanor of Aquitaine married Henry II; stayed so for three centuries; Basque fleet fought alongside our navy. But it

Basque fish soup; baudroie (angler fish); grilled gambas (prawns); piballes (small fried eels); fresh tunny and anchovies in season from fishing fleet at St Jean-de-Luz; Spanish Rioja wines from 18F; meals around 80F. Shut Sunday evening, Monday, part July, part Oct.

Hotel Loustau, pl République, (59)56.16.74: inside a neat, solid white building, dark beams, white roughcast walls, brown tiles, high-backed chairs – all Les Landes style. Jean Chicoye, patron-chef, comes from the Pyrenees. His cooking is good and regional; his hotel pleasant; menu 40–60F (good value); restaurant shut Sunday; rooms 60–130F. Shut 20 Dec.–20 Jan.

Biarritz – Fronton Hôtel, ave Joffre, (59)23.09.49: and its modern attachment La Résidence are both comfortable; middle priced meals, good value; menu 35–52F; rooms 150E. Shut part March; mid-Oct.–mid-Nov.

Hôtel l'Océan, pl Ste Eugénie, (59)24.03.27: genuine Basque dishes – chipirons; poulet Basquais (cooked with tomatoes, peppers, served with rice); duck confit; good fish; menu 45–90F; wines from 20F; rooms 130–250F.

was last place in France to hold out against Wellington. Place de la Liberté is excellent, attractive shopping centre, with arcades. Bayonne is known for its cured ham, chocolates, Armagnac, Izzara (liqueur like Chartreuse), and salmon from Adour river; most attractive city with lovely cathedral and interesting museum of Basque culture. Local blacksmiths invented the bayonet. 8 km away is the elegant, though fading, resort of Biarritz, developed from a fishing village by Napoleon III for his Empress Eugénie, and beloved by our Edward VIII. Crowded high summer now. Hôtel Palais is original palace built by Napoleon III so that Eugénie could be near her favoured Spain. I remember when it was filled with film stars. Now it pulls rich Spaniards. Biarritz is surfing capital of Europe, so bathing is fun but can be dangerous; so can the beachside casino. Bayonne is 32 km from Hendaye and the Spanish frontier.

Alternative Route
Hostens to Perpignan

D111E
St Symphorien
D8 Villandraut,
D11 Bazas,
D655
Casteljaloux
(72 km)

Bazas – Relais de Fompeyne, rte Mont-de-Marsan, (56)25.04.60: pricey but famous for local dishes, including wild pigeon (palombe), and river lamprey 'à la Bordelaise' (eels, sliced, cooked with leeks, garlic, in red wine); lamprey cooks and tastes like meat, not fish; odd that Henry I should have loved them enough to die of overeating them! Very nice dining room; flower garden; menu 75–130F; rooms 125–155F. Open 15 March–15 Oct.

Casteljaloux – Les Cadets du Gascogne, pl Gambetts, (58)93.00.59: I've found them! Joël Malvard and his young wife, formerly of the Palladium, Alvignac in Dordogne and Parc Hotel, St Céré. Two of my favourites! Installed as chef-owners of white old house, with pretty flowered terrace. He is a fine chef (ex. Prunier); uses local ingredients (trout, chickens, duck and duck liver); still offers his famous choice of desserts; menu 55, 75, 110, 180F; rooms 65–180F.

Cordeliers, rue Cordeliers, (53)93.02.19: comfortable, friendly logis; in quiet cul-de-sac in town centre; no restaurant; rooms 50–160F.

La Vielle Auberge, rue Posterne, (53)93.01.36: old beams, strings of garlic dangling from sideboard groaning with bottles. I can

Villandraut castle is a splendid ruin, built in 1264 by Pope Clement V, a local boy, ex-Bishop of Bordeaux and the Pope who moved to Avignon; big spender who weakened the Church. He was buried in nearby Uzeste (D110, 5 km). His name was Bertrand de Got.

From Uzeste D11E goes to Pont-de-la-Trave (4½ km, pretty views river Ciron, dam, ruined castle); D9 to Moulin de Cossarieu (road partly metalled – 15th-century fortified mill in lovely isolated position), then ruins of 15th-century Château de Cazeneuve; to Bazas by D9.

Bazas: perched above Beuve valley, Roman origin; Gothic cathedral started 1233; outer vault shows five foolish virgins, instead of usual seven; rue Fondespan, with medieval houses, leads to medieval gateway.

Casteljaloux: pleasant but slightly industrial; a few old wooden houses with projecting upper storeys. ('Jaloux' comes from old word meaning 'exposed, perilous'. A pity – a 'jealous' castle sounds more fun.) Country of the Three Musketeers.

see the Three Musketeers
drinking here! Huge open
fire; 70F menu particularly
good value; choice of 30
cheeses; menu 50F
(weekdays), 70F, 100F; rooms
60–90F. Shut Sun. eves,
Mon.

D655 Lavardac,
D930 Nérac,
D930 Condom
(51 km)

Nérac – du Châteaeu, ave
Mondenard, (45)75.90.110:
regional specialities;
comfortable rooms; menu
45–110F; house wine 14F;
rooms 65–130F. Shut
October.

Condom – Relais des
Chasseurs (Chez Note), bd de
la Libération, (62) 28.13.33:
little bar-restaurant near
river used by locals; very
cheap meals; enormous
portions; soup bowl, pâté
dish, left on table to help
yourself; second helpings of
meat offered; locals from
offices, shops, garages use it.

Continental, ave Foch,
(62)28.00.58: renovation has
robbed me of my bedroom
window-box flowers. Town's
meeting place; old-fashioned,
solid; good solid meals
include confits of duck,
chicken, cassoulet with duck;
nice wine list; very fine old
Armagnac; menu 45–90F;
rooms 70–120F.

Table des Cordeliers, rue
Cordeliers (61)28.03.68: if
you fancy eating in church,
there is no better place!
Beautiful dining room in
14th-century chapel with
Gothic-style bays; I have had
superb meals but have not

Very pleasant run through
forest. Vianne, 3 km from
Lavardac on D642, is a
'bastide' village fortified by
the English in 1284; beside
river; outer walls almost
intact with gates and towers;
fortified church; houses
mostly rebuilt. Lavardac was
bastide, fortified by French
against the English, but no
fortifications remain.

Nérac: charming market
town, once owned by Albret
lords, kings of Navarre,
including Henry IV of France;
their splendid castle was
partly demolished in the
Revolution; remaining wing,
with arcaded Renaissance
front, is a little Henry IV
museum. Here Marguérite
d'Angoulême wrote
Heptameron, a rival to
Decameron, and Henry IV
had a lively, licentious court.
Shakespeare set *Love's
Labour Lost* here; first folio
mentioned 'Navarre – a park
with palace'. Shady riverside
walk; old town across the
river far more interesting
than modern town. Nérac
was a Protestant stronghold.
When Henry IV cynically
turned Catholic to get the
French throne ('Paris is worth
a Mass'), many Nérac
citizens went into exile.

Condom
continued

tasted cooking of new chef. He gets top marks from experts. Michelin-star prices; try cold oyster consomé, many other interesting dishes; menu 90F (weekdays) 100–200F; rooms 120–170F. Shut Mon.; Jan.

Condom: delightful medieval town on a hill, dropping to river Baise, is the centre for Armagnac – a spirit similar to Cognac, made from white wine, but matured faster. Condom provides Ténarèze Armagnac, as opposed to Haut and Bas Armagnac. Low-grade Armagnac is for cooking; high-grade is better than all but best Cognac: One of very best comes from Château de Cassaigne, (D931, D208, 4 km), former castle of Condom's bishops, called Monluc; Condom's riverside quays once were crowded with boats carrying Armagnac; now a few pleasure boats; splendid market. Larresingle (3 km W on D15) is tiny bastide behind strong walls, moat; church, inn, old houses still inhabited.

D654 La Sauvenet, D148 Réjaumont, Mérens-les-Vals, Lestangue, little road right to St Lary, left on D930, N124 Auch (51 km)

Auch – De France, pl Libération, (62)05.00.44: Alas, I have never met André Daguin, nor eaten in his hotel, but the loss is mine. The French call him a modern D'Artagnan. My friends call him a human dynamo-inventive, a great guy to be with; and built like a rugby player, they tell me! He is, it seems, a brilliant cook, too, and the 'France' has two stars from Michelin.

A lovely route, but hilly and narrow roads; alternative (easier) direct Condom – Auch on D930, N124 (44 km). Mérens' horses, small in stature, black all over, of some of the oldest stock in Europe, remain pure with the help of Tarbes stud. Auch, old capital of Gascony, on banks of river Gers, is the town of D'Artagnan of Dumas' *The Three Musketeers*; he was Charles

So menus at 114–180F not out of place. A Relais Gourmand of Relais et Châteaux Hôtels de France, whose guide calls him 'Champion of Good Humour'. Large and lovely bedrooms and 'best breakfast which can exist', says a famous French gourmet. Some British and Scandinavian hotels might argue with that. Rooms 160–495F. Restaurant shut Sunday evening, Monday out of season; 2 Jan.–1 Feb.

Lafayette, rue Lafayette, (62)05.31.39: down to earth! Excellent Gascon dishes– real family cooking at its best by Huguelle Meliet; lovely Garbure (Gascon soup-stew of vegetables including haricot and broad beans, cabbage, garlic, herbs, chestnuts, with bits of preserved goose, duck, ham, pork and sometimes turkey; swilled from earthenware pot – a toupin – with wine); menu 46–120F.

de Batz, born around 1615 at nearby Château de Castelmore; served in French Guards regiment; took name D'Artagnan from mother's family to be better received at court. He carried out delicate assignments for Louis XIV, not all military; became captain-lieutenant of the first Company of Musketeers and died at the siege of Maestricht (1873). His 'Memoirs' (fictional) were published in 1700, giving Dumas the idea for his book. He was a typical heroic Gascon; but in French 'Gascon' means boaster or line-shooter. Auch has a cathedral with a glorious 15th-century coloured glass. Also 232-step monumental staircase down to statue of D'Artagnan – and a D'Artagnan tower! Older town on cathedral side of river.

D926 Saramon, Lombez, Carbonne, D627 Rieux, Montesquieu; D628, D119 Pailhés; D628, N20 Foix (161 km) (if weather bad or car or driver tired, easier route from Lombez is: D632 St Lys; D12 Muret on to N20 direct to Foix – 156 km from Auch)

Beautiful mountainous route. Lombez: interesting old cathedral among maze of old tiny streets; river Save valley.

Montesquieu: pretty little hideaway with shaded boulevards. Rieux – charming town. (sorry *city* – Pope Jean cut up huge diocese of Toulouse and gave Rieux a bishop and cathedral); many old houses.

Foix
continued

Foix – Hôtel Audoye-Lons, pl Georges Dutilh, (61)65.01.25: fine old coaching inn; excellent value. Small simple dining room with traditional cooking, plus restaurant with balcony overlooking Ariège river, with lovely mountain views, serving local specialities. Open fireplace; old cowshed cunningly converted into snack bar. Excellent cassoulet; duck dishes; house wine 18F. Rooms 100–160F.

Phoebus, cours Irénée-Cros, (61)65.10.42: have not been here since new chef-patron took over; local specialities; above Ariège river; menu 30, 45F; Shut Monday.

Foix: a miner's town until 1931; in 1293, Count of Foix given mineral mining rights (mostly iron) for this part of Pyrénees; iron was brought to Foix by mule. Gold was panned, too, professionally; a few amateurs try it for fun now. Foix has a museum of mineralogy. Tungsten mines of Salau still important. Area famous for myths and legends. 6 km on D1: underground river of Labouiche; 3500 m (3800 yd) stretch, of which you can go 2500 m (2700 yd) by boat, with two 'transhipments', 70 m (230 ft) underground, interesting and beautiful; stalactites and stalagmites in shapes of flowers and strange animals; pretty waterfall. Open Easter – 31 Oct. Gaston Fébus (1331–1391) Count of Foix, was poet, troubadour, famous huntsman; Fébus means 'brilliant' – he added the name himself! But he killed his brother, then killed his only son during an argument. He kept 600 hunting dogs, and at 60 fought a bear. He dropped dead returning from a bear hunt. A later Duke Gaston IV was given the city of Carcassonne for arranging a treaty between Aragon and France. Their castle still overlooks the town from a rock.

**D117
Perpignan
(136 km)**

Tourist office: Quai Lattre-de-Tassigny, (68)34.29.94; central and useful. Many hotels, restaurants. Sans Celma, rue Fabriques-d'en-Nadal, (68)34.21.84: great value; specializes in fish landed here; menu 35F. Shut Saturday evening, Sunday.

Restaurant Relais St Jean, rue Cité Bartissol (very near cathedral), (68)51.22.25: Catalan specialities, including paella; menu 50–60F. Shut Saturday.

Poste, Restaurant Perdrix, rue Fabriques Nabot (by castle), (68)34.32.53: passed from father to son for 150 years; simple, very convenient; Catalan cooking (lots of tomatoes, onions, aubergine, rice, chick-peas; some garlic; good guinea-fowl; clovisse (small clams); menu 35–70F; rooms 50–120F. Shut mid-Jan.–mid-Feb.

Old favourite of mine, but it does get too crowded now in high season with traffic for Spain, and holiday-makers from 'man made' Languedoc-Roussillon coast. Still attractive for café life. Many old, historic buildings. Capital for centuries of the Counts of Rousillon and the Kings of Majorca (their royal palace can be visited). Majorcan kingdom lasted only 68 years, with three kings. Louis XI occupied Roussillon, but Perpignan revolted, wanting Catalan rule; the King of Aragon entered in 1473. Besieged by the French, Perpignan held out until Aragon told it to capitulate. Twenty years later it was ceded to Spain. Catalans revolted against Madrid, and Richelieu seized the chance to grab Perpignan.

Route 2 North

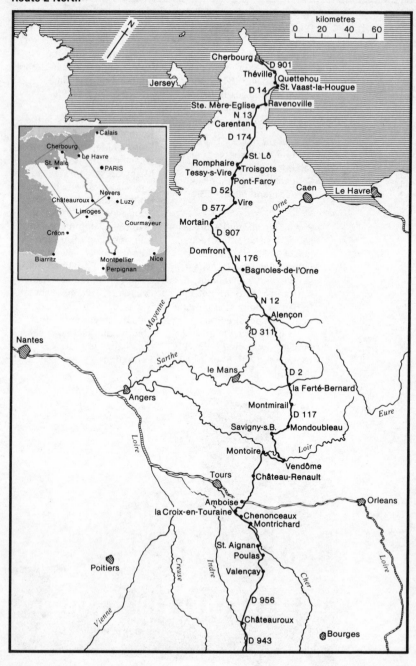

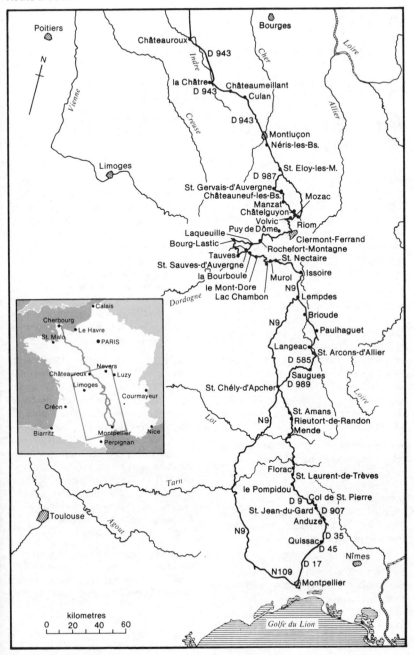

Route 2
Cherbourg/Le Havre through Dordogne, Auvergne to Montpellier
(for Cap d'Agde)

A gentle route at first, through fertile, pretty country, but ending with fairly hard driving through magnificent scenery – a chance to see some of the most sensational scenery in France. For bad weather, or if you fancy easier driving, I have given alternative routes which are still spectacular.

The route takes the lesser-known east side of the Cherbourg peninsula to the parkland of Normandy, and crosses the Loire at Amboise to see the superb château of Chenonceaux. The mountainous Auvergne route goes through little villages and towns with welcoming inns with reasonable prices. Do not go through the glorious Corniche des Cévennes without checking weather conditions.

Around Le Mont Dore is ski country which *in winter you can reach only with snow chains and experience even on main roads*. The Dordogne river trickles through Le Mont Dore, runs through the middle of the main boulevard in La Bourboule and rushes through ravines near Tauves.

This starts as a butter and cream route through Normandy, with superb cheeses. If the cheese, cream and oysters get too much for you, stop in the middle of your meal for a Trou Normand – a glass of Calvados, the apple spirit. It works for me!

Loire is a land of orchards and kitchen gardens, so you get lovely vegetables (including superb cabbage), tasty river fish, beautiful plums, pears, peaches; game, pork and all pork charcuterie, including sausage, hams, rillettes (try rillettes de Tours). Plenty of ducks, too, and goose country starts here; it reaches its climax further south where goose and duck fat are used for cooking most things and preserves (confit) of goose and duck are on every pricier menu.

Auvergne is pig country. Most cooking is in pork fat. Cured mountain ham rivals Ardennes ham; they make sausages, salt pork; try Friands de Saint Flour (sausage meat pâté rolled in leaves); Potée Auvergnate (soup-stew, varying in each village but always with pork, cabbage and potatoes). Auvergne claims to have the original coq au vin, ahead of Burgundy. Mountain cows give superb cheese; try Bleu d'Auvergne; also Cantal (a bit like cheddar). Lovely fungi – mouilles, cèpes.

Local red wines are better than the white or rosé, not very exciting, but cheap and palatable. Côtes du Forez red and St Poucain white have quality.

Cherbourg

La Vauban, quai Caligny, (33)53.12.29: locals as well as hordes of British flock to Claude Deniau's two-faced restaurant: to the 'snack' for a 50F meal with superb help-yourself hors d'oeuvres and the dearer à la carte restaurant for dishes of Normandy – ham in cider, boudin brochet, civet of lobster, scallops in cider, various crêpes flambés in Calvados (the apple spirit); huge platter of seafood would make a meal. Price high, wines rather dear. Frankly I would stick to the 'snack'. Shut Friday; February.

Le Cotentin, quai Caligny, (33)53.56.22: brasserie ideal for quick first/last meals; restaurant above; menu 40, 60, 100F. Can be noisy.

Pleasant port with attractive harbour, sandy beach. Market – fruit, vegetables, flowers, some clothes – in pl de Gaulle Tues, Thurs, Sat. mornings. Continent Hypermarket, Quai de l'Entrepot, near harbour. In J. F. Millet museum, works of Millet, peasant who painted country scenes so truly; also Flemish school paintings including Van Eyck, Van Dyck and Rembrandt, and a Botticelli. Fish market off rue au Blé. In Hitler's War, retreating Germans blew up harbour, but British frogmen cleared debris and mines and it became main Allied supply port.

West 5 km at Nacqueville is a fine château in a lovely setting of wooded hills and a river. At Gruchy on north coast is the house where Millet was born.

**D901 Théville,
D355 Le Vast,
D26 Quettehou,
D1 St Vaast-la-
Hougue
(30 km)**

St Vaast-la-Hougue – Hôtel France et Fuchsias, rue Maréchal Foch, (33)54.42.26: the fuchsias are winning; they have climbed round bedroom balconies to roof, turning hotel walls red when in bloom. M. Brix runs a farm, producing pork, veal, chickens for Mme Brix to cook in the hotel near by. Shellfish and fish straight from the port; red or white house wine costs 25F; menu 45, 60, 80F – or, if in good form, try 120F gastronomic menu, including huge dish of

St Pierre-Eglise, 2 km from Théville on D901 – attractive 18th-century château replacing older one.

Le Vast: charming village with rapids on river Saire. Quettehou church flanked by 15th-century belfry (on Valognes road). Sea and coast views from cemetery are superb.

St Vaast-la-Hougue: delightful little fishing port with pleasure yacht moorings; seamen's chapel by jetty (11th century), apse painted white as navigation

St Vaast-la-Hougue
continued

shellfish (whole crab, langoustines, prawns, shrimps) and half a lobster. Pleasant bedrooms, some simple, 69–150F. Shut 10 Jan.–5 Feb.

aid; La Hougue once separate isle, joined by isthmus with beach alongside; muddy sand and rock at low tide, when you can walk to tiny isle of Tatihou. Vauban built fort on Hougue in 17th century after English won sea victory near by. Louis XIV had got together an Irish-Catholic Army to invade England and put James II on the throne but the English Navy thrashed his fleet (1692). Edward II landed his troops here on way to Crécy. Huge oyster parks off Tatihou.

D14 Ravenoville, D15 Ste Mère-Eglise (24 km)

Ste Mère: centre of livestock-breeding area; inland from Utah beach where US forces landed on D-Day 6, June, 1944).

N13 Carentan N13, N174 St Lô (41 km)

Carentan – Auberge Normande, bd Verdun, (33)42.02.99: excellent dishes if not true Norman. Gérard Bonnefoy believes in light fresh dishes which can be used quickly; simple, good 39F menu (we liked true Norman omelette stuffed with Camembert, mushrooms and cream); excellent 59F Nouvelle Cuisine menu; also 89F menu with superb gâteau of salmon or of lobster with saffron sauce; makes award-winning cider, too. Simple rooms 48–92F. Shut Tuesday, part Oct., Feb.

Carentan: big cattle market; dairy centre.

St Lô historic city called Capital of the Ruins after terrible battle for it between Americans and Germans. US battalion commander Major Howie swore he would be first to enter but was killed just outside, so his unit carried in his coffin and put it on the ruins of a church belfry. A monument to him has been built there. Complete modern town, including spectacular modern belfry. Ramparts remain. Tapestries (16th century) in Fine Arts museum.

St Lô – L'Univers, av Briovère, (33)05.10.84: in one of St Lô's big modern buildings but long, not high, remarkable value. Alain Foucart (owner-chef) cooks well; try mussels in vermouth; noix de veau Normande (veal topside in cider, Calvados, cream); grilled lobster 'diable'; fish kept in seawater tank; wines splendid value – Bordeaux 25F; Muscadet, Cahors 32F; menu 38, 52, 78F. Views over ramparts; rooms soundproofed 55–160F. Shut Sunday in winter.

Terminus, av Briovère, (33)05.08.60: André Masse runs hotel, Madame Irène cooks very nicely; same modern set-up as l'Univers; meals very good value; family cooking – French style; rampart views; menu 45–55F (no wonder locals go there!) rooms 70–120F.

Famous stud with 250 stallions (mostly English and Norman) though most only there mid-July to mid-Feb. Visits 10–11.30 am; 2.30–5 pm.

D28 Romphaire, D159 Troisgots, Tessy, D21 Pont Farcy, D52 Vire (42 km)

Troisgots – Auberge Chappelle sur Vire, (33)56.32.83: unimpressive from outside, but big plans for future; good value; wood-fired grill; good seafood; menu 52–100F; wines from 20F; rooms 60–80F; nice countryside; near river.

Vire – Cheval Blanc, pl du 6 Juin 1944, (31)68.00.21: some fine old Norman dishes with cream and Calvados in a fine Norman-style corner building on a roundabout (tall hedge to cushion noise);

Troisgots: only 50 people live here but pilgrims have come since 12th century. I *still* cannot find out why! Statue of Virgin inside 15th-century church.

Vire: on a hillock commanding the rolling countryside, so fortified since 8th century though almost annihilated in 1944 fighting. Steep valley is called Vaux de Vire. Olivier Basselin, local 15th-century worker-poet, wrote drinking songs which a 17th-century poet

Vire
continued

excellent duck Normand; also Nouvelle Cuisine in pricey menu; permanent painting exhibition; menu 50–165F; rooms 74–170F. Shut Friday evening, Saturday lunch.

France, rue d'Aigneaux, (31)68.00.35: one-star hotel; reasonable prices; the place to try Vire speciality – andouilles, black sausage of chitterling, rich in herbs; good faux-fillet of beef, too; menu 32–80F; rooms 55–110F.

published under title 'Vaux-de-Vire' – where we got the word 'vaudeville'. Bocage, local countryside of small fields, hedges (haies), rocky outcrops, unsuited to US tanks in 1944, forcing Americans to learn 'commando' fighting. Called 'War of the Hedgerows'.

D577, D977
Mortain
(25 km)

Hôtel des Cascades, rue Bassin, (33)59.00.03: looks like English corner pub; quiet; reasonable; good chef; try trout in vermouth, veal

Along hillside above river Gance, Mortain is new, but being in granite, looks old. St Evroult church, 12th century, but founded 1082 by William

brawn; sole Normande; menu 35–85F; rooms 51–115F. Shut Sunday evening, Monday.

At St Hilaire-du Harcouet (14 km on D977) – Hotel Le Cygne, rue Waldeck Rousseau, (33)49.11.84: Henri Lefaudeux has many British supporters, some of whom wrote to me. Alas, I have not yet tried his cooking but a British chef praises it highly to me. Norman dishes; menu 40–130F; wines 30–200F; rooms 80–170F (bath or shower, WC).

the Conqueror's half-brother (Count Robert). Contains church treasures.

Abbaye Blanche, on Vire road, a convent from 1120, has fine cloisters. Became missionary centre, now a seminary.

Grande Cascade (waterfall in woods) by path from Abbaye Blanche avenue.

D907 Domfront (24 km)

De France, (33)38.51.44: remarkably good value; little old hotel with gardens, tennis, sauna, private fishing; a French auberge of tradition; real old Norman dishes – sole Normande, andouillettes; house wine 16F; menu 36.50–69F. Rooms 65–137F.

Poste, rue Maréchal Foch, (33) 38.51.00: pleasant modern Logis run with charm and efficiency by Yvette Le Prise, pure Norman cooking with some of my favourites – Poulet Vallée d'Auge (chicken in cider, Calvados, cream); caille (quail) à la Normande; super lobster terrine; menu 45F (lunch), 77, 95, 120F; rooms 55–140F. Shut 5 Jan.–25 Feb.

Impressive sight – walls of Domfront castle keep and medieval ramparts of the town crowning a rock 70 m (200 ft) above the Normandy plain. Castle built 1011 by William de Bellême, military engineer, but William the Conqueror took it few years later. It had 24 towers then. Here, too, Captain Montgomery of the Scots Guards was stripped of honours before his execution. Fighting with France against England, he had accidentally killed the French King Henry II in a jousting match, making Catherine de Medici a widow and robbing Diane de Poitiers of her lover. To cap it, he had become a Calvinist and bravely defended Domfront against overwhelming Royal forces until his 150-man garrison was down to 15 wounded, starving men.

D908, D386
Bagnoles-de-
L'Orne (12 km)

Resort 1 March–30 Sept, with all grades of hotel and restaurant. Nearly all shut in winter. Tourist office at station very helpful.

At St Michel-des-Andaines (2 km N. on D908) – La Bruyère, (33)37.22.26: open all year; restaurant shut Monday. Real old village inn; wood and chintzy décor. Logis; 2-star national; menu 45–90F; rooms 90–150F. Known for local dish – tripe cooked on skewers over open fire.

Attractively well-groomed, very French spa. On a small lake formed by river Vée before it plunges into a gorge. Surrounded by lush pastures, hills and forest. Great spring gushes 11,000 gallons of water an hour at 81°F (27°C). Used for circulatory and glandular treatment. Usual spa backcloth of neat restaurants, smart shops, calm hotels. Inevitable casino; pedalos on lake. Story goes that Hugues de Tessé freed his sick old horse Rapide in the forest rather than kill him. Weeks later Rapide appeared, cured and refreshed. So Hugues followed hoof track to the 'magic' curing spring. Baths open early May – end September.

D916, N176,
N12 Alençon
(47 km)

Au Petit Vatel, pl Cdt-Desmeulles, (33)26.23.78: gourmand's 'petit paradis'. Pricey but worth every franc. Balzac wrote often of Alençon's gourmands, and chef Michel Larat, now also patron, preserves tradition. Regional dishes, plus modern inventions like mussels in spinach, peppered lamb, snails in mustard sauce. Everything meticulous, from fresh vegetables perfectly cooked to wide choice of sorbets; menu 85–118F. Shut 15 Aug.–28 Feb.

Alençon, market town on the Sarthe river, is famous for 'point d'Alençon' lace started in the 17th century to stop ladies of the court importing lace from Venice. You can see it in Museum de Peinture and Ecole Dentellière (lace school) but not see it being made.

Many lovely buildings, including the Préfecture, 17th-century palace of the Guise family. Notre Dame church, 14th-century flamboyant, has magnificent stained glass and a very flamboyant porch. Town has good open-air swimming pool.

3 km E on N138 – Château de Maleffre, (33)31.82.78: lovely château in parkland with lake. True retreat. Rooms 65–180F; eat with the family, Mon.–Thurs. evening only, 80F.

North is Ecouves forest of mixed trees with deer and wild boar; glades for picnics and good place to stretch your legs. Here French tanks under General Leclerc defeated Nazi panzers in 1944 and at Carrefour de la Croix de Medavy stands a memorial tank.

D311, D2 La Ferté-Bernard, D7, D36 Montmirail, D117 Mondoubleau (87 km)

Montmirail – Relais des Maîtres Poste, (43)93.65.11: simple, old posting inn; no bedrooms to let. Open wood fire for grills; beams; stone floor. Weekday plat du jour 30F; menu 58–100F. Wine a bit pricey; patron's wine 35F; Muscadet 48F; meals good value. Shut Wednesday.

Mondoubleau – Grand Monarque, (54)80.92.10: ancient 'relais de diligence' (public stage coach) and looks it. Super! Big arch into coach courtyard; inside fine old wooden furniture and décor; true period piece; menu 34–135F; rooms 52–72F. Shut Sunday evening, Monday.

'Ferté' means small fortress; Bernard is in lush valley of river Huisne. You can park outside 15th-century towered gateway, walk under it and through narrow shopping street to market square. Food and wine market Monday morning.

Montmirail: once important seat of seigneurs of Bas-Perche; now tiny hamlet; fine 15th-century castle, turrets and towers; no visits – private residence.

Mondoubleau: impressive remains of castle (built 10th century). Keep leans sideways; from inside, look up and think you are falling over. Baillon (5 km on D86) pleasant old village beneath restored 16th-century château.

D921 Savigny, D5 Vendôme (24 km)

Grand Hôtel du Vendôme, faubourg Chartrain, (54)77.02.88: nice atmosphere; cosy rooms, quality furnishing; local regulars praise it; menu 50–100F; rooms 125–235F. Shut Sunday, Monday in winter.

Vendôme: sort of little town I like to wander round; nothing special to see, and the old abbey church of St Trinity is higgledy-piggledy mixture of architecture from 11th to 16th century, but it has atmosphere. River Loir

Vendôme
continued

Hôtel du Château, pl Château, (54)77.20.98: most pleasant old-style bar-restaurant with rear overlooking river; menu 40–100F; rooms good value 55–115F. Shut Monday.

Auberge Madeleine, pl Madeleine, (54)79.20.79: bedrooms look on to courtyard; simple rooms but value; good cooking– try porcelet (sucking pig); chicken with crayfish sauce; menu 38–82F; rooms 50F.

Chez Annette, faubourg Chartrain, (54)77.23.03: nice old-fashioned sauces; menu good value, carte dishes rather pricey; menu 45–75F; no rooms.

(without an 'e') divides here into several arms, spanned by many bridges. Inevitable attractive hilltop castle; too much urban building at bottom of hill. Honoré de Balzac went to school at Oratorian's College in 1807. Always in trouble for rebellion, he spent much time in the punishment cell, reading in peace. Now it is a lycée – I hope with rebellious students who read what they want and become magnificent writers.

D917 Montoire
(19 cm)

Cheval Rouge, pl Foch, (54)85.07.05: Robert Velasco, owner and renowned chef, is 'Maître-Cuisinier de France'. Try his cooking and you will know why. Such generous portions, too, that I was warned to go easy on his well-known hors d'oeuvres. Full use of local ingredients in season – especially salmon. Little shaded terrace; many Loire-area wines with nice Bourguiel. Menu 62–150F; rooms 54–135F. Shut Tuesday evening, Wednesday; February.

Lavardin – Auberge Paysanne, (54)85.02.72: bar-restaurant run by artist Jean-Pierre Digne; his paintings on wall; menu 45–72F; wines 30–260F. Garden leads to river Loire.

At Montoire, on 24 Oct. 1940, Marshal Pétain, 1914–18 War hero, embittered old man, met Hitler and sold out France for a 'peace' which was not. Such a nice place for a 'sell-out'! Ruined castle; Chapelle-St-Gilles has famous murals, some 12th-century.

Lavardin, up river, is tiny photogenic hamlet; fine old buildings, truly romantic castle ruins. Climb ladder of keep to sentry walks for magnificent view. Called 'the most French of French villages'.

D9 Château
Renault (20 km)

Lion d'Or, rue République, (47)56.96.50: looks like British pub, but cooking is very French, old-style. Duck and goose dishes include confit d'oie. Terrace. Menu 40–125F; rooms 50–120F. Shut parts February, June.

Electronic and chemical industries have come to small town where rivers Brenne and Gault meet.

D31 Amboise
(23 km)

Château du Pray, Chargé (2.5 km by D751 NW, (47) 57.23.67: hotel-restaurant in lovely 13th-century château with turrets; superb park, gardens and terrace; views of Loire; pricey but good value for such splendid surroundings, furnishings and food. 'Châteaux Hôtels Indépendants' member. All Loire specialities – salmon, trout, duck; excellent

See it from north bank or the bridge. Château largely demolished after Revolution, but what is left impressive and interesting. Charles VII stole it from Counts of Amboise, Louis XI gave it to his queen. Their son, later Charles VIII, brought back from Italy in 1495 Italian artists and craftsmen who changed French artistic styles. In 1498 Charles

Amboise
continued

patîsseries; menu 95, 120F; rooms 210–240F. Shut Jan.

Auberge du Mail, quai Gen. de Gaulle, (47)57.60.39: some delightful 'simple' dishes, like filet en Chevreuil (beef fillet cooked like venison – larded, marinated, roasted); liver confit in Vouvray wine; also most unusual dishes – trout stuffed with Roquefort with a creamed port sauce. Young chef-owner, François Le Clos, already building big reputation; menu 60–115F; remarkable wine list with vintages back to 1893; rooms 70–150F. Shut January.

La Bréche, rue Jules-Ferry, (47)57.00.79: near station; popular with locals; straightforward dishes; good value; rillette, tongue, ray, good terrine, salmon; nice cheeses including Tomme, goat's cheese; garden tables; menu 38–50F; rooms 44–105F.

cracked his head on a low lintel and died. Louis XII continued the work. Francis I turned it into centre of court junketings, with magnificent festivals, balls, masquerades, tournaments, even fights between wild animals. He brought Leonardo da Vinci here and the great artist finished his life at the nearby manor house.

Catherine de Medici, widowed queen, brought her boy-king son, Francis II and his girl wife Mary, later Queen of Scots, here when Protestants were rising up after St Bartholomew's Day massacre.

A foolish Protestant arranged for others to meet him at Amboise to start a revolt in 1560. Betrayed to powerful Duke of Guise ('Scarface') they were tortured, broken and hanged from castle balconies, still writhing in agony for days. Royals and

Bellevue, quai Charles Guinot, (47)57.02.26: views over Loire; at foot of Château; solid-looking, white-painted hotel with bits added; terrace; comfortable bedrooms; try excellent scallop and leek tart; magret of duck with green peppers; shellfish crêpes; menu 60–90F; wines 25–65F; rooms 85–150F.

La Bonne Etape, rte Chaumont, (47)57.08.09: good food; Loire fish; duck 'à l'orange'. Pretty garden, menu 65–90F; no rooms.

Auberge de la Ramberge, across Lire on two bridges at Posé sur Cisse, on Château – Renault road, (47)57.27.58: little inn with outstanding cooking; excellent fish, including shad, sandre and anguille (Loire eel); menu 50–150F; superb terrines (wild duck, wild boar, venison, hare, scampi, smoked salmon); good long list of Loire wines; rooms 70–150F. Shut 1 Nov.–1 March.

Court would come out after dinner to watch them. But the royal family were destroyed too – the boy king, Francis II died within months, his brother Charles IX, after a bloodstained reign, died in terror and remorse. Duke of Guise and Henry III both murdered and Mary Stuart was beheaded.

In Clos Lucé (15th century) are da Vinci's bedroom, copies of his drawings, and models of machines he invented. Hôtel de Ville has fascinating museum of the Post, including letters, envelopes and postage stamps.

D31 La Croix-en-Touraine, D40 Chenonceaux (14 km)

Chenonceaux – Au Gâteau Breton, rue Bretonneau, (47)29.90.14: tourist restaurant with remarkable value. Menu at 28F offers hors d'oeuvres; roast beef and haricots verts or ¼ chicken, rice creole; salad; fruit or ice. Menu at 39F excellent, with wine! Menu 28–50F; wine from 15F.

Château de Chenonceaux is the most beautiful castle I have ever seen; more, it is the most beautiful *house*, for it was designed by a woman, Katherine Briconnet, between 1513 and 1521 to be lived in; not by a man to withstand attack or siege. Another woman, sexy Diane du Poitiers, mistress of Henry II (who kept her in funds by levying a large tax on church

Chenonceaux
continued

Du Bon Laboureur et du Château, rue Bretonneau, (47)29.90.02: *the* famous Chenonceaux restaurant 'gourmand'; prices reasonable for such quality; river fish used extensively – pike mousse and quenelle; crayfish; sandre; little eels; also well-known local duck and chicken; super vegetable soup; alas, wines are too dear; menu 75–135F; charming rooms 110–210F (half pension only in season). Shut 1 Nov.–1 April.

bells), added a lovely garden and bridge between the château and Cher river banks. When Henry was killed accidentally in a jousting match, his wife Catherine de Medici took Chenonceaux from Diane and banished her to the draughty pile of Château Chaumont, which she soon left. Catherine had the splendid two-storey gallery built on the bridge, and laid out the superb park. She held incredible parties, with mermaids, nymphs, satyrs and cavaliers welcoming guests from moat. The stories of intrigue, love affairs and politics of Chenonceaux could not possibly be told in this space. See it for yourself and read a book on it – very rewarding. Open daily. Son et lumière performances in summer (mid June – mid Sept., start 10 pm but check this); also has wax museum with scenes from its history.

N76
Montrichard
(8 km)

Bellevue, quai du Cher, (54)32.06.17: 3-star, on river bank; part modernized; much praise for hostess Mme Ginette Dauzet; traditional cooking; menu 60, 84, 120F; rooms (bath, WC) 195F. Shut Tuesday in winter; 15 Nov. – 15 Dec.

La Tête Noire, rue du Tours, (54)32.05.55: cosy; short walk from river; traditional cooking; menu 50F (weekdays), 85, 115F; Touraine wine 30–50F; rooms 75–160F.

Old houses and streets (rue Nationale) more attractive than ruined castle. Church of Ste-Croix, with lovely Romanesque door, is where poor Jeanne de France (aged 12, hunchbacked, crippled and twisted face) was married by Louis XI to Louis of Orleans, heir to the throne. When he became Louis XII he discarded her by a disgraceful legal trick to marry Anne of Brittany, widow of Charles VIII. He wanted to keep Brittany.

La Bûcherie – La Strada, (54)32.13.10: Búcherie is grille-crepêrie; Strada is restaurant in beamed 11th-century chapel; menu 40–75F; large carte.

Another church at Nanteuil (330 yards W of Montrichard) has statue of the Virgin where pilgrims come on Whit Monday. Its power is to cure fear! In swamps near by lived in the Dark Ages a monster who fed on cattle and children. A young monk waded in alone carrying only a veil from the Virgin's statue and led the monster to the church using the veil as bait. People still come to pray for courage. Wine kept to mature in quarries upstream.

over river Cher, left on D17 St Aignan (17 km)

Grand Hôtel, quai Jean Jacques Delorne, (54)75.18.04: over-looking river; handsome, arcaded buildings; good period furniture; meals very good value. We had 65F menu with asparagus (or avocado); sea bream in Bercy sauce (wine, shallot); coq au Gamay (chicken in red wine); dessert (choice); excellent 85F menu too; river fish, game; menu 48-100F; rooms 48-155F. Shut 15 Dec.–1 Feb.

Fine old town of wood and plaster houses and shops. Renaissance château; private home, but you can climb monumental staircase to courtyard to see lovely views over Cher valley and Choussy forest. 11th-century church with wall paintings of 12th-15th centuries. River beach on island reached by causeway; grass banks for sunbathing; boats, attractive little town.

D17 Poulas
D33, D37,
Valençay
(21 km)
D956
Châteauroux
(43 km)

Valançay – Lion d'Or, pl de la Halle, (54)00.00.87: reasonable prices, good value; menus 37.50–95F; wines from 12.50F; rooms 55–120F; Restaurant shut Jan., Feb.

Châteauroux – Restaurant Jean Bardet at Hotel Elysée, rue J. J. Rousseau, (54)34.82.69: Jean Bardet is acclaimed by every guide; how right! Light Nouvelle Cuisine without the usual nonsense of mixing the unmixable for show. None of the fashionable 'curried cucumber with minted raspberry ice-cream' touches. Beautiful light dishes, some traditional dishes, too. Superb desserts. Menu 68–165F; rooms 135–210F.

Continental, ave Verdun, (54)34.36.12: good value, cheap bar-tabac-restaurant-hotel. Plat du jour 25F; menu 38–45F; rooms 55–75F.

Du Parc, av Paris, (54)34.36.83: modern; comfortable; reasonably priced; good old style cooking; trout in almonds; veal escalope in cream sauce; confit of goose; menu 42–80F; rooms 62–125F. local wines rather pricey. Restaurant only shut November; Saturday in winter.

Valençay is called a 'financier's château', like most in Loire Valley, built for love, parties, intrigue and show, not defence, despite its keep and turrets (all harmless). Built by penniless aristocrat who married financier's daughter; fell into hands of Scottish whiz-kid financier John Law of Lauriston who became Finance Minister of France, sent himself, his companies and nearly France bankrupt with his banking theories; then Talleyrand got it – 'middling bishop, but very eminent knave'. The ultimate 'Vicar of Bray' – following every cause and leader who was on top, from French Revolution to Napoleon, to French kings. 'Patron of Time Servers and Turncoats'. A bribe-taker in Mafia manner.

Park has flamingoes, peacocks, parrots, llamas.

Châteauroux: industrial town. Became English as part of Eleanor of Aquitaine's dowry when she married Henry Plantagenet (Henry II of England) in 1152. Castle and title of Duchess of Châteauroux given by Louis XV to youngest of three Mail sisters, each of whom became his mistress.

D943 Nohant,
La Châtre
(36 km)

Nohant-Vic – Auberge Petite Fadette, (54)31.01.48: typical old village inn catering also for visitors to George Sand's

Visit house where writer George Sand spent her childhood and teenage years.

house; try 'poulet au sang' (local speciality); menu 50–80F; rooms 50–110F. Shut Tuesday.

Châtre – Poste, Basse-du-Moulet, (54)49.05.62: nice, truly rustic restaurant serving straight local dishes (andouillette, oeufs en cocotte; poulet au sang; ris de veau); menu 50–150F; wine from 12F.

Lion d'Argent, (54)48.11.69: hotel offers weekends with tuition at its car-racing school 'Ecole Formula 3'; menu 50–120F; rooms 55–160F.

Auberge du Moulin-Bureau, (54)48.04.20: lovely creeper-clad restaurant beside river, 2 km from La Châtre; mill mechanism still in bar; beamed dining room; open fire; river fish, including fish soup; good trout; menu 45–90F. Shut Tuesday evening, Wednesday.

She came back to its peace and quiet to write, and died here in 1876. A charming house, it looks as if she has just popped out for a few minutes. Dinner is laid, Chopin's piano awaits the Master's touch; in her bedroom is the 'desk' where she wrote some of her masterpieces – a shelf in a doorless cupboard. Even the kitchen, with its old utensils, is interesting. Drawings for theatre and marionettes by her son Maurice Sand. Her name was Aurore Dupin de Franceuil. She caused a scandal in Paris when young by dressing like her boy friend – cropped hair, frock coat, top hat; stormy liaison with poet Musset; then with composer Chopin. Her house called locally 'château'. Shut Tuesday.

La Châtre, on a hill, has a museum of George Sand in Chauvigny castle; also collection of coiffes – headdresses of area.

D943 Château-
meillant, Mont-
luçon (62 km)

Châteaumeillant produces
nice red wines from Pinot
Noir and Gamay grapes.
VDQS (Vin Delimité de
Qualité Supérieur) – two up
on Vin Ordinaire.

Montluçon: factory town on
river Cher, but attractive and
old with narrow streets. 15th-
century castle occupied by
préfecture.

N144 Néris les
Bains, St Eloy-
les-Mines 4 km
later turn right
on D987 St
Gervais-
d'Auvergne
D227
Châteauneuf-
les-Bains (58
km) (if winter
conditions are
bad, stay on
N144 to Riom)

Néris – Le Garden,
(70)03.21.16: Le Garden has
a jardin – quiet and pretty,
with terrace. Pleasant hotel;
Bourgundian cooking
(fondue, coq au vin); menu
42–80F; house wine 24F;
rooms 100–130F.

St Gervais – Hotel de la
Place, (73)85.72.04: neat little
Relais Gastronomique (they
eat well and plenty in
Auvergne); menu 40–70F;
rooms 70–75F.

Castel, rue Gare,
(73)85.70.42: try mountain
ham (raw), local trout; menu
40F (weekdays); 60–90F;
wine from 23F; rooms 55–
150F. Shut part January.

Châteauneuf – du Château,
(73)86.67.01: delightful old-
style Logis with period
furniture; local dishes and
ingredients; chicken in
crayfish sauce; trout from
river Sioule, coq au vin
(Auvergne people claim they,
not Burgundy, invented it).
Menu 38, 65F; wines from
10F; rooms 50–150F. Shut 1
Oct.–30 April.

Néris: old town stands
above valley where spa is
situated. Into the Auvergne,
still known to many Britons
only for Stevenson's *Travels
With a Donkey*, and by-
passed by the French.
Rugged beauty; dramatic
views; volcanic peaks, many
of bare rock with fertile
valleys and hidden villages.
Turbulent countryside.
Streams from hill springs run
to lakes, warm in summer.
Castles of robber-barons
abound, ruined by Richelieu.
Superb run but check
conditions.

St Gervais: wonderful views
on horizon of des Dômes
and massif of Monts Dore;
best seen from terrace of
12th-century church.
Attractive little resort.

10 km on D987, D62 –
Viaduct des Fades, 290 m
(302 ft) high, tallest railway
viaduct in Europe; lovely
valley.

Châteauneuf-les-Bains: has
14 cold springs, 8 warm,
treating rheumatism,

Hôtel des Meritis, (73)86.67.88: delightful position off road, by river and spa baths; fine garden; terrace; peaceful; nice old building; quite simple but excellent value; home-made rabbit terrine; Auvergne ham; 'friture' of river fish; Sioule trout; coq au vin; tripeux; menu 31, 53.50F; regional wines (St Pourcain; Chateaugay); rooms 45–70F. Shut 1 Oct.–30 April.

anaemia, and 'drying out' alcoholics. 15 million bottles of it's water sold each year. Most attractive resort in valley by river Sioule (jumping with trout); from hamlet Pic Alibert lovely views from beside Virgin's statue; views too from St Cyr beside ruins of old church, by loop in river.

D227 Manzat, Châtelguyon, Mozac, almost to Riom (33 km)

Châtelguyon – Le Cantalon, St Hippolyte, (73)86.04.67: on edge of resort; quiet; garden; mountain and country views; good value; Auvergne specialities; menu 35–55F; wines 10F litre of red; house wine 15F; rooms 56–90F. Shut 1 Nov.–1 March.

La Grilloute, ave Baraduc, (73)86.04.17: Jacqueline Brandibat has cooked Auvergne dishes here for 20 years; regular loyal customers (local and visitors); terrines; trout in wine; sole flambé à la crème; prices most

Beautiful run continues. Châtelguyon: important summer resort on Sardon river; old houses; fine parks; thirty springs, rich in magnesium; spring water at 27–38°C (80–100°F) for treatment of liver and intestines; at Calvaire (cross) on site of old castle, orientation table; good walks; car-tour centre; several castles near by.

Château de Chazeron (3 km D78E) – attractively fierce-looking; 17th-century additions to feudal castle; handsome steps and terrace. Open 1 May–31 Oct.

Châtalguyon
continued

reasonable, including carte; menu 50–65F; closed Tuesday; 10 Oct.–15 May.

Manoir Fleuri (1 km on D78E), (73)86.01.27: high up, in open country, wonderful mountain views; quiet; flower garden; no restaurant; very comfortable; rooms 66–145F. Shut 15 Oct. – Easter.

Château Davayet (NW on N685, D15, 5.5 km), delightful old house of Louis XIII period with furnishings, pictures, arms and fittings of the time; park, chapel; pavillion with souvenirs of the Revolution.

Mozac's old abbey church (12th century) has many treasures including early Limousin enamel work and 12th-century sculptures of historic as well as artistic interest.

Riom: pleasant old town, surrounded by nice tree-lined boulevards; lovely fountains including Adam and Eve (16th century). Museum Mandet has works of Breughel, Hals, Watteau, Titian, El Rosso.

D986 from Mozac to Volvic (7km)

Château Tournoël (32 km along D15 towards Châteauneuf), superb romantic ruins on spur of rock; 12th century; enough left to be a dwelling; worth seeing. Gorgeous view from terrace.

Volvic: open cast mining of andesite, a fine-grained rock from volcanic lava – light, tough, acid-resistant, used in building, artistic works and industry; gives some Auvergne buildings a violet colour.

4 km take left D941 to outskirts Clermont-Ferrand, right

Clermont-Ferrand: former capital of Auvergne; two superb churches – Gothic cathedral, and basilica; old parts of city interesting but too large to be detailed here.

on D941 past
Puy de Dôme
to meet N89,
right to
Rochfort-
Montagne,
Laqueuille
(42 km)

Much industry. Home town
of Michelin tyres; grew from
little factory started by Scots
woman to make rubber balls
for her children and friends.

Puy de Dôme: one of chain
of Dôme mountains which
stretch 30 km, with 60
volcanoes – the highest (1465
m), and oldest, best known.
A holy mountain for
centuries, first for the
Auvernes people and their
god Lug; then Romans, who
built a temple to Mercury; in
12th century a little Christian
chapel built to St Barnabé,
St Paul's companion. When
chapel disappeared, locals
believed it was inhabited by
sorcerers. Blaise Pascal sent
his brother-in-law up in 1648
with a barometer to prove
the weight of air
(atmospheric pressure
decreases with weight). Drive
up (small fee), but road
blocked by snow Dec. –
April. Magnificent panorama
from top, showing volcanoes
of mountain chain, mostly
with big craters. On good
days you can see 11
départements making up an
eighth of France. Visibility
changes minute by minute.
Spectacular scene at sunset.

N89 Bourg-
Lastic, D987
(former N687)
Tauves, left on
D922, right on
D996 to St
Sauves-
d'Auvergne,

Le Mont-Dore – winter and
summer resort, so many
hotels and restaurants.
Tourist office, ave Gen.
Leclerc, (73)81.18.88.

Bourg-Lastic: in pastures and
pine forests, good fishing.
Road to Tauves winding,
mountainous, very beautiful,
through Gorge d-Avez, with
superb views; but only take it
if you have reasonable
weather and time (24 km –
see alternative in column 1).

N496 La Bourboule, Le Mont-Dore (71 km) (in bad weather, take D922 from Laqueuille to St Sauves d'Auvergne)

Hôtel de l'Oise, ave de la Tour, (73)65.04.68: good traditional cooking; coq au vin; trout; entrecôte with Auvergne blue cheese. Pleasant hotel on hillside; garden-terrace with fine mountain views; friendly. Menu 50, 70F; house wine 22F; rooms 80–160F. Open 15 May–30 Sept.; 20 Dec. – Easter.

Le Panorama, (73)65.11.13: modern mountain-style, lots of pine; bright; views; three-star, good duck dishes; salmon; menu 60–110F; wines from 24F; rooms 85–190F. Shut mid-April to mid-May; 1 Oct. – 20 Dec.

Bourboule: 850 m (about 2500 ft) above sea level; spa and resort in valley of Dordogne (upper Dordogne has hydro-electric dams, which is why it is no good for carrying wine further down now). Bourboule springs (hot and cold) have more arsenic than any others in Europe; also sodium; used to treat respiratory troubles (including asthma), skin troubles, allergies. Attractive valley; parks, casino.

Le Mont-Dore: another spa. Waters used to treat respiratory troubles. 1050 (about 3450 ft) up; hot springs known to Romans; remains of their baths inside present thermal building. Fine mountain views, from casino in particular; winter spots centre.

D996 Lac Chambon, Murol, St Nectaire, Issoire (51 km)

Murol – Du Parc, (73)88.60.08: local Auvergne and mountain dishes: Teyssier family proudly boast 'cuisine bourgeoise très soignée'; menu 50–70F; wine from 12F; rooms 75–160F. Shut 1 Oct.–31 Jan.

St Nectaire – La Bel Air, (73)88.50.42: older hotel with modern annexe; family atmosphere. Try potée Auvergnate – super soup-stew of meat and vegetables (in very old times, it would include a cabbage, leg of pork, lump of bacon, turnips, hock of veal, side of beef, boiling fowl, simmered over log fire for five hours); also

Lac Chambon is a large, shallow lake produced by a volcano; 877 m (2877 ft) up, pretty escarpment to north, 100 m (328 ft) high, called Saut de la Pucelle. A shepherdess, trying to shake off enthusiastic molesting by a seigneur, jumped over it without damaging herself. To convince disbelievers she tried again. Alas, she died. Murol Château has had a mixed history from 13th century, having belonged to the great d'Estaing family and been a brigand's lair.

St Nectaire: during Wars of Religion, beautiful girl who lived at castle, Madeleine de St Nectaire, joined

coq au vin, trout in almonds; good pâtisseries; menu 43, 65F; rooms 52–120F. Shut 5 Nov.–20 Dec.

La Paix, (73)88.50.20: attractive country-inn style; large garden; local dishes (potée Auvergnate; salmon crêpe; good pâtisseries); menu 45–70F; wines from 20F; rooms 55–110F. Shut Nov., Dec., March, April (open for groups).

Issoire – La Pariou, ave Kennedy, (73)89.22.11: modern; neatly furnished; Logis. Charcuterie (area speciality); coq qu vin; trout in almond cream; good value; menu 36–60F; wines from 25F; rooms 75–112F. Shut part Sept., part May.

Protestants, beat the King's Lieutenant of Haute-Auvergne in battle and killed him with her own hand. Another spa (25 May – 30 Sept.), within 10 minutes of ski slopes.

Issoire: on Couze river; little village in lush country which became small industrial centre in World War II – now makes much of France's car electrics. Splendid old Romanesque church; 15th-century mural of the last judgement must have scared peasants stiff. Château de Parentignat (4 km back on D996) – elegant 18th-century Louis XIV château; lovely furniture; good paintings; marble staircase; tapestries of Auvergne countryside. (Open 1 July–30 Sept. Shut Wednesday.

N9 Lempdes, N102 Brioude (34 km) (NB: In snowy weather, check at Lempdes on route ahead. If necessary, drive direct on N9 Lempdes to Montpellier.)

Brioude – La poste et Champanne, bd Dr Devins, (71)50.14.62: good value; very modern, comfortable annexe in garden; restaurant takes coach parties; Auvergne dishes. Menu 40–70F; rooms 60–100F. Open all year.

Julien, rue d'Assa, (71)50.14.62: good cheap little restaurant for Auvergne specialities; menu 37–50F. Shut October.

La Vieille Auberge, (71)50.15.93: creeper-clad old Logis; simple; good value; menu 35–45F; rooms 55–90F. Shut Sunday out of season.

Brioude: agricultural market town; salmon fishing industry; salmon have to jump dam in swimming up river Allier; old houses; 12th-14th-century church with 13th-century frescoes (Triumph of Virtue).

N102 Vieille Brioude, D585 Langeac, St Arcons-d'Allier (38 km)

Reilhac (3 km before Langeac on D585) – Hotel du Val d'Allier, (71)77.02.11: simple inn; menus change meal to meal; try 'parfait' chicken pâté; pike mousse, snails; menu 30–68F; rooms 62–95F.

Winding route follows lovely valley of river Allier – beginning of spectacular Gorge d'Allier.

Langeac is in fertile farming stretch.

Alternatives – (from St Arcons) D585 direct by Saugues (15 km) or beautiful, winding, rougher route (not for winter) – left on D48 Prades, D301 St Privat-d'Allier, D589 Monistrol-d'Allier, Saugues (about 46 km)

Prades – Chalet de la Source (on D585 to St Julien), (71)74.02.39: old-style mountain Logis with excellent cooking by Henri Mollon; try special sausage in wine: cèpes (delightful fungi) in Provençale sauce; local salmon; salmis de pintadeau (guinea fowl in wine); good value weekday 55F menu; superb gastronomic 140F menu; others at 75, 100F; wines from 25F; rooms 75–150F. Shut 30 Sept.–31 May.

St Privat – Vieille Auberge, (81)57.20.56: pleasant mountain inn with good

Alternative route through Prades goes into wilds of Auvergne, winding, sometimes narrow roads (not for winter or bad visibility); magnificent, really rugged scenery in gorge of river Allier. Well worth extra time and effort. View from D48 before Prades, just after St Julian, look left – isolated chapel at foot of great rock.

Prades is charming, shut-in village.

Monistrol is in one of best positions in whole Allier valley. Magnificent views.

Saugues is a market town.

cooking; potée Auvergnate; duck 'à l'orange'; do try Dalle régence (soufflé of calves' brains and mushrooms – delicious); house wine 18F; menu 33–70F; rooms 45–85F. Shut part Oct., 1 Jan.–1 March.

D589, D989 St. Chély-d'Apcher (41 km) N9, N106 St Amans, Rieutort-de-Randon, Mende, Florac (82 km) (total 123 km)

St Chély – Jeanne d'Arc, ave Gare, (66)31.00.46: rather grey-looking inn with far from grey welcome; regional dishes, especially excellent charcuterie; menus 30–60F; rooms 70–90F.

Florac – Du Parc, ave Jean Monestier, (66)45.03.05: nice rustic hotel; meals excellent value; 45F weekday menu includes chicken 'chasseur' or kidneys in Madeira; try also local duck, salmon, trout; menu 45–100F; rooms 70–165F. Shut Sunday evening, Monday out of season; 1 Dec.–1 March.

Mende: centre for touring Gorges du Tarn; 730 m (2400 ft) above sea level on ridge above river Lot. Attractive; cathedral built 1365, damaged by Protestants (including bell weighing 20 tons – biggest in Christendom). Old streets down to river, 14th-century bridge. Brave, fanatical Protestant leader Capitaine Merle (penniless aristocrat – 'brave as 50,000 devils') took Mende in revenge for massacre of Protestants by Catholics on St Bartholomew's Day.

Zoo (7 km on N107 at Chastel Nouvel) has wolves, lynx, bison, etc. in pine woods. (1 June–30 Sept.)

Round Corniche des Cévennes (in bad winter weather very difficult, so take D907 direct) D907 St Laurent-de-Trèves D983, then D9 on right to Le Pompidou, Col de St Pierre, D260, D909 St Jean-du-Gard (53 km)

St Jean-du-Gard – L'Oronge, (66)85.30.34: delightful inn – 17th-century Relais de Poste – balconies from bedrooms look on to courtyard where meals are taken in summer; otherwise in old beamed dining room; most bedrooms have WC and bath or shower; try pintadeau aux cèpes; river fish; menu 35–90F; rooms 70–160F. Shut 20 Jan.–1 April.

Superb route above gorges and valleys with wonderful views. Very winding. One of the great roads of France on a clear day. Experts say that late afternoon light is best.

St Jean-du-Gard: little old town with clock tower and picturesque old bridge with six arches, rebuilt after being swept away in 1958. Here Robert Louis Stevenson, in his Travels With a Donkey, parted with Modestine, his wilful donkey companion.

D907 Anduze (14 km)	At Mialet, near Anduze (8 km on D129 to Générargues, left on D50) – Hôtel des Grottes de Trabuc, beside river, (66)85.32.81: nice country cooking; menu 44–65F; wines 13–37F; rooms 65–110F. Open 1 April – 30 Sept.	Anduze: green oasis among arid rock; beside a deep cleft; old tortuous streets.
D35 Quissac (19 km)	(to Nîmes, Arles, Avignon, Aix en Provence, Côte d'Azur)	Museum of the 'Désert' (8 km on D129 to Générargues, left on D50, D50A to Mas Soubeyran). Out here in rocky 'desert' Protestant resistance movement operated when made illegal from revocation of Edict of Nantes (1685) until Edict de Tolérance (1787); remarkable stories of persecution, courage, of poor peasants; museum in house of Roland, Protestant leader, includes room of history of thousands sent to slave galleys. Now shrine to French Protestants.
D45, D17 to Montpellier (40 km)	(for Sète, Agde, Perpignan, Spain)	

Route 3
Le Havre/Dieppe to
Dourdan, through
Burgundy, Savoie to Nice

A route for wine-tasters, lovers of mountain scenery and gourmets.

Dourdan is a little place south-east of Paris. Route from Le Havre takes in the charming town of Pont Audemer and crosses pleasant Norman scenery through the green Risle valley. Dieppe route is through the lovely Lyons forest which few tourists know. You run into the crowds at Fontainebleau, but worth it to see the forest and the palace. You cross the Loire at Sully, stop for good wine-tasting at Sancerre – a gem; from Nevers, quieter, lonelier country across to Mâcon – quite rugged.

Through foothills of the Alps to Grenoble, then on Route Napoléon, considered quite a test of a car with cable brakes and old-time steering when we went to Cannes in the 1940s. Impressive scenery, with a few desolate stretches, and some splendid scenery, especially around Digne and Corniche Sublime. After Castellane, you start coming into tourist country at Grasse, but very pleasant. Few know the grandeur and wildness of the Route Napoléon these days.

Mâcon is a few miles from Lyons, capital of French gastronomy, and Bourg en Bresse is not only famous for its chickens, but also its cooking. In Burgundy, try Ecrivisses à la Nage (crayfish in the wine and herb court-bouillon in which they were cooked); Pruneaux au Bourgogne (prunes stewed in wine). Poulet de Bresse is not a phrase used lightly for chicken; they are protected by law and lead a nice life, fed well on corn and allowed to wander fields, with a lead ring round one leg.

Cooking in the Savoy and Dauphine may be a little less sophisticated but is often very tasty; dishes like Gratin de Queues d'Ecrivisses – poached crayfish tails in cream sauce with crisp crust of breadcrumbs and butter. Various Tome cheeses are splendid; best known in Britain is Tome aux Raisins – cow's milk cheese in mixture of grape skins, stalks and pips which flavour it. But few of the cheeses on this route surpass those of Normandy at the start.

Savoie wines are mostly white, and not to be compared with white Burgundy or Sancerre. Mâcon red may not be quite so good as true Beaujolais – but I have never refused it.

Route 3 North

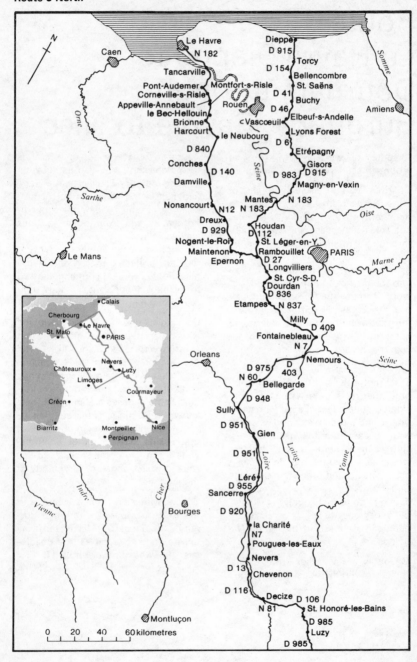

Route 3 South

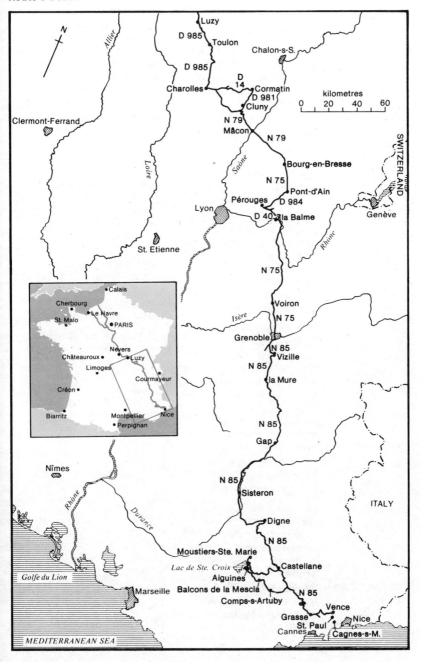

Le Havre

Badly-off for hotels except chain hotels for businessmen, and not in the top league for meals. Cheap, quick, filling meals are available from the line of restaurants on quai Southampton opposite Townsend booking office.

Monaco, rue de Paris, (35)42.21.01: Max Lucas, once maître d'hotel on liner *France*, and his young Breton chef offer enormous choice with wide price-range. Near dock gates; very popular. Try jugged duck in Bouzy wine, cassoulet of lobster Neuberg, kidneys in Calvados; usually has superb oysters; Norman apple soufflé; menu 55–150F; rooms 85–145F. Shut late Feb., early Sept.

Mon Auberge, rue Gen-Sarrail, (35)42.44.36: Odette Mailly cooks superbly but has only six tables, so book ahead. Evenings only; menu 52F; à la carte dishes include turbot with wonderful Dieppoise sauce of cream, shrimps, mussels and wine, excellent terrines of rabbit and duck, and apple tart, Normandy style. Shut Sunday, early August.

La Chaumette, rue Racine, (35)43.66.80; small, popular, expensive, thatched roof, fake beams amid Le Havre's concrete and glass; very good for fish and duck; dishes according to what is fresh in the market and 'the knowledge and inspiration' of

A modern town with 'son of Corbusier' architecture, planned after terrible wartime destruction. Avenue Foch is like a modern version of Champs Elysées, with many shops at expensive Paris level. Auguste Perrett's place de l'Hotel de Ville is one of Europe's largest squares. Arcaded rue de Paris, leading from the square towards the port, is useful for window shopping in rain or wind; windows of elegant clothes, tempting food. Huge concrete Church of St Joseph has eight-sided belfry 116 m (348 ft) high, and interior has an awesome lantern tower and remarkable inside lighting effects by coloured glass set in the walls; interesting building.

The Musée des Beaux-Arts, in glass and steel, facing the sea, has splendid light to show off Impressionist paintings, including seventy by Dufy, others by Sisley, Boudin and Pissaro.

the chef-patronne Christine Frechet. You must book; menu 120F. Shut Saturday, Sunday; late August.

La Petite Auberge, rue St Adresse, (35)46.27.32: used by locals; good fish; good value; menu 58–75F. Shut Monday, August.

At St Adresse, suburb NE – Beausejour, pl Clemencau, (35)46.19.69: right beside sea, with panoramic views; many superb fish dishes; live lobsters; menu 70–145F; wines 40–800F.

N182, D982 Tancarville Bridge (toll) (29 km) D180 Pont-Audemer

Pont-Audemer: three superb restaurants here – Auberge du Vieux Puits, Le Petit Coq and La Fregate. All very dear. La Fregate, rue La Seule, (32)41.12.03: cheapest. Lovely crab soup and moules à la crème; menu 85F plus carte; wines 45–350F. Shut Aug.; Sun. eves, Monday.

Au Rendez-vous des Chauffeurs, rue Notre Dame, (32)41.04.36: where I usually eat. Next door to Vieux Puits – a Relais Routiers. Splendid value menu at 28–45F. Simple, cheap rooms.

Little port on several branches of river Risle. One of my favourite hideaways for 43 years; many of its old wood and brick riverside houses luckily survived war damage; so did streets and courtyards off rue de la République, and St Ouen church, started in 11th century. Its superb Renaissance stained glass by no means clashes with modern windows by Max Ingrand, with their unusual use of colour. The 17th-century Auberge du Vieux Puits, once my favourite, now a bit film-set inside, with Michelin rosette and prices beyond me. Food as good as ever.

N180
Corneville-sur-
Risle, D130
Appeville-
Annebault,
Montfort-sur-
Risle, Le Bec-
Hellouin
(22 km)

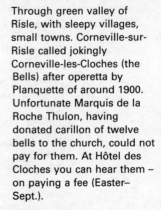

Through green valley of Risle, with sleepy villages, small towns. Corneville-sur-Risle called jokingly Corneville-les-Cloches (the Bells) after operetta by Planquette of around 1900. Unfortunate Marquis de la Roche Thulon, having donated carillon of twelve bells to the church, could not pay for them. At Hôtel des Cloches you can hear them – on paying a fee (Easter–Sept.).

Appeville-Annebault: inside 16th-century church is collection of Brothers of Charity staffs.

Montfort is pretty - willows overhanging stream; forest to its streets; overlooked by ruined castle built by King John of England.

Bec-Hellouin (just off road on left) – Benedictine monastery with English links since William the Conqueror. The Italian Langfranc studied here. For fixing William's marriage to his cousin with the Pope, William made him Archbishop of Canterbury and virtual ruler of England when William was warring in Normandy. Another Italian Bec graduate, Anselm, followed him. Another Bec old Boy was Gundulf, Bishop of Rochester, Kent, designer of Tower of London. Abbey restored 1948 (shut Tues). Museum of vintage cars beside abbey entrance (open 15 March–30 Sept.)

D130 Brionne
(6 km)
D137 Harcourt,
Le Neubourg
(15 km)

Logis de Brionne, pl St Denis, (32)44.81.73: high-grade Logis de France; reliable 'cuisine du marche' – fresh seasonal food, so menus change; good game and duck dishes; good wine list; menu 40–85F; rooms 60–120F. Shut Sunday evening, Monday lunch, part Oct., 5 Dec.–15 Jan.

Aub, Vieux Donjon, rue Soie (32)44.80.62: old, timbered restaurant; interesting courtyard; log fire; outstanding value, especially 40F weekday menu; good choice; nice touches such as individual copper dishes and casseroles; highly recommended; menu 40–120F; rooms 70–90F. Shut Monday, Sunday evening out of season; part Oct., part Feb.

Le Neubourg – Soleil d'Or, pl du Chateau, (32)35.00.52: former Logis; nice fish ragôut with crayfish; ham braised in wine; menu 36F (weekdays), 50, 78F; rooms 82–180F.

Sprawling market town; pleasant; on little isles formed by branches of river Risle; watched-over by ruins of a castle-keep (12th century).

Harcourt: castle was original seat of one of oldest families in France (d'Harcourt). English took it in 1418. Various owners until taken over by French Academy of Agriculture in 1828. Grounds open to public (except Dec., Jan.), planted with rare trees; marked walks through park.

D601 left at Rouge Perriers leads to Ste Opportune-du-Bosc and Château Champ-de-Bataille, given to Harcourt family after their other château, Thury-Harcourt destroyed in 1944. Lovely, 17th-century; huge courtyard; inside superb furniture, tapestries, paintings, historic relics. (Shut Wednesday.)

D840 Conches-en-Ouches
(17 km)

La Grand'mare, ave Croix de Fer, (32)30.23.30; charming Logis with 10 pleasant rooms; opposite small lake; good value; patron-chef Jean Dubois cooks very well; try mussels in cream sauce, apple and Calvados soufflé, crab soup; menu 55–150F, rooms 60–95F. Shut Tues.

You pass on the way Château de Beaumesnil, a 17th-century house, reflected in its moat, in a classical French park; farm maintained since 1640; ponds, labyrinth of yews made from foundations of medieval dungeons. Curious line of owners, from Harcourt family

Conches-en-Ouches *continued*	La Toque Blanche, pl Carnot, (32)30.01.54: fun restaurant with Norman cooking; old Norman building with staff dressed in Norman costume; menu 60–89F.	to Lord Willoughby (a present from Henry V), Marquis de Nonant, Grand Duke Dimitri of Russia and Jean de Furstenberg. A gorgeous house.
D140 Damville, D51, then immediately right on D50 to Nonancourt, N12 Dreux (39 km)	Dreux – Auberge Normande, pl Metezeau, (37)46.74.51: a splendid classical chef who stands firm against fashionable gourmets, who urge him to give up creamy, alcoholic sauces and take to the light and fairy. Try his tournedos à la Royale – like Rossini with port and crayfish; turbot with scallops and vermouth; good Norman cooking for gourmands and gourmandisors – epicures and gluttons; menu 72–120F. Shut Sunday; August.	Dreux: busy market town; once a frontier town between Normandy and France. Constantly besieged.
D229 Nogent-le-Roi, D983 Maintenon, D906 Epernon, Rambouillet (48 km)	Rambouillet – at Gazeran, 4 km on D906: Villa Marinette, 483.19.01: delightful creeper-clad inn with pretty flower garden; near forest. Ile de France cooking (Paris-style) mixed with Alsatian; good tourist menu 45F; gastronomic menu 100F; wines from 25F, Shut Tuesday evening Wednesday; 16 Aug. – 15 Sept.	Maintenon: the imposing château, built in Middle Ages, was bought by Louis XIV for the widow Françoise Scarron – 'Madame de Maintenon' – his mistress, later his morganatic wife. Lovely furniture and interesting family portraits. Park laid out by Le Nôtre; shut Friday in summer; open only Sat., Sun. afternoons in winter. Epernon: ancient hillside town with winding streets, above two rivers that meet. Rambouillet: Francis I, rival of our Henry VIII, died here in the château (built 1375). In

17th century the Marquise gave great fêtes of art and poetry here. A financier bought it, but Louis XIV made him give it to Count of Toulouse, Louis' son by Mme Montespan. Louis XV liked the Countess and visited her here weekly. Louis XVI built the dairy for Marie Antoinette to play at being milkmaid; Napoleon rearranged apartments and his bathroom is there. Now it is summer residence of the President of the Republic. But you can visit it when he is not there – except Tues.

Rambouillet Forest, nearly as big as Fontainebleau and wilder; lakes, pretty villages; wild game (deer, boar, duck, pheasant).

N306, D27
Longvilliers, St Cyr-sous-Dourdan, D838 Dourdan
(24 km) Route continues from Dourdan on p. 90

D27 goes alongside Parc Animalier des Yvelines – part of forest made into game sanctuary, with hides for photographers and observation. 12 km of paths. Open Saturday afternoon Sunday, Tuesday for 'chasseurs photographers' (photograph-hunters) who pay 30F.

Alternative route Dieppe to Dourdan

Dieppe

Step off the Sealink boat and you immediately get the flavour of France, bistros opposite; a fish market; and pavement cafés for a plate of shrimps or moules marinières to a full meal. Grand 'Rue is a pedestrian area, with shops selling a wide variety of things from expensive fashion shoes to cheap chickens and including a Prisunic chain store. On Saturday mornings, fishermen and farmers bring their produce to market – oysters, butter, farm pâté and prawns are sold from stalls. Sea front has wide lawns, beachside pool and casino. Dieppe Castle, where Canadian soldiers in 1942 climbed the sheer cliff face, has a museum with navigation equipment, ivories and paintings, including works by Walter Sickert, who lived here. At Varangeville (8 km) is a clifftop village church with superlative colourful modern window by Braque. His grave, designed by pupils in his style, is in the churchyard. You can visit Ango Manor, strange 16th-century home of the corsair chief Jean Ango, a French 'Drake' who became Governor of Dieppe after destroying 300 Portuguese ships. Pourville has a museum of the 1942 Dieppe Raid, including tanks.

Restaurants and hotels

Windsor, bd Verdun (sea-front), (35)84.15.23: Claude Lambert keeps up standards splendidly. Excellent Normandy dishes (cooked in cream) and sole à la Dieppoise (cooked in white wine with mussels, crayfish, mushrooms and cream added); super scallop pâte; true Norman apple tart; cream gâteaux with Calvados. Sea views from dining room; menu 63–90F; rooms 75–170F. One of my favourites. Shut 15 Nov.–18 Dec.

L'Univers, bd Verdun, (35)84.12.55: Mme Tilquin's family have owned this comfortable hotel for generations and Jean Tilquin is a great chef. Try scallops, escalope Normande, tournedos crepette, best cod (morue fraîche) I have tasted, magnificent seafood platter, outstanding Muscadet; extensive wine list; menu 70–100F; rooms 140–280F. Shut most of December and January.

La Marine, arcade de la Poissonerie, (35)84.17.54: modern; younger locals use it, excellent value; try mattelote Marine (plate of fresh, local fish and shellfish); sole or turbot Dieppoise; creamed mussels, estouffade (beef in red wine and herbs); mirliton (apple and almond tart); good service; reasonable wines; menu 39, 55F (good value), 72F. Shut Tues. eves, all Weds.

Marmite Dieppoise, rue St Jean, (35)84.24.26: a cliché in Dieppe – locals and tourist-regulars flock to simple-looking restaurant where fish is cooked superbly and chicken in cider very well. Willing service. 110F gastronomic menu; 40, 63F menus not served Friday, Saturday evenings. Shut Sun. eves, Mon.; 20 June–4 July.

Normandy, rue Duquesne, (35)84.27.18: outstanding value in replica old Norman farmhouse. Tables close: bustling service; candlelight in winter; huge choice even on cheapest menu; specialities – chicken in cider, escalope à la Normande, shellfish pancake, apple and Calvados sorbet; good cheap wines for 21F, menu 36.50, 52, 76F. Shut Jan.

Du Port, quai Henri IV, (35)84.36.64: still popular with locals, especially for fish soup and turbot terrine with langoustine sauce; menu 53–85F. Shut Thursday.

Best place to find good, really cheap meals is no longer quai Henri IV (opposite Sealink boats) but past fish market on arcade de la Poissonerie. Several old bistro-style bar-restaurants with menu outside from 25F. Old-style names, too, like La Victoire. A more modern ambitious restaurant here is:

La Moderne, (35)84.12.33: two floors, modern décor; good fish; also try guinea fowl in cider; menu 40, 56 (good value), 86F; wines from 22F. Shut Tuesday evening, Wednesday.

Useful, inexpensive overnight hotel (with restaurant) is the old Richmond, rue Commandant-Fayolle, (35)84.22.33.

Pourville (4 km) – Au Trou Normande, (35)84.27.69: Jean-Jacques Baton has left my little old favourite, Patron Vaillant is in the kitchen. I'm told he cooks well and gives value. Specialities: scallops, brill (barbue); menu 42–66F. Shut Sun. eves, Mon.

Puys (3 km) – Domaine à Dumas, (35)84.15.70: inn called Auberge du Vieux Puits which I knew as a boy has joined the upper classes. But Alexander Dumas *did* live here. Menu 80–190F; menu of day 110F; wines now from 40F; rooms 73–126F.

D915 Torcy, D154 Bellencombre, St Saens, D38, D41 Buchy (51 km)	Buchy-Gare – Hôtel du Nord, (35)34.54.82: local café-restaurant with simple rooms; Norman country cooking; value; menu 34–62F; house wine 26F; rooms 44.70F. Shut Sunday evening, Monday.	Road along quiet Varenne valley, with farms and brick manor houses, bordering Eawy Forest; lovely beech trees; into Forest of St Hellier, to little town of St Saens.
D41, D146 Elbeuf-sur-Andelle D46, N30 Vascoeuil (18 km)		Into valley of swift-flowing Andelle river, to Forest of Lyons. Vascoeuil Castle, where Andelle joins river Crevon, photogenic setting, surrounded by half-timbered thatched cottages. (open 1 Apr.–10 Oct.)
D115 left through Lyons Forest on to D321 to Lyons-la-Forêt (12 km)	La Cappeville, rue Cappeville, (32)55.11.08: live lobster tank; open grill; try civet of lobster, kidneys in cream and Calvados (Normand); scallops 'au Noilly' (in vermouth sauce); menu 55–130F.	Old hunting ground of Dukes of Normandy – down to 40 square miles. Magnificent old trees. French guerrillas used the forest as refuge from English in 100 Years War; French Resistance centre in World War II. Lyons-la-Forêt-old woodman's village grown into tranquil town with 1000 population. Lovely, old, timbered buildings, prettily restored and colour-washed. Fine old market hall.
D6 Etrépagny D14 Gisors (30 km)	Gisors – Moderne, pl Gare, (32)55.23.51: classical dishes; try kidneys in Madeira; menu 65, 115F; rooms 90–165F. Shut Sun. eves, Mon.; mid-July to mid Aug.	Gisors; damaged in 1940 but still historically interesting. Another castle 11th-12th century; built by William Rufus; tree-lined promenade. Gardens. Gisors overlooks river Epte.

Hostellerie des Trois Poissons, rue Cappeville, (32)55.01.09: three fish are truite Normande (trout in cream, Calvados and cider); raie à la moutarde (skate in mustard sauce); barbue Hollandaise (brill in sauce of butter, egg, lemon and wine). Some complicated dishes, but also country favourites; menu 48–90F; rooms 40–70F. Shut Mon. eves, Tues.; 10–30 June.

D915, D983 right Magny-en-Vexin, Mantes-la-Jolie, Houdan (60 km) (From Magny, D86 leads through beautiful Aubette valley – 12 km return)

Magny-en-Vexin – Cheval Blanc, rue Carnot, 467.00.37: attractive restaurant with flower-boxes; good reliable cooking; try roast veal Orloff (creamy onion sauce and cheese); kidneys in port; asparagus feuilleté; house wines 25F; menu 50F (weekdays), 70F. Shut Wednesday; August.

Mantes-la-Jolie – Les Glycines, rue Lorraine, 477.04.13: family-run hotel with interesting variety of dishes; try turbot Miroton; cassoulet Castelnaudry; Charlotte Mousse de Macon; menu 70F; rooms 75–150F.

Les Acacias, bd Maréchal-Juin, 643.05.67: pleasant, simple modern hotel-restaurant; good traditional cooking; try duck with green pepper, tournedos Rossini; also pintade (guinea-fowl) in raspberry sauce; menu 50–120F; rooms 80–120F.

Mantes-la-Jolie: historic little town, battered in World War II, much rebuilt in local stone. But new factories by the Seine hit you first as you drive in. William the Conqueror burned it down after being insulted by Philippe I of France. Then he fell off his horse and died six days later at Rouen. Here, too, Henry IV, Protestant leader, became a Catholic to get the crown of France. He told Protestant supporters that without his 'conversion' there would no longer be a France, through feuding and warring. Mantes Church of Notre Dame (built 1170) has beautiful Navarre chapel with old and modern stained glass.

Houdan: farming centre; breed of chicken named after it. Enormous 12th-century castle-keep, with four turrets.

D983, D112, D12F, St Léger-en-Yvelines, D936 Rambouillet, D27 Longvilliers, St Cyr-sous-Dourdan, D838 Dourdan (51 km)

For information on Rambouillet-Dourdan, see same section on Le Havre – Dourdan route, begins page 84.

St Léger is charming village with 12th-century church. Once had a royal castle where Philippe Auguste of France, having married Ingeburge of Denmark in 1193 because she might one day inherit the English throne, shut up his bride the day after the wedding; three years later, he married Agnes of Bohemia. The Pope declared it void and excommunicated him. Agnes died of sorrow. Ingeburge was held in Guinette tower, Etampes, for 12 more years; released on Pope's insistence and became Queen again at the Louvre Palace.

From Dourdan D836, N191 Etampes (18 km)

Etampes – is 80 km (50 miles) from Paris; the restaurants rely heavily on Parisians who drive out and locals who work in Paris, hence some have Parisian prices and summer closures.

L'Europe (A l'Escargot), rue St Jacques, 494.02.96: good value but inconvenient closing; known for snails and lamb; menu 35–40F; rooms 55–90F. Shut 25 June–25 July; 15 Sept.–6 Oct.; restaurant shut Wednesday.

At Chalo-St-Mars (7 km on D21) – Les Alouettes, 495.40.20: country auberge, attractive décor, imaginative dishes; menu 70F but many dishes carry supplements; try local duck with turnips. Shut Wednesday, Thursday; 10 Aug.–10 Sept.

Etampes is in very attractive position on Chalouette river, with riverside walks; many lovely old buildings. In 14th century was seat of ruling regent, Abbé de St Denis, while Louis VII was fighting a Crusade, and it rivalled Paris. Lovely drive in Chalouette valley through very pleasant villages – Chalo-St-Mars, Moulinex, Chalou (D21, D160).

At Brerville (D49) is L'Epi d'Or, France's first youth hostel (opened 1929).

D837 Milly,
Fontainebleau
(38 km)

Most restaurants and hotels are dear and touristy. These are exceptions:

Ile de France, rue de France, 422. 21.17: praised by France's leading food and travel writers and by many of my readers – but *not* all. Food is Chinese by a chef from Hong Kong but, unlike here in Britain, loaded towards the French ('spicy Imperial-style frogs' legs' and trout in Chinese wine); one of France's greatest experts finds it good. Certainly not dear – menu 29.50F (with wine), 48, 65F. Louis XVI dining room, nice flower garden. Bedrooms fairly awful when Charles Glise arrived 5 years ago, now decorated, all with own bath or shower and WC; rooms 80–150F; family rooms (4–5 people) 200F.

Le Dauphin, rue Grande, 422.27.04: large helpings, keen service, good straightforward cooking; menu 45–70F; house wine 24F; shut Wednesday; February.

Grand Café, 422.20.32: bar-restaurant; useful for cheap meals, 31–50F menu with choice (main dish – pork, chicken, sausage or beef stew).

Milly: old town on edge of Fontainebleau forest. Its fine buildings include market halls made entirely of oak. Chapel of St Blaise-des-Simples (12th century) restored in 1958. Tomb of Jean Cocteau (1889–1963) writer, artist and above all, playwright. He decorated the chapel in 1959 with lovely drawings of the Crown of Thorns and the Resurrection.

5 km north is Château de Courances, magnificent 17th-century building in a park laid out by Le Nôtre; you can visit it on Saturdays, Sundays and public holidays. Charming drive to Fontainebleau through the wild forest of pines, oaks and beeches; notices name some aged trees as if they were dogs, while others bear legends like 'Stag and Boar Crossing'. Rocks used as climbers' training grounds with torrents rushing between them. The Château, not so impressive as Versailles, has as much historic importance and atmosphere. Louis VII began it, but the flamboyant Francis I made it into a palace, and brought in Italians to decorate it. Louis XIV had the garden laid out, Napoleon I converted part of the château as his living quarters, imprisoned the Pope here, abdicated in the Red Room, and said farewell

Fontainebleau *continued*		to his Old Guard in the courtyard; on most weekdays you can also see Napoleon and Josephine's rooms and those of Pope Pius VII. The Château abounds in secret nooks and crannies and back staircases, ideal for intrigue – or parties.
N7 Nemours (15 km)		Nice position in valley of Loing; 12th-century castle, rebuilt 15th century; interesting tapestries.
		Du Port family, economists, left Nemours for US in 18th century, started Du Port industrial empire – chemical, nylon now, also nuclear.
D409, D975 Bellegarde (39 km)	L'Agriculture, pl Ch. Desvergnes, (38)90.10.48: very good value; salmon; sandre (Loire fish); guinea-fowl in Sauvignon wine; blanquette of veal; estouffade de boeuf (top rump stewed slowly in pot with wine, herbs, veg, pork); menu 30–80F; house wine 22F; rooms 40–100F. Shut October.	Market garden, rose-growing and corn in fertile country. Bellegarde is built round enormous square; fine 17th-century paintings in church.
N60, D948 Sully-sur-Loire (21 km)	L'Esplanade, rue Fg St Germain, (38)35.20.83: opposite Château; pleasant garden, terrace and pretty glassed-in terrace. Specializes in fish from Loire and sea. Owner-chef Philippe Brossard is former chef at Georges V in Paris. No need to say more! Menu 62–126F; rooms 80–115F.	Much rebuilt after war damage but very pleasant; river spanned by long, graceful suspension bridge. Dark and forbidding fortress-château with broad, deep moats, beside river; towers and sentry walks; but inside walls is pretty Renaissance pavilion. At the Château, after victories, Joan of Arc persuaded the Dauphin to go to Reims to be crowned King of France. After failing to

Pont de Sologne, rue Pont de Sologne, (38)36.26.34: bar, brasserie, restaurant; hotel; if you like strong cheese, do try assiette gourmande de crottins; it means 'dung' but is a sharp, dry goat's milk cheese; excellent fish; try pocheteau Grenobloise (deep-sea ray with capers and lemons); menu 52F and 120F, gastronomic; rooms 47.50–135F.

take Paris, she returned to Sully and was kept waiting a month. Finally she rode away to be captured and burned.

Voltaire found refuge here with the Duke of Sully when he had to flee the Court for making epigrams too biting and true. The Duke, a liberal who loved new ideas, built him a theatre; he wrote comedies and tragedies to be performed in it.

D951 Gien
(23 km)

Gien: a town of flowers and a pottery factory, 160 years old. Church dedicated to Joan of Arc was destroyed (1940); modern church in pink brick (specially baked in wood-fired kilns) and black. Coloured windows by Max Ingrand, great modern stained-glass artist; pottery capitals to pillars show episodes from Joan's life. In rue Lejardinier are some medieval houses. In 1429 through Golden Lion Gate, now gone, seven riders (one a 'young boy') rode weary and sodden. Joan was on her way to save France. Château (1484) contains International Hunting Museum (superb tapestries and paintings, fine Desportes collection).

D951 Léré
D751, D955
Sancerre
(67 km)

Sancerre – Auberge Alphonse Mellot, pl de la Halle, (36)54.20.53: 'Auberge Dégustation' – inn for wine-tasting; Mellot family own vineyard (La Chatellerie) and cellars, and sell most Sancerre wines. 'Menu-Dégustation' 40F – terrine,

Sancerre – delightful, walled town on steep hill with narrow, steep roads and pretty little houses, capped by terrace with lime tree shade and views over the Loire you will never forget. A huge curved viaduct below

ham omelette, crottin de Chavignol goat's milk cheese (see opposite column). Collection of old wine-making equipment.

Hôtel du Rampart, (36)54.10.18: outstanding value; comfortable bedrooms; patron-chef Paul Decreuze cooks traditionally and well, try coq au vin; salmon or trout in Sancerre sauce; lamb stew; veal brawn; all local specialities; menu 37, 75, 95F; house wine 25F; good Sancerre 50F; rooms (all with bath, WC). 95–120F. Good views.

At St Thibault-St Satur – L'Etoile, quai de Loire, (48)54.12.15: lovely position overlooking Loire: elegant restaurant; good local cooking; hotel needed face-lift on our visit in '82. Grills over wood fire: good Loire eels; coq au vin; rooms (mostly simple) 65–118F. Shut Wednesday out of season; 15 Nov.–1 March.

La Roch, (48)54.01.79; floating restaurant on boat; specializes in Loire eels in red wine; 'small fry' from Loire; menu 60–90F. Shut Tuesday, open weekends.

L'Auberge, St Thibault, (48)54.13.79: built 1610; country furnishing; restaurant leads to flower-garden; meals good value; pleasant bedrooms; try trout in Sancerre wine; chicken in Sancerre; ficelle Auberge (stuffed pancake); pâté

takes a road to by-pass St. Satur, a very old village.

In 1534, Protestant Sancerre withstood for seven months a Catholic siege; people ate powdered slates and leather. Finally gave in but remained Protestant. 16th-century Protestant church and old Catholic church. Sancerre known for its dry white wine made from Sauvignon grapes (delicious as aperetif, with fish, fowl or just for drinking); also makes red and rosé with Pineau d'Aunis grapes (very old-fashioned).

Chavignol – 3 km before Sancerre on D955, on to D183 at Fontenoy; wine-growers' village making Chavignol Sancerre; also 'crottin de Chavignol' (goats droppings of Chavignol) splendid strong goat's milk cheese.

In Sancerre is rue Macdonald. In 1746 band of Scots fled with Prince Charles after defeat at Culloden; settled at Sancerre. One was a schoolmaster from Uist; his house is No. 3 rue Macdonald. His son Etienne went away to military academy, became one of Napoleon's Marshals and Duke of Taranto.

St Thibault-sur-Loire (D955 before reaching Sancerre, D4 – 5 km): on Loire banks: Fête on 16 August with river races and fun is famous in France. Large island

d'amandes (almond paste – local speciality); menu 40–85F; house wine 32F; rooms 71–130F. Shut Tuesday out of season.

upstream where goats are grazed; ferried across each morning on huge punt-raft: provide goat's milk cheese. Lively village; fisherman's chapel to St Roch, protector from pestilence, and of fishermen.

D920, D7 La Charité-sur-Loire (26 km)

A La Bonne Foi, rue Camille Barrière, (86)70.15.77: restaurant in Guenault family for three generations. Excellent fish, especially trout, sandre, from Loire; menu 47–116F. Shut Monday.

D7 here still busy in summer, but not like pre-motorway days. Charité built in amphitheatre down to Loire: lovely river scene with handsome 16th-century stone bridge. Name came from 11th-century monks who

La Charité-sur-
Loire
continued

gave best alms to pilgrims
on long route to
Compostella. Joan of Arc
failed to take it from
Burgundians – beginning of
her end. Fine view of town
from bridge. Local wines of
Charité worth tasting.

N7 Pougues-
les-Eaux,
Nevers (24 km)

Central, (86)68.85.00:
pleasant Logis with bright
blinds, flowers in window-
boxes, pavement terrace.
Nice, old-fashioned meals –
tournedos, snails, frog's legs,
chicken livers: five menus
between 40F and 120F
(gastronomic); rooms 80–
121F. Shut 15 Nov.–15 Dec.

Nevers – Auberge Porte du
Crous, rue P. du Croux, (86)
57.12.71: very nice, pretty,
quiet; terrace overlooking
gardens with tower and
ancient city wall. Charming
welcome. Fish direct from
Atlantic coast or from the
Loire. Meal prices inevitably
higher but still good value;
menu 84–141F; rooms 89–
95F. Shut August.

Hostellerie La Folie, rte des
Saulaies, (86)57.05.31:
modern swimming pool;
Logis; very good value;
menu 42–89F; rooms 80–
160F.

Pougues: little spa with
views into Loire valley;
waters used to combat
stomach illness, liver trouble,
diabetes; inevitable casino
(why do the sick make life
worse by gambling away
their money, too?).

Nevers: where Loire joins
river Nièvre; famous for fine
china. On hill, dominated by
cathedral and ducal palace.
Italians introduced china-
making in 16th century.
Turreted Porte du Croux
(14th-century tower gate) is
superb. Collection of Nevers
china in museum (shut
Tuesday). At Convent of St
Gildard, bd Victor Hugo, in
chapel, is a macabre display
– body of St Bernadette in
glass cask (the girl who saw
visions at Lourdes and
became a nun here in 1867).
Certified 'uncorrupted', but
darkened and wax-covered.
New church dedicated to her
looks solid as a Nazi West
Wall bunker, but interesting
inside. Old Nevers lives
alongside new tower-blocks
and supermarkets.

D13 Chevenon
D13, D116
Decize (39 km)

St Honoré – Hôtel-
Restaurant Henri Robert, ave
Gen. d'Espeuilles, (86)
30.72.33: highly praised by

Decize: built on an island in
the Loire river on a steep hill
where the Dukes of Nevers
once had their castle, it has a

D81, D37, D106
St Honoré-les-
Bains, D985
Luzy (49 km)

French guides; Martine Pouthier has been called 'perfect hostess'. Old manor house; charming grounds; dishes of Morvan, Burgundy, Nièvre; fine cooking; try as starter oeufs en Meurette (poached eggs in red wine, onions, mushrooms, bacon); also Saupiquet Decizois. Good wine cellar (wines from 35F); menu 50–110F (40F full meal for children); rooms 50–160F. Open 1 May–30 Sept.

Hôtel du Morvan, ave Jean-Mermoz, (86)30.74.44: splendid 'Grand Hôtel' in thermal park; excellent cooking; Charollais beef; coq au vin; crayfish; lobster; trout; live lobster tank; menu 50–100F; house wine 29F; rooms 70–140F. Open 4 April – 30 Sept.

Luzy – Hôtel du Morvan, ave D'Dollet, (86)30.00.66: same name as in Honoré, different hotel; but another good coq au vin; escargots; escalope Normande; fromage blanc à la crème; menu 30.50–80F; house wine 25.50F; rooms 51–75F.

lovely half-mile promenade of massive plane trees. On route, Chevenon castle, poised to control the valley. Built in 14th century by a commander of Charles V regime: later centre for looting and brigandry, typical of the Wars of Religion in France. Decize was home of St Just, enthusiast of guillotine in Revolution, Margaret Monnet, composer of 'Irma La Douce' and many Edith Piaf songs, and of Charollais cattle, best of beef.

St Honoré: Romans found this spa (as usual!); waters contain sulphur, arsenic, radioactivity; used for treating asthma, bronchitis. In lovely country – just after town on D985 is beautiful view over Lake of Seu.

Luzy: little town in pleasant, wooded countryside.

D985 Toulon,
Charolles
(54 km)

Charolles – La Poste, ave Libération, (85)24.11.32: delightful white hotel in town centre; known for Charollaise entrecôte steaks – 300 g (nearly 12oz) a person; fish mousse; Bourguignon snails; stuffed veal escalope (excellent); Rhône wine 20F; menu 60–100F; rooms (all with shower/bath) 75–95F; good value.

Charolles came under Dukedom of Burgundy, not France, for centuries; then under Hapsburg ownership; then Counts of Bourbon-Condé until 1761. Last count, Charles, relieved boredom by shooting from his castle at tilers working on roofs of houses within range. Caused deaths and injuries; got royal pardon each time from Louis

Charolles *continued*	Moderne, ave Gare, (85)24.07.02: entrecôte Charollaise, sauce marchand de vin (steak in butter, red wine, meat stock, shallots) – succulent, good cooking; garden with swimming pool; quiet. Menu 60–140F; rooms 75–200F. Shut Sunday evening, Monday out of season. At Viry, 7 km NE – Le Monastère, (85)24.14.24: delightful little restaurant in quiet, pleasant village; in 15th-century building; menu 35, 55, 60, 69, 100F; wines from 14F. Shut Wednesday except July, Aug.	XV. Finally Louis offered a pardon to anyone killing him in reprisal! Castle now ruined. Each Wednesday, sale of Charollais cattle – France's best beef cattle, often crossed now with our breeds in Britain.
D79, D983, D14 Cormatin, D981 Cluny (40 km) (in bad winter weather take N79 from Charolles to Mâcon)	Cluny – Moderne, pont de l'Etang, (85)59.05.65: old hotel successfully renovated; nice terrace and dining room by river; 25-year-old chef Patrick Deschamps gets high marks for imagination and enterprise for his new dishes; but cooks old favourites too, like oeuf meurette; lotte à l'orange; menu 50–130F; wine list very good, mostly pricier wines, some delicious Burgundies; rooms 80–160F. Shut Monday except high season; February. L'Abbaye, ave Gare, (85)59.11.14: comfortable and good value for one-star hotel; big sitting-room; quiet except for 'musique d'ambiance'; serves especially nice boeuf Bourguignon among typical	Cluny: small town which in Middle Ages was a religious, political and artistic centre called by one Pope 'the Light of the World'. Founded in AD 910, the Abbey of Cluny gradually extended its influence over most of Christendom; the abbot was often more powerful than the Pope. By 14th century abbots preferred their house in Paris to the Cluny abbey. Cluny was a natural prey in Wars of Religion; pillaged, devastated. Main hall survived until Revolution, when it was closed, sold for demolition. Meanwhile the job as Abbot had become a lucrative sinecure given by the King to favourites, such as Richelieu and Mazarin. Cloisters, now housing a national art and craft school,

local family dishes (coq au vin); menu 55–100F; wines reasonable (Mâcon, Beaujolais 32F); rooms 54–135F.

are among remains. Some abbey stone was used for stables – now part of French National Stud with 90 stallions between March and July; a few at other times.

D980, N79
Mâcon (26 km)

Pierre, rue Dufour, (85)38.14.23: a discovery; charming little restaurant; delightful décor amid old stone, leather and pictures; good local cooking and dishes from other countries; excellent value; menu 45–70F; in pedestrian area.

Au Rocher de Cancale, quai Jean-Jaurès, (85)38.07.50; specializes not in local beef or Bresse chicken but fish, including shellfish, kept live in seawater tank; but cooked excellently, at reasonable prices; fine 65F menu; good trout pâté; also sabayon au porto (egg yolks whisked with port and cream); menus 50, 65, 73, 135F. Shut Saturday lunch; Sunday evening, Monday, 1–15 Aug.

Génève, rue Bigonnet, (85)38.18.10: modern, like block of flats, in nice garden; very well run; soundproofed rooms; you are expected to have dinner if staying overnight. Plats du jour according to best ingredients available each day; good pochouse (mixed fish from river, stewed with herbs); menu 62–79F; daily small-meal suggestions 39F; rooms 67–194F. 15 June – 15 Sept.: half-board 132–173F per person.

French Romantic poet Lamartine was born in Mâcon (1790); brilliant writer who went into politics and diplomacy. Fine view of town from 14th-century bridge over Saône river; wine stores at west end. In Louis XIV's reign (1660), a Mâconnais of giant size, Claude Brosse, took two barrels of his Chasselas wine to Versailles – past highwaymen and robbers, 33 days on mud-tracks, on a bullock cart. There he sold it personally and directly to the King. So all fashionable courtiers drank it and Mâcon was made. Red wine slightly inferior to neighbouring Beaujolais, above 'ordinaire' status. White (Pouilly-Fuissé) is fine, gentle wine, not so tasteful as Meursault nor so grand as Chablis Grand-Cru, but far above most dry white wines we find in ordinary restaurants. Good, slightly cheaper wines are Mâcon-Vire (especially Clos-du-Chapitre) and Pouilly-St Veran. To visit Pouilly, go back on N79, take D54 left, then D112 (7 km). Chasselas (3 km further) produces wine and table grapes.

N79
Bourg en
Bresse (34 km)

An area producing splendid fresh dairy products and poultry, so mostly the cooking is simple, the result often delectable. Chicken is usually cooked in cream and white wine. Bleu de Bresse cheese is another local speciality.

Mail, ave du Mail, (74)21.00.26: though Auberge Bressane facing the church is more famous than Mail, it is dearer. French experts say that cuisine here never falters. Wines from 40F, strong in Burgundy and Bordeaux; menu 60–120F; pretty garden; pleasant bedrooms 65–130F. Shut Sunday evenings; Monday; part July, Jan.

Revermont, rue Ch. Robin, (74)22.66.53: nice simple corner restaurant with rooms; popular with locals for good cooking of Bressane dishes; value; menu 30–87F; rooms 50–80F. Shut Monday.

De France, pl Bernard, (74)23.30.24: real old 'Grand' hotel; restaurant popular locally; menu 55–78F; rooms 60–210F. Restaurant shut Sunday.

Savoie, rue Paul-Pioda, (74)23.29.24: good local cooking; choice of 5 menus 35–100F. Shut Wednesday evening, Thursday; part August.

One can tire of looking at old churches in France, but the church at Brou, suburb of Bresse, is one of the prettiest – a meeting of Gothic, Flamboyant and Renaissance design, dainty rather than magnificent; the choir stalls, carved by the best local craftsmen, are remarkable. One shows a master enthusiastically beating the bare bottom of a pupil. The nearby tombs were carved by craftsmen brought from Flanders, Italy and Germany. Superb windows. The story of the Brou Monastery is, alas, too long and complicated to tell here, but worth reading – a story of an orphan princess used for political power from babyhood, divorced, widowed but so intelligent that she became Regent of the Netherlands and Franche-Comté – wise, liberal, loved by the Comptois people: Marguerite of Austria, daughter of Emperor Maximillian.

Bresse makes fine rustic furniture from cherry, pear and apple trees, and is the market for the great Bresse chickens and dairy produce.

From here you motor through the foothills of the Alps and some nice scenery. Lovely mountain scenery with a waterfall at Artemare (Cascade de Cerveyrieu).

N75 Pont d'Ain
(19 km)

Mas Pommier (2 km N on N75), (74)39.08.42: my favourite old farmhouse, now popular not only with my readers but the French who drive miles to eat here. Excellent value. Whole room devoted to 40 hors d'oeuvres dishes and choice of sausages hanging on wall. Try salmon; trout; quail, with crayfish sauce; or, of course, roast Bresse chicken; menu 35, 42, 60, 83F; rooms 35–70F. Shut Tuesday evening, Wednesday out of season.

Alliés, (34)39.00.09: more good local cooking, plus good wines 28–180F; menu 60–120F; rooms 80–190F. Shut November.

D984 Pérouges
(22 km)

Ostellerie du Vieux Pérouges, (74)61.00.88: one of France's oldest auberges; historic 13th-century inn; superb old furniture and pots and drinking vessels. Not cheap, but an experience. Old dishes of Bresse and

A treasure – pure medieval village, free for centuries of overlords and its people successful craftsmen. It decayed last century, being far from a railway; buildings fell down or were knocked down and it seemed certain to disappear. Saved by a campaign of artists;

Pérouges *continued*	Pérouges; mid-afternoon you eat galette (flan) of raspberries and cream with a mug of cider; menu 95–180F; rooms 220–450F. Far too pricey but someone has to help keep up this magnificent village.	preserved and repaired. 90 people lived here in 1910; now has 500; not a museum piece – craftsmen work here again; but so authentic it has been used as a film set (*Three Musketeers, Mister Vincent*).
N84 (East) D40, D65 La Balme; back on D65, right on D65G, N75 Voiron (87 km)		Grottes de la Balme – open caves known in Middle Ages; most impressive. Used as hideout in 18th century by Louis Mandarin, smuggler and outlaw. Voiron: makes skis, cloth, silk and paper; also distills Chartreuse liqueur with monks from Grande-Chartreuse monastery high up the mountain. Monks collect mountain herbs for this strong liqueur. Visits and tastings in Voiron caves (in winter, weekdays only).
N75 Grenoble (26 km)	12 km from Voiron, left turn at Voreppe on N520E to Pommiers-la-Placette (7 km) – Hôtel du Col, Col de la Placette, (76)50.04.65: fine views round here; good solid mountain dishes – sauté chicken; fillet steak; pork chops; gallantine of guinea-fowl; carafe wine 11F a litre; nice Savoy Gamay rouge 32F; menu 39–105F; rooms 61–125F; very pleasant hotel, way off the tourist tracks. Le Rabelais, ave Jean-Jaurès, (76)46.03.44: splendid value; 34F menu offered us chicken-liver mousse pâté; chicken suprême; creamy mountain	Grenoble, once one of my favourite bigger cities – different from any other except perhaps Innsbruck; it has been greatly industrialized and hugely modernized in its buildings. The big 1968 Winter Olympics village added final touch. But surrounding scenery is gorgeous, air exhilarating, University founded in 1339 keeps the city lively and up to date (including its nuclear school!) so it is not boring, and young people don't want to leave it. Magnificent views of Belledonne and the other surrounding ranges from top of cable-car at Fort Bastille –

cheese; try sole soufflé in crayfish sauce; gratin Dauphinois (potatoes baked brown with cream); roast quail; menu 34–77F; wines from 19F. Shut Friday evening, Saturday.

Splendid Hôtel, rue Thiers, (76)46.33.12: excellent overnight hotel; no restaurant; interesting décor; our bedroom had black walls; comfortable and cosy; rooms 65–152F, good value.

Chaumière Savoyarde, rue Gabriel-Peri, (76)87.29.71: pleasant 'rustic' dining room; Savoyarde cooking; generous portions; but why poularde Angevine up here? Some Anjou wine salesman must have talked fast; genuine 'pieds et paquets' (tripe rolled into packets, cooked in wine, tomatoes with sheep's trotters); menu 42, 55F; house wine 26F. Shut Sunday evening; August.

now a restaurant. Grenoble belonged to Burgundy, then the German Empire. Dukes of Albon next owned city and whole Dauphiné – sold it to France on condition King's eldest son was called 'Dauphin'.

Organised Resistance against Nazis here was so successful that Germans had to drop an SS Para battalion to combat them. Whole city of Grenoble awarded Legion of Honour. Resistance and Deportation Museum at No. 14 rue Jean-Jacques Rousseau. Museum of writer Stendahl is in town hall.

Museum Beaux-Arts has paintings by Renoir, Monet, Picasso, Léger, Modigliani, Utrillo, Matisse.

N75, N85, Vizille, La Mure, Corps, Barrage du Sautet (63 km)

At Claix (8 km S of Grenoble by N75; D269 to right) – Les Oiseaux, (76)98.07.14; good value meals; country dishes; family atmosphere; Relais du Silence, promising calm, peace, quiet; pretty situation; menu 48–80F; wine from 18F; rooms 90–155F. Big swimming pool in summer.

Vizille: on river Romarche; imposing château, built 1611, now a summer residence of President of France; fine park; tapestries, furniture, fireplaces of 17th century (shut Tuesdays). Trout farm in grounds produces enormous fish. Lovely route past lakes of Laffrey. At village of Laffrey troops sent to arrest Napoleon, who was marching to Paris after his escape from Elba, cheered

Vizille *continued*		him and joined him (March 1815). Napoleon said: 'Until Grenoble, I was an Adventurer; at Grenoble, I was Prince.' This is the 'Route Napoleon' – in reverse. Route becomes rather tough from lakes to La Mure.
N85 Gap (40 km)	Hotel-restaurant Le Pavillon; Motel Le Carina, (92)52.02.73: very comfortable; reasonably priced; modern rooms; all in Carina have bathroom, WC and some in Pavillon; pleasant meals; speciality sauerkraut; trout with morilles (mountain fungi – lovely); menu 50–80F (includes pichet of red wine); rooms (for 2 including breakfast) 108–190F. Shut 24 Dec.–10 Jan. Good full board rates.	Important commercial town. Old centre surrounded by new buildings; dry and hot in summer until evening, though 800 m (2400 ft) up. First town on Napoleon's march to Paris, to receive him warmly.
N85 Sisteron (48 km)	Les Chênes, Route de Gap (92)61.15.08: fine views, charming garden and terrace for summer meals; neat bedrooms; most with WC, shower or bath; local products, Provençal cooking; menu 38–85F; wines from 18F; rooms 75–140F. Shut Wednesday out of season. At Salignac (D4 across river, second left, signposted – 8 km) – Grand Cèdre (92)61.29.26: in beautiful country, woodland setting, pretty little hideaway hotel where they bake bread, grow vegetables for table, make all dishes fresh, according to	Old town of narrow, steep streets, some arched, climbs from river Durance up to the old citadel, built over centuries; 14th-century chapel was destroyed when Germans petulantly bombed the town in retreat in 1944. Fine views over town from chapel site.

season. A gem. Family atmosphere; menu 40–65F; wines – Ventoux 20F, plus many Provence; rooms 53–95F. Shut 15 Nov.–20 Dec.

N85 Digne (40 km)

L'Aiglon rue Provence (92)31.02.70: pleasant hotel and restaurant; try terrine of hare or wild boar; local trout or crayfish; menu 40–105F; rooms 65–136F. Shut Friday; Jan., Feb.

La Chauvinière, rue l'Hubac, (92)31.40.03: remarkable value; worth climbing a few steps; on 28F menu you could get duck in green peppers, curried lamb, wild rabbit in mustard sauce; on 46F menu, roast quail, guinea-fowl, kidneys in garlic cream sauce; menu 28, 46, 80F; Jean-Louis Chauvin could make me a Chauvinist pig. Shut Monday out of season; part Nov., part Feb.

Central, bd Gassendi, (92)31.31.91: no restaurant; comfortable beds; rooms 70–160F.

An oasis 610 m (2000 ft) up in wild mountain country, described as poorest, least populated, most desolate of the Alps, with peaks denuded and white. Luckily our road follows valleys of the river Durance, beautiful, and river Bleone, with rugged backcloth. The Durance has two hydroelectric dams on this stretch. Famous Mediterranean light, beloved by artists, said to be at its best in mountains here. Natural hot springs used to treat rheumatic sufferers. (Thermal baths 3½ km SE.)

N85 Castellane (54 km)

At Col des Leques, (10 km before Castellane on N85) – Les Peyrascas, (92)83.61.28: 2-year-old hotel-restaurant at summit of mountain road, 1149 m (3766 ft) up. I have not tried it, but must be most welcome to tired drivers and over-heated cars. Good reports on bedroom comfort and value meals (especially 55F 'Menu du Jour', changed daily). Lamb 'au Roquefort';

Mountainous route. Castellane is a large village on Route Napoleon by river Verdon; overlooked by the Roc, 180 m (600 ft) high crag crowned by chapel, built 1703. Centre for tours of Grand Canyon of Verdon, one of most striking natural features of French Alps. River has scooped series of steep gorges in soft limestone – some 610 m (2000 ft) deep.

Castellane
continued

quail; ½-litre Provence wine 12F; menu 45, 55, 90F; rooms with bathroom 130–150F. Shut part Jan., part Nov.

At La Garde (6 km past Castellane on N85) – Du Teillon, (92)83.60.88: delightful old-style auberge with shady garden in attractive village; local products; game, guinea-fowl; trout; menu 39, 50, 80F; rooms 70–130F. Shut March 1–31 Oct.

Motorists can see into depths in places. Best way is on foot by marked paths: takes 8 hours and you need tough walking shoes and gear. Until 1928, when paths were made, this was walk for experienced speleologists and explorers.

Diversion: (good weather) to tour Canyon du Verdon by Corniche Sublime – Castellane, D552 Moustiers Ste Marie (45 km); D552, D557 Pont d'Aiguines (6 km); D19, D71 along Corniche Sublime to Balcons de la Mescla (28 km – wild spot; view of rivers Verdon and Artuby fighting on their way through Canyon); D71 Comps-sur-Artuby (16 km – small spa with hotels, restaurants – try Hotel Bains); D21 to rejoin N85 (Total of diversion 111 km).

From Castellane N85 Grasse (63 km)

Maître Boscq, rue Fontette, (93)36.45.75: tiny restaurant in picturesque street in old town near Place aux Airs flower-market. 'Old beams, old brass and some good liquor,' says Patrick Boscq, chef-owner, who collects traditional local recipes and cooks in the good old-fashioned French manner. Try courgettes stuffed 'en fleur' (very tender); le fassum (cabbage stuffed with meat, veg and rice – including one stuffed with partridge); local torteaux (large crab) with herbs; super chicken dish; special 51F menu (with drink) very good; menu of Grassoisses dishes at 61F, outstanding. Provence wines

Into old Côte d'Azur tourist country, but delightful. Tiny republic until 12th century. In 18th century local lad called Honoré Fragonard went to Paris to become a painter. Come the Revolution, he fled back to Grasse with five perfumes made for Mme du Barry which she didn't like. In Grasse he sold them for a few francs; over 100 years later American banker Pierpoint Morgan paid a fortune for them. Grasse had become capital of French perfume industry. It rewarded Fragonard with a memorial and museum of his paintings. A Count of Grasse, a royal Admiral, joined the Americans in War of

from 23F; full list. Shut Sunday.

Les Aromes on N85 after Grasse (93)70.42.01: looks right for Provence – white, pantiles, blinds, attractive terrace for summer eating; pleasant, friendly little hotel. Plat du jour may be faux-filet of beef with capers, chicken Washington, fish, escalope for 30F; on main menus, steaks cooked various ways before your very eyes; shoulder of lamb in honey; menu 30–85F; wines from 22F; big, comfortable bedrooms; quiet; rooms 122.50F. Shut 30 Nov.–1 Feb; restaurant shut Saturday.

Independence; Congress rewarded him for his help, but in 1782 he was captured, flagship and all, by our Royal Navy.

Napoleon's sister, Pauline (the naughty one), made it fashionable in 1807 when she left her husband Prince Borghese and came here to look for consolation. Later Queen Victoria spent some winters at the Grand Hotel. Perfumeries open to visitors include Fragonard, rue Fragonard.

D2085, D2210
Vence (27 km)

Les Muscadelles, ave Henri-Isnard, (93)58.01.25: variety – Belgian, Provençal, Indonesian, South African dishes, plus good choice of cheese: menu 60–90F; rooms 85–180F; pretty flower garden. Shut 15 Oct.–15 Nov.

La Closerie de Genets, impasse Marcellin-Maurel, (93)58.33.25: an oasis in crowded Vence; in centre yet quiet, with gardens. Good value: plat du jour 35–45F; menu 50–60F; can eat in garden in summer; menus based on fresh products from markets each morning; fresh fish cooked simply. Speciality: Niçoise 'Aigo-Bouido' (fish and garlic soup like bouillabaisse). Rooms 70–140 F (many overlook garden and have sea views).

Vence: must have been heaven before it became fashionable; still beautiful, but so crowded in summer. About 305 m (1000 ft) up. 9 km from sea, 40 km from winter snow-slopes; lovely surroundings; beautiful old buildings with narrow streets, fountains, arches. Delightful at all seasons.

Place du Peyra and its fountain – absolutely superb. So are simple, poignant drawings by artist Henri Matisse on white walls of Chapelle du Rosaire – and the superb decorated windows (open only Tuesdays, Thursday). D. H. Lawrence died here in 1930 (Villa Robermond). Galerie 'Les Arts' has superb modern paintings – Chagall, Dufy, many others.

Vence
continued

Restaurant shut Nov., Dec.; Monday, Tuesday, lunch.

La Farigoule, rue Henri-Isnard, (93)58.01.27: in old town with garden and terrace; nice ambiance; mixture of traditional Provençal dishes: rabbit in wild thyme, fish soup, quail with grape, daube Provençale, and unusual suckling pig with ratatouille in anis; menu 50–60F. Shut Friday; 15 Nov.–15 Dec.

D2 St Paul de Vence (5 km)

Morateur, rue Grande, (93)32.81.91: my favourite since I was a lad: Poirier family still run it. Higgledy-piggledy décor and ornamentation among old beams, pillars; same old-style solid dishes – kidney ragôut, ris de veau, Mediterranean fishes; leak tart (super version); menu 60F. Shut Sunday evening, Monday out of season; July, August to avoid crowds.

Like a fortified feudal village – almost intact; parts of walls breached. Withstood several sieges. Charming. For long, a hideaway of painters, many of whom paid for meals or settled bills at La Colombe d'Or with paintings; others gave them to the owner, M. Roux, so this hotel-restaurant is an art gallery, with works of Braque, Picasso, Rouault, Matisse, Dufy, Modigliani, Utrillo, Leger and others.

Fondation Maeght (NW) – very modern buildings; museum of modern art.

D2, D36
Cagnes, D36,
N98 Nice
(20 km)

Route 4
Calais/Boulogne through Champagne, Jura, Annecy to Mont Blanc

From Calais and Boulogne, it passes through 'unknown' country of sleepy hamlets, wooded hills, and fish-filled waterways between the busy N43 and N1 roads. It crosses fine country north of Paris through old royal hunting forests to the lovely city of Laôn, once capital of France, and the Champagne hills. A stop at Rheims to see the superb cathedral and taste the magnificent nectar of Messrs Moët et Chandon or their rivals. Then into the glorious country of Franche-Comté, which we call Jura; a land of mountains, fast rivers, woods, little spas and delightful towns almost totally unknown to Britons. It is tempting to drive to Geneva and use the motorway to St Gervais, but that stretch through Annecy, over Col des Arivis to Megève, *which you cannot drive in winter,* is just as gorgeous in summer sun.

Fresh fish of Boulogne or Calais, some of the finest in France, appear far inland along this route, with freshwater fish from the many streams of Picardy, wild duck, which makes such gorgeous pâté, and superb vegetables. Mostly a Flemish-cooking area for good hearty dishes like delicious leek and cream tart, smoked sausages, stews cooked in beer, hochepot (a sort of pot au feu made with mutton and bacon) and Potée Flamande (bacon,

ham, sausage, potatoes, cabbage and sprouts). Champagne has a lovely coq au vin made with local red Bouzy wine. Its chalky soil favours pigs and sheep, and you can still get real, tender mutton. You can also taste real Brie cheese.

You hear cowbells in Franche-Comté, symbol of the local dishes. Fine beef in the valleys, superb cheeses in the mountains, but the whole area is famous for pork, with many fine sausages; true mountain ham is magnificent. Mountain streams bring trout, pike, eels, salmon trout and crayfish. Pochouse – freshwater fish stewed in wine – can be delicious.

It is a White-Winesman's route. Franche-Comté (particularly the part truly called Jura) makes vin jaune – yellow wine kept six years in cask, a little like sherry and used a lot for cooking. Whites made from Chardonnay grape are the best, rosé from Arbois is smooth, like a pale red; reds are very ordinary; Vin Fou (mad wine) is cheap, refreshing, sparkling, not comparable, with Champagne. 'Let us not talk about Champagne, let us drink it,' one of the Mercier family said to me. Drink it *now.* Alas, two bad harvests have brought a shortage, prices are rising above inflation. Don't forget the still white wine – splendid!

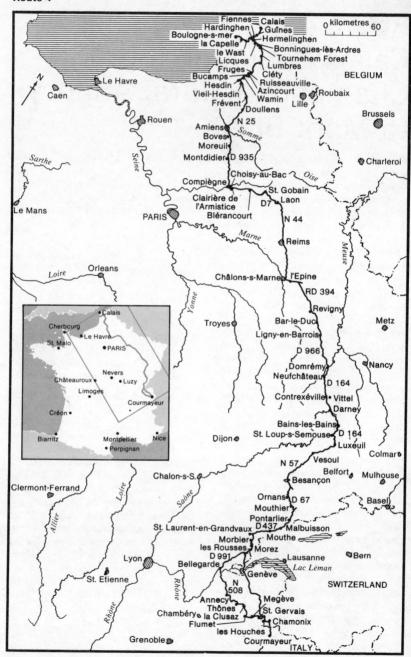

La Feuillandine, pl d'Armes, (21)97.32.57: when the famous Hamiot family sold their brasserie in Boulogne, Dad joined Grandad at the gastronomic Atlantic Hotel in Wimereux; grandson Eric started this simple, attractive little restaurant in Calais; already making an impact with menu 'marché' – fresh ingredients bought daily; short menu of good dishes. Mother Jacqueline shares cooking; menu 51F; carte reasonable. Shut Sunday.

Le Channel, bd Résistance, (21) 34.42.30: very popular with British tourists; service efficient, food reliable; open kitchen promotes customer confidence; good fish; menu 33, 52, 110F. Shut Sunday evening, Tuesday off season; 15 Dec.–15 Jan.

Coq d'Or, pl d'Armes, (21)34.79.05: new owners have settled down; back in favour locally; several menus 45–100F; 77F menu good value; Shut Wednesday.

Sole Meunière, bd Résistance, (21)34.43.01: next door to Channel; more formal, traditional; once one of the best fish restaurants in N. France – now smaller, cheaper, but still strong on fish; menu 39–100F. Shut Monday, Sunday evening, out of season; 20 Dec.–26 June.

Signposts from ferry encourage you to hurry round the town, but there are genuine local grocers, greengrocers and wine shops; many are around pl d'Armes, a medieval square until destroyed in last war; rebuilt in functional style. Cheese shop across square offers 200 cheeses; super fresh fish shop for moules or oysters to take home. Locals mostly shop in streets higher up, beyond railway station (bd Lafayette, bd Jacquard). Outside Flemish town hall is Rodin's statue to the burghers who defied the English under Edward III; on islet in the harbour, the Green Jackets (Rifle Brigade) stood against Nazis in 1940. War museum in German naval HQ bunker includes British wartime newspapers. Hypermarket at Marck sells *almost* everything. You can wheel your trolley into the café and have anything from coffee and brandy to a meal – if you fancy eating in a supermarket.

Calais has large beach used by locals, not Britons. From Blériot Plage, 2 km on D940 Blériot took off from beach on first Channel flight in 1909. A memorial also to Lambert, who ditched in Channel, earlier and was picked up nonchalantly smoking a cigarette. Must have been a calm day!

Calais *continued*	Moulin à Poivre, rue Neuve, (21)96.22.32: my first meal here six years ago was superb; now it varies – some good, some not so good; my friends agree. Perhaps we expect too much, but carte is not cheap. Simple menu at 40F is good value. Shut Sunday, Monday lunch.	
	At Blériot Plage (2 km on D940) – Des Dunes (21)34.54.30: charming old country inn has sprouted modern dining room; cooking still excellent; try salmon rillettes; sea food; sole in champagne; menu 38–140F; rooms (being renovated) 78–105F. Shut Monday; early Oct., Feb.	

D127 Guînes,
Fiennes,
Hardinghen
(18 km)

Guînes – Lion d'Or in main square; old, simple bar-restaurant; looks like a film set for World War I; menu 39, 65F.

Guînes: looks left over from World War I, with small shops in old squares, old fashioned cafés. When Britain owned Calais, Guînes was English front-line, nearby Ardres was French line. Between them (on D231) Henry VIII met Francis I in an ostentatious show of wealth and pomp to discuss an alliance 'Field of the Cloth of Gold'. They tried to out-do each other in everything. Henry alone had 5000 followers from Court, dressed in velvet, satin and gold; Francis used 6000 workmen to prepare the site; Cardinal Wolsey, the English organizer, sent over, among other items, 2,014 sheep and 4 bushels of mustard! D127 passes through Forest of Guînes, with hillsides covered in oak, beech, hornbeam, and birch – lovely walks. High on a hill to the left is a memorial to Col. Blanchard; in 1785 he and an American, Dr Jeffries, left Dover in a balloon and landed here – first aeronauts to cross the Channel.

Boulogne (to Hardinghen)

Brasserie Alfred, pl Dalton, (21)31.53.16: old wood, gingham tablecloths; deserved success means my old favourite packs them in tight; service slower, too, but cooking as good as ever; menu 70, 150F (gastronomic); wines good value. Shut Tuesday.

Chez Jules, pl Dalton, (21)31.54.12: younger locals eat here; plastic look – good value; try farandol Boulonnaise (plate of several fishes); menu 53–60F. Snacks. Shut 1–2 pm daily.

La Charlotte, rue Doyen (next to 'Alfred'), (21)30.13.08: tiny; enterprising fish dishes; try fish terrine; sole in mint; menu 68–100F, wines pricey. Shut Sunday.

Chez Zizine, rue Amiral-Bruix, (21)31.43.24: looks a bit run-down, but that is part of the simple act. Superb value for fish; few tables; something of a fashion with Britons, so book, menu 40F. Shut Sunday.

More interesting than Calais. The port from which Caesar invaded Britain has stimulating vitality and is constantly invaded by British day-trippers until early evening. Good place for shopping, for cheaper meals. Fish market on quayside daily, and food and flower market outside old St Nicolas church in pl Dalton – Wednesday and Saturday, 6 am –1 pm. Its main interest, which people hurrying southwards miss, is old Ville Haute (at top of Grande Rue); surrounded by 13th-century walls with 17 towers. Walk round the top of walls for superb views; castle where future Napoleon III imprisoned in 1840 after landing from England to start a doomed coup, and Britain's Unknown Soldier lay in state in 1919 on way to Whitehall burial. Cathedral has a Roman crypt where England's Edward II married a French princess. Their son claimed the French throne and started the Hundred Years War.

Boulogne
continued

Club (formerly Hamiot), opposite fish market, is no longer run by Hamiot family, but locals, as well as tourists, still use it, including families on Sundays; English critic condemned it on one plate of moules marinières; I have had at least 40 plates of it here with no complaints. Cheap meals of local dishes, especially fish.

Union de la Marine, bd Gambetta, (21)37.38.83: large, cheap, good value; menu 30–50F, wine 14F, opposite fish market.

De la Plage, bd Sainte Beuve, (21)31.45.35: friendly; useful overnight; menu 50–60F; rooms 65–100F. Shut Monday.

La Ménéstrel, rue Brécquerecque, (21)36.60.16: good Relais Routiers; clean rooms, noisy street; good cooking, excellent value. Try fish soup, steak poivre; menu 35–50F; wines 19–48F; rooms 50–60F. Shut December.

Magnificent cathedral dome dominates Boulogne. From Gayette tower, de Rozier, first man to make a successful balloon journey, tried to balloon across Channel in 1785; he lies in nearby Wimille cemetery.

Good shops, especially in rue Faidherbe and turnings off. Sandy beach, where bathing started in 1789, has casino with indoor pool. On D940 Wimereux road see Calvair – huge cross dedicated to sailors. Chapel (open) of nearby Château Souverain Moulin in Wimereux Valley has three tapestries by great modern master Jean Lurçat.

N42 La Capelle
(8 km)

Auberge de la Forêt, (21) 31.82.05: attractive period furnishing; specializes in fish and home-made foie gras; menu 68F (includes wine) 83F. Shut Tuesday, Sunday evening out of season. Sells its special pâté foie gras to take away.

Edge of forest of Boulogne; oaks, ash; walks, rides; picnic tables.

After 7 km, left on D127 to Le Wast 6 km; after Le Wast, turn right still on D127 (*not* on D127E to left) to Hardinghen (22 km)

La Wast: favourite place of Boulogne people; fine country village; 12th-century church has unusual Roman portal.

From Hardinghen left on D191 Hermelingen, Licques, D217 Bonningues-les-Ardres D225 through Tournehem Forest to Lumbres (30 km) D192, D193 to join D928 at Cléty, D928 Fruges Ruisseauville, left on D123 to Azincourt (35 km)

Lumbres – Moulin de Mombreux, (21)39.62.44: difficult to find, but many do, so book! Lovely water-mill in unlikely spot near factory chimneys (unseen once in mill grounds). We found it 16 years ago when Jean-Mare Gaudry slipped in quietly from l'Oasis at Napoules (3-star Michelin) and offered true gastronomic cooking in remote Pas de Calais village. It remains a revelation. Magnificent rich, thick, 'alcoholic' French sauces; everything beautiful, especially vegetables; little choice; menu 100, 160F; rooms vary in size and price: 55–100F shut Sunday evening, Monday.

Trou Normand on N42, (21)39.63.65: village inn; wood tables, check cloths; country dishes – trout, rabbit, guinea-fowl, local chicken; menu 50–75F; simple rooms from 45F. Shut Sunday evening, Monday.

These little roads take you through a hidden, almost secret countryside which few Frenchmen know and fewer Britons. Attractive, with hamlets, old village churches and wooded slopes. An escapist's route.

Licques is the market centre for hamlets; was Spanish under Charles V's empire, as were many places around here.

Lumbres: on river l'Aa; old squares, narrow streets, trout fishing, market, but also paper mills, cement works.

Fruges: little town with old houses, huge reconstructed church and statues of St Augustine and St Monique.

Azincourt is our 'Agincourt' where in 1415 our Henry V's small army, racked with sickness, beat a French army three times its size. The ground is simply and poignantly marked with a cross.

Right to
Bocamps and
back to D928
Wamin,
through Hesdin
Forest to
Hesdin (18 km)

Hesdin – La Chope, rue d'Arras, (21)06.82.73: happy, old-style auberge to which people (including myself) return year after year; not much to look at, but try Mme Samper-Deman's cooking! Mostly Flemish, but something from all over France. Do try tarte Flamiche (tart with leek, cheese and cream). Nice choice of cheaper wines. Locals drink here. Clean rooms. Menu 42–90F; rooms 83–111F. Shut Thursday except July, August.

Des Flandres, rue d'Arras (21)06.80.21: modernized Logis; local businessmen use restaurant, big open grill: I had superb Canche trout in almonds; menu 40–82F; rooms 47–160F. Shut 20 Dec.–10 Jan.

Charming forest with picnic tables. Hesdin in an attractive old town at meeting of two rivers; Renaissance church and pleasant market square. Town hall is former palace of Marie of Hungary, sister of Charles V, in 16th century; ballroom is now a theatre.

D110 Vieil-
Hesdin, D340
Fillièvres,
Monchel-sur-
Canche,
Frévent D916
Doullens

Fillièvres – Auberge du Vieux Moulin, (21)04.83.42: modernized, next to old mill by river, so splendid Canche trout; local meat; excellent faux-filet beef and old-fashioned pot-au-feu; good value; menu 38F (weekdays), 52F (Sunday lunch); rooms 64–68F. Another 'Village Fleuris'.

Doullens – Aux Bons Enfants, rue d'Arras, (22)77.06.58: attractive old Logis with mostly Flemish cooking: try flamiche Picarde; ficelle (stuffed pancake); poulet du Comté (chicken in Gruyère cheese sauce); plat du jour (changes daily) 30F; menu 48–95F; rooms 60–100F. Shut Saturday.

Vieil-Hesdin: old town where medieval Counts of Artois lived; destroyed by army of Charles V in 1553; now a pretty village. Route to Frévent known as 'road of the villages of flowers' (Villages Fleuris). Take D102 at Conchy (4 km) to Château de Flers. (Louis XVI, in brick and stone), former home of Barons of Flers; family chapel; riding stables and school in out-buildings.

Frévent on river Canche; plastic factory, but also nice gardens and attractive town.

Le Sully, rue d'Arras, (22)77.10.87: I have not yet tried it, but well recommended to me. Known for lapin Flamande: flamiche Picarde; menu 35F (in week): 45–80F; rooms 55–69F. Shut Monday in winter; 13–30 April.

At Pommera (5 km on N25) – La Faisanderie, (21)48.20.76: lovely old farm with wood fire; looks like classic old French inn. Wonderful meals by highly creative chef: Chef Jean-Pierre Dargent uses many old traditional ingredients such as nettles, blanched; menu 55, 75, 115F.

Doullens: many old Picardie buildings have survived. Here in March 1918, when German counter-attack by Ludendorff threatened to split British and French armies. British Commander-in-Chief, Douglas Haig, suggested diplomatically a single command under French General Foch ('If General Foch consents to give me his advice, I shall listen willingly'). The alliance was saved, the war won.

Interesting museum Lambart in old convent (antiques, folklore, paintings). Doullens is known for macaroon biscuits.

N16 Amiens (30 km)

Hôtel St Roch, pl Foch, (22)91.38.69: a Relais Routiers where they speak English, cook local specialities and offer low price meals with good choice; try coquilles de

Amiens lost 700 houses in 1918, 4700 during World War II but much that is old and beautiful survives. Velvet has been made here for centuries: so have duck pie, macaroons and pancakes.

Amiens
continued

poisson; ficelle Picarde; trout; faux-filet of beef with peppers; choice of 25 desserts; menu 29.50, 42, 57.50F. Provence rosé wine 14.60F; rooms 42–68F. Open 6.30 am until 1 am except Sunday evening. On rather busy corner.

Les Voyageurs – le Mermoz, rue Jean-Mermoz, (22)91.50.63: renovated even to the white napkins; good cooking; try leak and cream tart, turbot terrine, salmon, duck; menu 55F (in week), 75–150F. Shut Sunday evening.

Joséphine, rue Siere-Firmin-Leroux, (22)91.47.38: Louis Pollene has cooked in this period house for 35 years. He believes in traditional cooking with cream, sauces; grills over wood fire, and is not afraid of the frying pan; the people of Amiens love his cooking; menu 60–75F. Shut Sunday evening, Monday; August.

Cathedral is one of largest in France. Built 1220–69; famous statue of Christ on pillar of middle door; interior regarded as architectural 'miracle'. Roof 42 m (138 ft) high supported by 126 slender pillars. Wonderful rose window 35 m (115 ft) in diameter: 110 choir stalls, magnificently carved. About 60 per cent of Amiens was rebuilt from 1946 onwards and it is a well-planned city. On canal du Hocquet where, every Tuesday, Thursday and Saturday is held Market on the Water at 7–8 am big black boats come to the quay to sell vegetables and fruit. East of the city are the 'horti-lonnages – market gardens where fruit and vegetables are irrigated by streams into which the river Somme divides here.

N334 Boves
D935 Moreuil,
Montdidier
(36 km)

Montdidier – Hôtel de Dijon, (22)78.01.35: reasonable value; friendly; menu 40–90F; rooms 46.50–120F.

Montdidier: was always in trouble; sieges, sackings, burnings through history. When French troops freed it from Germans in 1918, they found little but ruins. A pleasant town was rebuilt. Law Courts survived which have an interesting 16th-century Flemish tapestry.

D935
Compiègne
(32 km)

Hôtel de France et Rôtisserie du Chat qui Tourne, rue E. Floquet, 440.02.74: the cat who turned the spit to roast a chicken belonged originally to a mountebank who performed here in 1665. Now it turns by electricity. Charming old hotel; fine cooking, but not cheap. 'Repas' 39.50F menu 76.50F gastronomic menu 165F; rooms 84–160F.

Le Picotin, pl Hôtel de Ville, 440.04.06: traditional French cooking, pleasant; fair value; menu 40–70F. Shut Dec., Jan.

Flandre, quai République, 483.24.40: looks like a bank outside, a gentleman's club within; solid comfort; reliable traditional cooking; menu 48–58F; rooms 80–150F.

At Elincourt-Ste Marguerite (15 km by N32 N and D142) – Château de Bellingese, 476.04.76: a bit pricey but what a delight! 16th-century Louis XVI château in pink with turrets and grey-green roof; set in big park with lake; one of the 'Châteaux Hôtels Indépendants' as opposed to 'Châteaux Hôtels de France'. Lovely furnishings; excellent chef; try baron of lamb with aromatic herbs; turbot in champagne, wines 25–350F; menu 80–160F; rooms 190–230F. Restaurant shut Sunday evening, Monday.

In a huge forest 72 km north of Paris, Compiègne is rich in art treasures. Here Kings of France always had a hunting hideout. Louis XV had a new castle built – rather severe but elegant. Louis XVI, when Dauphin, first received his fiancée here. It became a barracks, but Napoleon restored it as his castle home and Napoleon III and Empress Eugénie held impressive hunts and balls. Rooms of Marie-Antoinette and the Napoleons retain their tapestries and furniture. Many Empire-period paintings including Boudins. Vivenel Museum has a vast collection of treasures spanning centuries, with superb Greek vases. Musée de la Figurine Historique has 80,000 lead, wood and board soldiers. I love the Vehicle and Tourism Museum, with 150 vehicles from a Roman chariot to a Citroën chain-track car and including diligences (stage coaches), a post chaise, superb sledges, a remarkable steam coach (1885), early cars.

N31, D546 to
Clairière de
l'Armistice
(5 km)

In this lovely glade, Marshal Foch, commander of Allied Forces, received the German surrender in 1918, in a railway carriage. In 1940 Hitler insisted on receiving the French surrender here.

D81 Choisy au Bac, D130 through Laigue forest to D934, then right to Blérancourt (32 km)

Choisy au Bac – Aub-des-Etangs du Buissonnet, 440.17.41: pricey but good; excellent cooking; lake, park; on edge of forest; carte only 100–150F. Shut Sunday evening, Monday.

Blérancourt – Hostellerie Le Griffon, (23)52.60.11: charming, restful inn with pretty garden at castle gates: Parisians drive out at weekends to eat. Menu sensibly governed by market and seasons. Try salmon Pojarsky (superb salmon 'fish cakes'): very good flamiche (leek, egg, butter and cream tart); menu 60–110F; rooms 70–150F. Shut Sunday evening, Monday.

Lovely forest run, mostly beeches. Blérancourt is a quiet hideout of knowledgeable Parisians on relaxing weekends. It was the centre of terrible battles (1916–1918). It was rebuilt by Ann Morgan, daughter of the US banker, Pierrepoint Morgan, as a symbol of Franco-American friendship, and its castle, dating from the 17th century, houses a Franco-American museum mostly of the Kaiser's war, including a superb T-Ford ambulance. Pretty gardens.

D5, D13 through St Gobain Forest to St Gobain, D7 Laon (31 km)

Bannière de France, rue F. Roosevelt, (23)23.21.44: friendly old inn with lots of polished wood and cosy rooms; meals excellent value; charming atmosphere. Menu 50F (includes wine), 85, 130F; well chosen wines; rooms 61–210F. Shut 20 Dec.–10 Jan.

Angleterre, bd Lyon (in lower town), (23)23.04.62: modern hotel, much nicer inside; comfort, pleasant décor; reliable cooking at sensible prices; menu 45, 75, 130F; rooms 65–190F.

La Petite Auberge, bd Brossolette (lower town) (23)23.51.79: bargain; rôtisserie – using wood fire cooking; good steaks, ham steaks, veal cutlets; menu 37, 51, 79F. Shut Saturday.

Forest mostly of oak, but other trees in the valleys; once frequented by wolves and wild boar; still plenty of game, and mushrooms; shallow lakes. St Gobain was an Irish hermit who settled here.

Laon: delightful old city, once capital of France (4th to 9th centuries), set high on a steep hill, with magnificent views, especially from medieval ramparts; worth an overnight stop to explore and enjoy its old buildings, streets, and rampart walks. Cathedral of Notre Dame (12th century) is one of the oldest Gothic cathedrals in France. From outside it is beautiful, inside it is magnificent.

N44 Reims (47 km)

Good restaurants mostly very dear (Boyer, ave d'Epernay, around 350F for a meal); too many tourist restaurants charging too much for mediocre cooking.

Restaurant Le Drouet, at Hôtel la Paix, rue Buirette, (26)40.04.08: 'Grand Hotel' – style restaurant giving very good value, good service; menu 60–95F. Shut Sunday.

Climat de France, la Neuvillette, (26)09.62.73: quiet, in pretty setting; menu 41–64F; rooms 130–169F.

The Kings of France used to be crowned here and I don't blame them. The cathedral is a masterpiece; it was begun in 1211, damaged in World War I, restored in 1938. 13th-century and modern (Braque) glass both magnificent.

Many of us don't go to Reims for church architecture so much as to visit the Champagne cellars. You might decide to put off this pleasure until you reach Epernay; I don't; I visit one cellar in each town. For some visits you need letters of introduction. Without introduction you can see

Reims
continued

these in Reims: Mumm – 34 rue du Champ de Mars; 45-minute tour. Veuve-Clicquot-Ponsardin – pl des Droits de l'Homme; nice historic story of the Widow. All offer tastings; hours vary but mostly 9–11 am, 2–4 pm weekdays. Clicquot opens Saturdays, Sundays except winter.

N44 Châlons Sur Marne (44 km)

Angleterre, pl Mon Tissier, (26)68.21.51: same owners as Armes de Champagne at L'Epine, different chef and menu; even lighter Nouvelles. I like filet de boeuf au Ratafia (unfermented grape juice and brandy). Attractive flowery terrace; menu 50, 92, 132F; rooms 98–192F. Shut Sunday, Monday evenings; 15 Feb.–15 March.

Here in AD 451, in a bloody battle in which 200,000 were killed, Attila the Hun, 'scourge of God', was beaten by Romans, Visigoths and Francs; he fled to Hungary and turned his hordes on to Italy.

N3 L'Epine D394 Revigny, Bar-le-Duc (53 km)

Aux Armes de Champagne, (26) 68.10.43: 'cooking takes time', says the carte, 'quality of a dish and speed do not always go together'. How very true. And the food here is worth waiting for. Hughes Hoverd, the chef, came from La Mère Poulard at Mont-Saint-Michel. He tends towards Nouvelle Cuisine with simpler, lighter sauces most carefully cooked; menu 53, 96, 140F; formidable wine list with vintage Champagnes; rooms 105–220F. Shut 10 Jan.–15 Feb.

Bar-le-Duc – Grand Hôtel du Metz et Commerce, bd la Rochelle, (29)79.02.56: very good fish, freshwater and

L'Epine has a basilica from 15th century, built because local people found a statue of the Virgin in a burning bush. Has two realistic gargoyles representing vice and spirit of evil.

Bar-le-Duc. Where the bicycle was invented – monument to the inventors Pierre and Ernest Michaux. Famous, too, for its pipless redcurrant jam! Though industrial, still has old interesting town rising 225 m (740 ft) from bank of river Ornain; 12th-century clock tower; old castle gate leads to esplanade with fine views. In St Etienne church (rue Grangettes) is an

sea; try salmon-trout braised in 'gris' (light rosé wine of Lorraine); sea bass flambé with fennel; menu 42.50–13F; wines 23–200F; rooms 53–150F (on three floors – no lift).

La Meuse Gourmande, rue St Mihiel, (29)79.28.40: Jean-Louis Chrétien, well-known in the business, opened recently small restaurant near the station; genuine regional cooking; very good value; lots of creamy sauces; try timbale of mixed mushrooms and other fungi (delicious); matelote Lorraine (fish soup-stew – very nice); or traditional meat dishes with good sauces: short, well-chosen wine list; menu 48F; carte around 100F for meal. Shut Sunday.

extraordinary macabre statue of a skeleton, by Ligier Richier (pupil of Michelangelo). It is the skeleton of René de Châlon, Prince of Orange, whose widow ordered it. He was killed in 1544 at Siege of St Dizier and is said to have requested a statue of himself three years after his death. I reckon he was misinterpreted! In 1916, Bar-le-Duc was centre of a supply route to the French Army holding Verdun – a route called la Voie Sacrée the Sacred Highway (or Road to Heaven, perhaps) for 650,000 French troops took it to one of the bloodiest battles of the war).

N135 Lignyen Barrois, D966 Domrémy-la-Pucelle, D164 Neufchâteau, Contrexeville (92 km)

Neufchâteau – Hôtel St Christophe, ave Grande-Fontaine, (29)94.16.28: modern dining room overlooks garden; nice meals at reasonable prices; menu 36F (in week), 50, 78F; rooms 82–180F.

Contrexeville – L'Aubergade, rue 11 Septembre, (29)08.04.39: Claude Obriot, no doubt, earned his Michelin star for really good, straight cooking of good fresh ingredients; prices inevitably high; menu 110–175F; wines 35–250F. Shut Sunday evening, Monday; 1–15 Mar.,1–15 Oct.

Domrémy-la-Pucelle: *never* tell a Frenchman that you have not heard of this tiny village. Joan of Arc was born here (16 Jan., 1412); and here she heard her 'voices' telling her to save France from the perfidious English. Her simple home is intact, though the 'coat of arms' of her family seems odd for a peasant girl. More poignant is an inscription 'Vive labeur – 1481 – Vive le Roi Louis'. House next door is a museum. Basilica de Bois Chenu is 1.5 km along D53 (Coussey road). Started 1881,

Contrexeville
continued

At Norroy (D13 from Contrexeville, right at Mandres-Sur Vair, 7 km) – L'Orei du Bois, (29)08.13.51: modern, in nice setting on border of forest, beside entrance to horse-racing track; quiet, period furnishings; good cooking, accommodating menu and price system, with alternatives of eating two or three courses. Quick meal 40F; menu 65–108F; local trout; quail; quiche Lorraine like mother never knew how to make; happy service. Shut Monday (mid-winter); November.

consecrated 1925, it is in the spot where she heard 'the voices'. Inside are frescoes by Lionel Royer recording Joan's life.

Neufchâteau: old town on hill above river Meuse: still has old houses; ramparts and fortifications destroyed by order of Richelieu.

Contrexeville: 335 m (1100 ft) up in Vosges mountains: old spa with mineral springs; casino and park. Richly wooded area: Lac de la Folie prettily placed in woods.

5 km on D429 – Vittel; spa; taste famous mineral water from the spring, not from a pub bottle! But local factory fills 3½ million bottles a year. Used for alleviation of gout, arthritis, migraine and liver ailments, and added to brandy and Scotch as well.

D164 Darney, Bain-les-Bains (43 km)

Darney – Hôtel l'Eléphant, (29)09.43.36: this modern Elephant is a Logis which looks more like a beehive. Nice views from terrace over Vosges countryside; enthusiastic and friendly service; modernity of dining room tempered with plants and flowers. Cuisine 'au natural' – best way to cook local fresh ingredients; try fish terrine, Vosges blue trout, local raw ham quail; good wine list; menu 45–130F; rooms 70–150F. Shut in winter (1 Nov.–26 March).

Darney: a Czech museum in its town hall! Here on 30 June, 1918, French President Poincaré proclaimed in the name of the Allies, before M. Benes and two Free Czech regiments, the independence of Czechoslovakia. Pretty little town on Saône river in hills, forests.

Bain-les-Bains: yet another little Vosges spa (for maladies of heart and arteries, and hyper-tension). Fine park on both sides of river Baignerot. Two baths, one on site of original Roman bath. Beautiful

Bain-les-Bains
Hôtel des Sources, pl Bain Romain, (29)36.21.08: very good value; pleasant dining room; family cooking with variety; menu 34F and 41F in week, 55F Sundays; house wine (red or rosé) only 12F; rooms 55–65F.

scenery, with quiet walks by river and through woods. Attractive place.

D164, D64 St Loup-sur-Semouse, Luxeuil-les-Bains, N57 Vesoul (57 km)

Luxeuil – Beau-Site, rue Thermes, (84)40.16.67: good cooking; try potée Lorraine; trout in 'yellow' wine of Jura; lapin à la moutarde (rabbit in mustard sauce – very nice). Flower garden; central for sport, thermal establishment, casino; all very good value; menu 50F in week, 55F Sunday; rooms 70–200F. Shut Sunday evening in winter.

Luxeuil: spa, well-known in France; hot baths (gynaecological treatment, rheumatism); in woods and pastures; old town with lovely old buildings. St Colomba of Ireland founded the abbey, dispersed in the Revolution; known for its strict physical punishments meted out to erring monks. Superb flamboyant Gothic house (15th century) built by

Vesoul
continued

Aux Vendanges de Bourgogne, bd Ch. de Gaulle, (84)75.12.09: very pleasant; comfortable; attractive décor; pavement tables; flowers on restaurant tables; remarkable value for such standards; 35F Plat du Jour menu with entrée meat and vegetables, dessert or cheese; other menus 47–100F; splendid trout and local Franche-Comtois dishes; house wine (red) 15.50F, rooms (comfortable) 65–160F. Restaurant shut 5–28 Aug.

Cardinal Jouffroy, favourite of Louis XI. Later inhabitants included Madame de Sévigné, poet Lamartine and Augustin Thierry.

Vesouls: lovely old houses from 14th–18th centuries; below a hill, La Motte, topped by a chapel with views to the Vosges and Jura mountains, sometimes the Alps, too. You must climb it on foot.

N57 Besançon
(46 km)

Restaurant Poker d'As pl St Amour, (81)81.42.49: I gather it means 'Poker Dice'. Known for its fine fresh fish and high standard of all ingredients, simple careful cooking; menus 55–126F; wines rather pricey. Shut mid July to mid August.

Terrass, rue Belfort, (81)83.40.45: reliable, complete renovation; comfortable bedrooms include some family rooms for four people; serves good charcuterie and cheese from the mountains near by; menu 44–115F; rooms 75–160F; Restaurant shut Sunday.

Julius Caesar remarked on its strategic importance; now people remark on its splendid position, with river Doubs wandering attractively in a loop round the fortified rock. Looks like huge old defence citadel but is capital of Franche-Comté province, has an archbishop, a university and is important politically and commercially; also a spa and holiday resort. Archbishopric under the Emperor Constantine, sacked by Barbarians in Dark Ages; rebuilt in 1031. Was variously part of Germany, Burgundy and Flanders. Louis XIV had Vauban, great military architect, build the citadel (open all year). So many interesting museums here that I suggest you go to Tourist Office, pl I're Armee Française (80.92.65). for list and times of opening.

N57, D67
Ornans
(26 km)

De France, rue Pierre-Vernier, (81)62.24.44.: famous old hotel; patron-chef Serge Vincent rightly proud of the cuisine; try blue trout, duck, house terrine; menu 55–95F; rooms (re-fitted 1981) 95–162F. Shut Monday; February.

Au Progrès, (81)62.16.73: neat, white-painted Relais Routiers and 1-star hotel; meals excellent value; menu 31–105F; rooms (quiet and well kept) 60–78F. Shut Sunday in winter.

Beautiful scene as river Loue runs between old balconied houses; see them from Grand Pont. Grotte de Plaisir Fontaine on D67, 5.5 km before Ornans (signposted on small road to left – to right if coming from Ornans); park car, walk. Lovely countryside all round here, D67 passes through ravine by rivers Brëme and Loue. Superb villages tucked beside rivers between wooded hills, rapids loved by canoeists; splendid fishing. Gustave Courbet, father of Realist movement in painting, born here 1819. Some of his works in his birthplace (open to public). His animal paintings are a delight.

D67 Mouthier-
Haute-Pierre,
on to N57
Pontarlier, N57,
right on D437

Pontarlier – Gai Soleil, at Doubs, 2 km, (81)39.16.86: evenings only; good value; menu 42, 65F; rooms 50–90F. Open mid-June to mid-Sept.

Countryside gets even better. Mouthier is lovely little place, under wooded slopes capped by sheer rocks, then more trees. Spectacular. Lods, its

Malbuisson,
Mouthe, St
Laurent-en-
Grandvaux
(63 km)
N5 Morbier,
Morez, Les
Rousses
(21 km)

Malbuisson – Auberge la Poste, (81)89.31.72: modern, but a typical Logis de France, with simple charm, run with enthusiasm and understanding; alas restaurant open only to hotel guests mid June to mid Sept. Excellent value; game in season; roast meat and duck; family cooking 'comme á la maison'. 200 wines at reasonable prices, from 18F – all French districts, including Corsica. Menu 40–70F; rooms 70–120F, half-board 3 days or more 130F.

Morez – Poste, rue République, (84)33.11.03: my spies give it high marks for value; traditional cooking; good choice; roasts; chicken in local wine; house wine 20F; menu 47.50, 73, 175F; rooms 80–133F. Terrace, garden. Shut 15 Nov.–15 Dec.

Les Rousses – Relais des Gentians, rue Pasteur, (84)60.02.79: happy hotel and restaurant, making most of mountain food: fresh crayfish; trout in yellow wine; chicken with fungi (Morilles, etc.); also poularde de Bresse; 'patio' room for snacks and drinks, with Andalucian theme, including girls in Spanish dress. Some bedrooms look like those of successful courtesans; most of hotel comfortably simple. Menu 55–150F; rooms 150–220F. Shut in June and October.

neighbour, red-roofed village hiding beside river; Vuillafans, near Ornans, has lovely bridge; Mouthier cherries used for making Kirsch liqueur.

Malbuisson: a summer resort on Lake St Point, 6 km long, for watersports; lake freezes in winter; cross-country skiing (langlauf), super summer fishing. Lake Romeray (8 km south) separated by Clay ridge, is prettier. Source Bleu (3 km north of Malbuisson on side road) – deep, pure water. Local lord returning from the Crusades found that his young wife had consoled herself with a lover. From the prison where he put her, she could see her lover-boy hanging from a gibbet. Her tears coloured the water blue.

St Laurent makes excellent cheese; rebuilt after being burned down in 1867, still looks a bit temporary. Centre for Pic de l'Aigle (11 km NW) 993 m (3258 ft) high, with views across all Jura, even to Mont Blanc in good weather.

Morez: famous for watches and spectacles (those you see through); pince-nez glasses were launched here; also makes morbier – firm, white cheese with a formidable smell.

Les Rousses: at 1100 m (3609 ft) – winter sports centre; nice forest for walks.

We are now coming into winter sport country. Route ahead includes some tough patches. In winter, unless you are a very experienced snow-and-ice, driver, and car is well equipped I suggest taking routes Les Rousses to Geneva (Switzerland), then motorway to St Gervais.) Better weather route from Les Rousses to Annecy is – N5 for 15 km, then right on D936 for 6 km; left on D991 to Bellegarde-sur-Valserine N508 Annecy (88 km)

Bellegarde – Belle Epoque, pl Gambetta, (50)48.14.46: looks like its name; small mock castle on a street corner, built 1900, furnished in style; comfort, calm in middle of town; good cooking of sound ingredients; menu 48–125F; rooms 85–159F. Shut Tuesday (out of season); January.

At Lancrans, 3 km on D991 – Du Sorgia, (50)48.15.81: pleasant, comfortable, reasonable prices; Logis de France; menu 38–70F; rooms 64–80F. Shut Monday.

At La Balme de Sillingy (30 km from Bellegarde 11 km Annecy) – Les Rochers et la Chrissandière, (50)68.70.07: comfortable hotel, and lovely 'residence' annexe in big attractive park; small heated swimming pool; delightful bedrooms. Menu 50–100F; rooms 85–150F. Shut November.

Bellegarde: quite a new town on the Lyon–Mont Blanc tunnel route at meeting of Rhône and Valserine rivers. Good touring base.

Annecy: in gorgeous lakeside situation with Alps around. But industry growth each year, and the old town is nicest. 11th-century castle was residence of Counts of Geneva; burned several times. Reconstructed 15th–16th centuries; not so much one castle as a group of fortified buildings of different periods. Boat trips round lake in season.

Annecy
continued

Annecy – Auberge Lyonnais, rue République, (50)51.26.10: absolutely delightful position, old house in old town on canal, surrounded by flowers in season; like quiet corner of Venice; good steaks, trout; menu 60–94F; rooms 135F.

Au Faison Doré, ave d'Albigny, (50)23.02.46: at end of delightful avenue; looks like small block of flats, but pleasant and cosy inside; quiet; among trees; 100 m from lake and big park. In same family since 1919. Fine, old-fashioned cooking of Savoy; try veal kidneys in Marc (spirit from wine grapes); fillet steaks in cream and green peppers; menu 60–95F; rooms 190F.

D909 Thones, La Clusaz, over Col des Aravis to Flumet (48 km)

La Clusaz – Hôtel Christiania, (50)02.60.60: comfortable, warm: mountain ingredients used in many dishes – salmon, lavaret (salmon-type fish from deep Savoy lakes); splendid Tomme de Savoie cheese, smooth, strong smell but a lovely mild flavour, made in farms and village dairies; menu 50–85F; rooms 90–155F. Shut mid-September to mid February, mid-April to mid-June. A pity!

Difficult route but very rewarding; Col des Aravis impassable because of snow from December to April.

A road of spectacular mountain and valley views; at Col de Bluffy is Château de Menthon, 15th-century replacement for old castle where Bernard de Menthon was born in 10th century – St Bernard himself, founder of the Hospice Grand St Bernard whose dogs (and monks) saved so many lives until the helicopter came to the Alps to rescue lost travellers.

Thones is in a huge dip at meeting of two rivers. At Glières, above Thones, is a cemetery of French Resistance fighters operating from these mountains.

La Clusaz: delightful village hugging its great church among lovely forests of pine and Alpine pastures with background of rugged rocky hills; walking country in summer; winter sports.

Col des Aravis – views become more and more breathtaking as you drive on. Towards end of May the mountain spring flowers bloom – gentians, even; greatest view is the foot of Croix de Fer, just off the road, on a rocky lane from Chalet du Curé.

N212 Megève (10 km)	Being a summer and winter resort, Megève has hotels, pensions and inns of all types, sizes and prices. A question of finding one which suits your taste and pocket and which has vacancies! Ask Office de Tourisme rue Poste, (50)21.27.28. Prices are 'ski-resort' high.	Altitude 1113 m (3650 ft). Oldest of French ski-resorts; still has far more ambience, interest and appeal than new custom-built resorts, which are all concrete, pistes, lifts and earnestness! A real farming village hidden among the ski-runs, launched as a resort in 1919. Splendid in summer, too.
N212, D909 St Gervais-les-Bains (11 km)	Again, consult for vacancies; Office de Tourisms, ave Mt-d'Arbois, (50)78.22.43. Thse are recommended for value:

Couttet, pl l'Eglise, (50)78.26.65: modern but traditional style and welcome; surprisingly good seafish for mountain area; also nice filling 'plats du jour' for mountain air and exercise – coq au vin, lamb sauté, beef Bourguignon; menu 45–110F; rooms 70–150F; full pension 130–160F; rear rooms have views of Aravis chain. | Brightest of the ski-resorts of Grandes Alpes, 807 m (2648 ft) above sea level, traditional base for climbing Mont Blanc. Spa for nearly 150 years; sulphur springs; treatment for skin and respiratory ailments; the air here is a joy to breathe. 'Le Tramway' takes you up mountains to Col du Voza, with grand views of the Mont Blanc range; also to Le Nid d'Aigle (2386 m/7827 ft) and views of the Bionnassay glacier. Le Fayet, the lower part of St Gervais, has an |

Gervais-les-Bains *continued*	La Maison Blanche, (50)78.25.77: most attractive Logis with mountain wood décor and panoramic views from pleasant dining room; 14 bedrooms with bath, WC. Quiet. Menu 50–80F; wines 23–115F; rooms 70–200F (some for 3 or 4 if wished).	interesting church (Notre Dame des Alpes) designed 1939 by Novarina, respected modern church architect; modern style combined with Savoy and 'chalet' style; lovely internal décor by artists of Swiss 'Society St Luc'.
N205 Les Houches, Mont Blanc tunnel (17 km) Chamonix (3 km further)	Chamonix – Office de Tourism, pl Eglise, (50)53.00.24. A pricey place. I have found good restaurants but too dear. Best value I found: Hotel Prieuré, Restaurant La Baita, allée, Recteur Payot, (50)53.20.70: daily change of menu according to market; menu 60F; enormous 'chalet' hotel; nice bedrooms with balconies; very pleasant; room prices include breakfast, tax and service; single rooms 120–165F; twin 156–230F; triple 165–290F. Variations are according to season. Shut 15 Oct.–15 Dec.	Mont Blanc (4807m/15,770 ft): best view of the whole grand *massif* said to be from Trelechamp, village reached on road past Chamonix to Argentière; from here, road is rugged and zig-zagging (about 12 km from Chamonix). Most popular route from France to Italy. Toll around 36–76F for cars. Chamonix (1037 m/3403 ft) is delightful winter and summer resort; also French capital of Alpine climbing, with famous company of guides; interesting Alpine Musuem (open 20 June–15 Sept.). Material on all major ascents and attempts. Wonderful mountain trips; by rack-railway (from near railway station) to Montenvers (1400 m/4594 ft. Cable-car to Plan d'Aiguille (2310 m/7578 ft) with splendid views; here cross a bridge over an abyss to another cable-car to Aiguille du Midi (3800 m/ 12,468 ft) with sensational views; a chair-lift now goes to 3842 m (12,600 ft) for incredible panorama of the Mont Blanc snows. You *must* take warm clothing and sunglasses. Cold is *intense*.

Route 5
Round Brittany

Before jet package holidays, Brittany was the favourite holiday area abroad for British families, and children of my generation met their first foreign friends on the beaches of Dinard, La Baule, Morgat or Benodet. It is still very popular with Parisian families and has renewed its popularity with the British since Brittany Ferries restarted the old St Malo ferry service, and the Cherbourg service of Townsend Thoresen and Le Havre service of Sealink have improved.

Most visitors to Brittany hug the coast, missing many treasures and uncrowded roads inland. The trick when touring is to hit the coast at key spots and enjoy uncrowded by-roads, villages, delightful waterways and low hills of the interior.

You never feel far from the sea in Brittany, even on gorse-covered moors or winding inland waterways. The sea rules life. Brittany has 700 miles of coast – sandy beaches, rocky headlands, tall cliffs, little coves reminding us of Cornwall, salt marshes, fens and hundreds of islands, some just little rocks. The Gulf Stream washes it, bringing gentle warmth to protected beaches; the Atlantic hurls fierce rollers at unprotected rocks.

Bretons regard France as another country, as the Welsh regard England. And it is – a Celtic country where ancient legends and history are interwoven so that you cannot untangle them. Armorica became Brittany gradually because the old Britons fled there from the Saxon invasion of Britain. Not until 1488 did France annexe Brittany – through the marriage of the Duchess of Brittany to the French King. And people there still talk of 'Frenchmen' as if they are foreigners.

For fishermen, sailing enthusiasts, and shellfish addicts like me, Brittany is a special joy. And the hotels have that old-fashioned friendly 'family' feeling of seaside hotels of my youth.

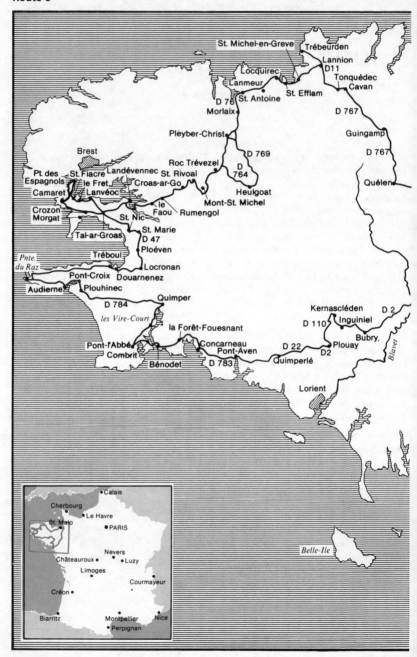

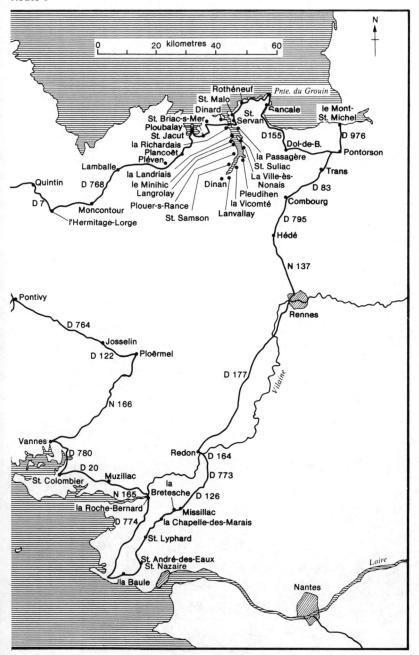

St Malo	See Route 1 (page 21).	
D301 St Servan (5 km)	See Route 1 (page 22).	

N137 right by airfield on D5 to La Passagère back to N137, right on D117 to St Suliac, D7 right to La Ville-ès-Nonais, road right to join D29 to Pleudihen, La Vicomte, N176 Lanvallay, D2 under cross-river viaduct to Dinan (36 km without diversions)

Pleudihen – at Mordreuc, down side road, L'Abri des Flots, (96)27.50.43: Auberge de France with incredibly good value meals; I had help-yourself vegetable soup; ham crêpe, pork chop in rosemary, jacket potato, French beans; cheese and dessert; for 24F including red wine (help yourself from a litre bottle) and mineral water. Small Sunday supplement; rooms (2 people) 50F; full board (1 person) 100F. Overlooking river Rance.

If arriving late and wanting to reach hotel, cross Rance estuary by D168, then right on D266 to Dinard (9 km) – see Route 1 – but tour of Rance is a 'must' and can still be done following day.

La Passagère – good views over river Rance.

At St Suliac, turn left at church, leave car 1 km further on, walk on footpath past old mill to point of Mont Garrot (more lovely views).

From La Ville-ès-Nonais, short detour to Port St-Jean bridge over river Rance with splendid valley views.

Pleudihen: famous for apples 'Doux Eveques', and cider; tidal mill on side road to Mordreuc, attractive hamlet on river bank.

La Vicomté (walk to point) is new snob area of Dinan; nice houses.

Dinan – see Route 1.

Lanvallay – views of old Dinan, ramparts, belfries.

D12 St Samson-sur-Rance, Le Minihic-sur-Rance, right on to D114 for ¼ mile, then D3 to La Landrais, back on to D114 to La Richardais, Dinard (34 km) D766 St Briac (9 km)

La Richardais – Le Petit Robinson, (99)46.14.82: popular locally; good fish – river and sea; menu 45–98F. Shut Tuesday evening, Wednesday (except July, Aug.); part Nov., part Jan.

Dinard – See Route 1

Le Minihic – old fisherman's cottages; La Landrais – park car; walk 1.6 km along Hures Promenade (old customs officers' walk) beside river.

La Richardais: church with fine fresco in green, brown, ochre of Stations of the Cross. Stained glass by the great modern artist Max Ingrand.

Allow 4–5 hours with sightseeing stops for tour round river Rance.

St Briac: pleasant resort; fishing; yachting harbour; beaches; coast views from Balcon d'Emeraude.

D5 minor road, then right on D168 Ploubalay, D168, D26 St Jacut, D62 left for short time on D786, then right on D768 Plancoët D28 Plèven (28 km)

Plancoët – De la Source, (96)84.10.11: 30F menu (except Friday evening, Saturday, Sunday). Also 45–90F. Try shellfish; home-made terrine of pike; veal sweetbreads (ris) in wine; couscous Thursday, Friday; rooms 55–70F.

Plèven – Manoir du Vaumadeuc, (98)84.46.17: expensive but superb; 15th-century manor of the Vicomtesse du Breil de Pontbriand; club atmosphere; medieval décor; magnificent

St Jacut: long peninsula continues into sea with islet of Hébiens; two safe beaches. Nice sea views; several crêperies (pancake cafés).

Pleyden: on edge of lonely Runadaye forest, beside long lake formed by river l'Arguenon.

Plèven
continued

furnishings; bar in 15th-century dovecote; bedroom furnishings are a delight. Châteaux Hôtels Indépendants. Two pavillions in same style. Excellent cuisine 'simple, without pretension'; ingredients from own farm; fine wine cellar; menu 130F; rooms 180–350F. Lake nearby 17 km (10½ miles) long; fishing (boats and tackle provided).

D28 Lamballe
(16 km)

At La Poterie (2 km on D28, left) – Auberge du Manoir des Ports, (96)31.13.62: delightful; I was a founder-guest about 5 years ago when it was being converted from 15th-century manor-farm; charming simple bedrooms; cosy dining room, open fire; park with shallow lake (étang) with fishing; excellent regional cooking; shellfish live from tank; Relais du Silence (calm, rest, silence); good value meals; menu 70F; rooms 180–250F. Shut February; Monday out of season.

Tour d'Argent, rue Dr Lavergne, (96)31.01.37: also delightful, in different way. Genuine small-town Relais with some bedrooms in nice modern annexe (500 yards); traditional family cooking; very good value; menu 35–90F; rooms 68–150F. Relais Routiers with 'casserole' for good regional cooking.

Charming little town of whitewashed houses on hillside; big market for pigs, cattle; fine old buildings; Gothic-Romanesque church on terrace overlooking Gouessant river valley; views. Old houses in pl du Martrai include 15th-century executioner's house (now Tourist Information Office and small museum). Only chapel survives of Lamballe Castle – pulled down by order of Richelieu because owner, Lord of Penthièvre, son of Henry IV, conspired against him; castle besieged in Religious Wars by 'Bras de Fer' – Calvinist captain La Nouë who had metal hook in place of lost arm. He was killed at siege. Henry IV said sadly: 'Pity that such a little fortress destroyed so great a man.'

Lamballe's one-way traffic system is difficult. Best known for its stud farm for

Angleterre, bd Jobert, (96)
31.00.16: 3–star, modern
interior; large dining room;
comfortable bedrooms; no
frozen foods; menu 50–85F;
also lunch snacks (omelette
18F, mussels 16F); house
wine 22F; rooms 60–160F.
Restaurant shut November.

Breton draught horses and
old style post-horses. Has
about 150 stallions; go out
daily in tandem, pairs or
fours, but sent away to stud-
stands mid-Feb. to mid-July;
also dressage school (40
horses), riding school.

D768
Moncontour
(15 km)

Hôtel de France (on D768
just past village),
(96)73.41.37: very good 55F
menu: 2 starters from
salmon terrine, duck pâté,
asparagus tips, Breton
terrine, sweetbreads and
mushrooms; main course –
quail, salmon, braised steak,
lamb Provençale, tournedos,
veal escalope chasseur;
cheese; sweet; wine 15–90F.

Attractive old fortified town
of granite where two valleys
meet. Six fine Renaissance
stained-glass windows in
church; alleys and stairs lead
down to ramparts. Place
Penthièvre fine example of
18th-century architecture;
Notre Dame du Haut (5.5 km
back towards Lamballe on
D768; right at cross-roads on
D6 Collinée, right on D6A –
ask for key at nearest farm) –
wood statues of healer
saints; go to them with good

Moncontour
continued

humble hearts and they will help, it is said; votive plaques marked 'Merci' show that some believers are left.

D44 Ploeuc, L'Hermitage-Lorge, D168, then soon D7 through forest of Lorge to Quintin (29 km)

Quintin – Hôtel du Commerce, (96)74.94.67: little country-style hotel with beams, pretty bedrooms; peaceful; Mme Le Gaudu gives smiling service; her husband cooks Breton-style; try excellent stuffed praires (type of clam); all fish excellent, often with good béarnaise or hollandaise sauce; coq au vin; potée Bretonne; menu 48–134F; good choice of wine from 18F; rooms 72.50–134F.

First right off D44 on D25A at Henon is Elevage du Rocher de Bremar – famous for duck and goose-liver pâté.

3.5 km south of L'Hermitage-Lorge, where D778 meets D7 to Uzel, is a noticeboard: 'This is Lorges, centre of Resistance for the Département, where 55 men of the Resistance, after torture, were murdered and buried in this wood by Nazi hordes. In the night, freedom listens to us.' A stone points to a dark pinewood on a hill.

Quintin: another charming old town; old houses rise in terraces from Guet river: riverside lake; very good fishing; 17th-century wing to castle; in church, a piece of the Virgin's girdle brought from Jerusalem in 13th century.

D28 Quélen, D767 Guingamp (46 km)

Guingamp – Relais du Roy, pl Centre, (96)43.76.62: 18th-century façade; Louis XIII dining room; impeccable service and table setting (Limoges china); excellent cooking with outstanding fish, from mussels in cider to soles aux cèpes and lobster. Not cheap, of course; menu 65F (weekdays), 100F (excellent value), 120F; rooms 160–250F.

Guingamp: countryside on route from Quintin seems almost empty – tiny hamlets, chapels, streams, pools, roadside crosses; green lanes, once roads for carts and horses, now overgrown except where tractors pass.

D767 Cavan, small road left Tonquédec Castle, D31b to join D11 into Lannion (30 km)

Lannion – Hôtel Bretagne, avè de Gaulle, (96)37.00.33: almost opposite station; meals good but disappointment in room and service; bedroom at 85F with bath smelt musty, no heating on cold night; in bar, full of locals, girl put chairs on tables at 9 p.m. to sweep up for the night. Menu 45, 65, 85F; rooms 60–100F. Shut Friday evening, Saturday; 25 Sept.–mid Oct.

At Le Yaudet (D786 towards Morlaix, then D88A 8 km), lovely little river port with beach – La Gavotte, (96)35.14.16: friendly little restaurant; favourite with locals; good value menus 35–90F; rooms 50F.

Château de Tonquédec – impressive skeleton on heights overlooking valley. Built 13th century, dismantled by order of Richelieu, an even greater demolition expert than our Oliver Cromwell. Two courtyards with two towers, a keep with walls over 4 m (13 ft) thick; climb 76 steps for views of fertile plains and deep wooded valleys. (Open early spring to 30 Sept.)

Lannion, port on river Léguer, with many old half-timbered houses, looking like a set for a musical on Old Brittany. Best of houses (15th-16th century) in pl Général Leclerc and alleys leading off. Staircase of 142 steps leads to Brélévenez church, built by Knights Templars in 12th century, but view from top is rewarding. Big golf ball on heath to North is radome of telecommunications centre – like ours on North Yorks Moors. This one links France to US.

D65 Trébeurden (9 km)

Family Hôtel, rue Plages, (96)23.50.31: well named; friendly, comfortable; typical old, tall, thin Breton building with balconies – in pink granite; will take one-nighters even in season, which many resort-hotels will not. Specialities: fish; shellfish; patîsseries; menu 45–90F; rooms 70–150F. Shut 15 Nov.–15 March.

Old Breton resort, still attractive but hilly. Overlooks bay littered with islands; prevailing westerlies give splendid sailing. Several fine sand beaches; harbour; rocky peninsula Le Castel attached to mainland by thread of sand; path along it – coast views. Long beach round peninsula.

Trébeurden
continued

Ker an Nod, rue Pors Termen, (96)23.50.21: right by sand beach; good sea views; nice hotel, good value; difficult to get one-night rooms mid-summer, but ask. Good seafood; light 'modern' sauces; wide choices of desserts; menu 60–110F; rooms 90–170F. Restaurant open March – November. Shut Tuesday, Wednesday lunch low-season.

Hôtel Ti Al Lannec, alleé de Mezo Guen, (96)23.57.26: old favourite of mine; delightful old manor standing on cliff-top with grounds down to sea (path through it but a hard haul back); terrace and dining room with wonderful views of sea and isles; Relais du Silence; old-style comfort. M. Jouanny, patron, chooses meticulously best product of local farms, markets and fishing boats; menu 85–240F; rooms (all with bath, WC) 160–235F. Open 15 March–30 Nov.

From Trebeurden to Trégastel and Perros Guirec called Rose Granite Coast; masses of rose-red rock divide the beaches, even pop up in fields and gardens.

RELAIS DU SILENCE

D65 back to Lannion, D786 St Michel-en-Grève, St Efflam, right on D42, D64 round Corniche l'Armorique to Locquirec, D64 Lanmeur small road (C4) right to St Antoine, D76 beside estuary of Dossen

St Michel – La Plage, (96)35.74.43: 100 years old; alongside beach with enclosed and open terraces overlooking sands. Super 70F menu of five courses, plenty of choice; 45F if you skip fish or meat course. Fish includes choice of oysters, moules marinières, scallops, sole or four other white fish; main course choice includes quail, duck in orange sauce, turkey, guinea-fowl, grilled steak; huge choice desserts; one of

One of my favourite areas of Brittany. St Michel-en-Grève: charming little beach resort, end of magnificent Lieue de Grève beach 4 km (2½ km miles) long, 2 km (1¼ miles) wide at low tide; trout streams run through little valleys into sea; wooded coast road past Grand Rocher (rock mass) 80 m (261 ft) high (steep path up – about half-hour return).

(Morlaix) river to Morlaix (50 km) join route here from Roscoff.

best value meals we have met recently; also good bar snacks (seafood, fish). Rooms 80–130F. Shut 3 Jan.–26 Feb.

St Efflam – hermit from Ireland (AD 470); beside his chapel is domed fountain.

Plestin church, 16th century, was mined and burned by Germans in 1944; rebuilt.

Locqirec – Du Port, (98)67.42.10: looking down on interesting harbour; small, very Breton. Warning to peace-lovers – jazz sessions in dining room sometimes. Menu 40–80F; house wine 15F; rooms 65–110F. Shut end Sept.–Easter.

Armorique, (98)67.40.06: most attractive creeper-clad hotel overlooking sands and harbour; very fresh and well-cooked fish and shellfish; superb lobster à l'Armoricaine (grilled in sauce of oil, wine, brandy, shallots, tomatoes, garlic – sometimes wrongly called 'a l'Américaine'); menu weekdays 40–80F, Sunday 72–110F; rooms 58–100F.

Armorique Corniche – road follows eccentric coast, heavily indented.

Locquirec: super little fishing port and resort; fine views by walking round the point; delightful walled harbour; sands; old church once belonged to Knights of Malta.

Morlaix: huge railway viaduct across Dossen estuary (known as Morlaix river) dominates old town. Fine old buildings, especially Grand'Rue (market). Once corsair headquarters (including Jean Bart, Duguay Trouin, Cornic). In 1522, corsair John of Coetanlem sacked Bristol; in reply, 80 English ships entered bay, sailors ransacked Morlaix

Morlaix
continued

Morlaix – Europe, rue d'Aiguillon, (98)62.11.99: dull-looking but pleasant inside; old staircase, 17th-century wood décor; local fish including shrimps and prawns from bay; talented young chef produces own dishes of interest and good flavour; menu 40–65F; rooms 75–195F.

while citizens were at Guingamp festival. English sailors drank too much; many were caught asleep in a wood by returning Morlaix citizens and massacred. So town's arms show a lion facing English leopard with motto: 'If they bite you, bite them.' Castle built at harbour entrance to discourage English.

D769 for short distance, then small road right to Pleyber-Christ, small road left back to D769 through Arrée mountains into forest of Ambroise, D764 right to Huelgoat (33 km)

Huelgoat – Ty Douz, rue Brest, (98)99.74.78: very good value restaurant; good cooking; excellent fish; try moules farcies (stuffed mussels); coquille de poisson; langoustines; on lake shore; menu 35–70F; wines from 20F.

Du Lac, (98)99.71.14: simple hotel by lake; busy road in front; back rooms quieter; menu 35–80F; rooms 50F (some with shower).

If not interested in churches stick to D769 – attractive road. Pleyber-Christ: arch dedicated to dead of World War I leads to Gothic-Renaissance church containing many treasures, including remarkable beams and carved chests.

Huelgoat is in unusual landscape of hills, rocks, hollows, streams and waterfalls; lovely trees – beech, oak, pine, spruce; fine fishing, including trout. See Chaos du Moulin (granite rocks in green setting); Grotte du Diable (path in loops down a hollow to river where it goes underground); trembling rock (100-ton rock sways on its base when pushed).

D764 Roc Trévezel, D785 Montagne-St-Michel, D785, D30 St Rivoal D42 Croas-ar-Go through Cranou forest to Rumengol, Le Faou (54 km)

Le Faou – La Vielle Renommée, pl Mairie, (96)81.90.31: fish and classical dishes; copious portions; delicious palourdes farcies (stuffed clams); good cheeses; langouste Cardinale (lobster in half shell, covered in lobster and truffle sauce, browned under grill –

Westward through Arrée mountains. Road left D36 leads to St Michel reservoir lake.

Trévezel: rock escarpment about 365 m (1200 ft) high looks like miniature Alps. Leave car by road, walk for wide panoramic views (½ hr

delicious); cider 13F litres; Gross Plant white wine (dry, rather like Muscadet) 30F bottle; menu 50F (not Sunday lunch), 75F, 130F; rooms 115–160F. Shut part September, part October; Monday out of season.

return). St Michel mountain: car park signposted; chapel and panorama at 380 m (1250 ft); peat bog at foot of hill – called locally 'Entrance to Hell' because of its winter grimness.

St Rivoal: open-air museum of old Breton houses; interesting.

Winding, hilly road through Cranou forest (oaks, beeches).

Rumengol: famous for its 'pardons' – festivals of forgiveness on Trinity Sunday; 15 August (Assumption Day). These pardons held all over Brittany; religious festivals still often followed by secular celebrations.

D791 Corniche road through Térenez, round Bay du Folgoat on small roads right to Landévennec, D60 back on to D791, right at Tal-ar-Groas on D63 to Lanvéoc, D55 to Le Fret, St Fiacre D355 Espagnols Point, Camaret-sur-Mer (57 km)

Views over Le Faou river, then whole Landévennec Peninsula and Aulne river.

Landévennec: ruins of old Benedictine Abbey and new one (1965). D60 is picturesque road. New Térenez bridge has central span 272 m (893 ft).

Le Fret: little port with boat service across Rade de Brest to big naval port of Brest.

Camaret
continued

Espagnols Point: in fine
weather remarkable views
over whole vast roadstead of
Brest. Named after troops
sent here in 1590 by Philip II
of Spain to help Liguers –
league of fanatical Catholics
– fight Henry IV.

Camaret – France, at the
port, (98)27.93.06: good
position looking over port;
newly furnished; good value;
50F menu offers soup,
shellfish platter or cassolette
of shellfish; trout with
vegetables in vermouth
sauce, cheese or dessert.
Other menus 78, 80F
(splendid seafood meal),
125F (very good); rooms 96–
198F. Shut December–March.

Camaret: little seaside resort
and lobster port; small beach
beyond natural dyke which
defends port from Atlantic.
After English, Spanish and
Dutch attacks, military
architect Vauban fortified it in
1689. Anglo-French fleet tried
to make landing but troops
were defeated by dragoons
and Breton 'Home Guard'
with pitchforks and scythes.
Worthy of Dad's Army! In
Camaret Bay in 1801,
American engineer Fulton
tried out a submarine (5 man
with pointed oars, speed 2
knots – stay down for 6
hours) Camaret has a naval
museum.

D8 Crozon,
D887 Morgat
(15 km)

Morgat: sheltered resort with
fine great sandy beach.
Tunny fishing boats.

Back through
Crozon on
D887, 15 km
onward take
D63 right
marked St Nic,
left at St Nic on
D108 to rejoin
D887 for
Ménez Hom

Locronan (2 km NW on small
road) – Manoir de Moëllien,
(98)92.50.40: proud old
manor house of 1642 with
tower; in ruins when Marie-
Anne Le Corre and her
husband restored it superbly;
delightful rooms, fine
furnishing; Relais du Silence;
Château Hôtels

Ménez Hom (330 m/1082 ft)
– windy moorland peak at
approach to Crozon
Peninsula, used for centuries
to defend Brest and area.
Germans dislodged by US
and Free French in siege of
Brest, 1944. One of best
viewpoints in Brittany. On 15
August, Folklore Festival at

Armorique. At
St Marie right
on D47 to
Ploéven, D63
Locronan
(46 km)

Indépendants; surprisingly low prices; family-style cooking; try duck fricassé in cider; brochette of scallops; salmon rillettes; fish ragôuts; menu 52–100F; wines 30F; rooms 160–180F (all with bath, WC). Most attractive place. Shut Tuesday evening; Jan., Feb., March.

Summit. (Hill reached by taking D83 – 1 mile – just before Chapel of St Marie or by parking by the chapel and walking 50 m (55 yds) to hill.) Chapel beautiful with ornamented altar-pieces.

Locronan: superb little town of old granite houses; once manufactured sailcloth, now 'Ville d'Art' with artisans working in glass; weaving wool, linen and silk (see weaving mill of old India Company in pl Eglise; Tour Carée workshop, rue Lann);

Prieuré, (98)91.70.89: in town, very attractive old granite house; jolly dining room; pretty flowery bedrooms; excellent shellfish; good value menus; 40, 50, 70F; rooms 55–100F. Shut October.

Au Fer à Cheval (1 km D63 SE), (98)91.70.67: newly built attractive country hotel; nicely, neatly furnished in modern style. Specializes in fish and shellfish; menu 47–98F; rooms: single 100F, double 150F, others 190F.

museum of contemporary art depicting Breton scenes, furniture, costumes. Lovely old square with well.

Armorique *continued*	Also, Restaurant Au Fer à Cheval, pl Eglise, (98)91.70.74: town centre; same owners; menu 40–110F.	

D7
Douarnenez,
Tréboule
(10 km)
D7, D784
Pointe-du-Raz,
D784 Audierne,
D765 Pont-
Croix, local
road south
Plouhinec,
D784 Quimper
(96 km)

Auberge du Rosmeur, rue Boudoulec, (98)92.08.45: very pretty old restaurant where André Mignon cooks well; carte; middle prices; good steaks as well as fish.

Le Frikou, rue Grand Port, (98)92.37.05: another little bistro with good fish; menu 39F (plus 5F if you choose platter of seafood), 69F.

Chez Fanch, rue Anatole France, (98)92.31.77: good cheap menus except July, Aug., Sept., when carte only, but prices fair. Good langoustines flambées à la crème, tunny fish with wine and cream sauce, moules marinières, lotte (monkfish or angler fish – ugly brute, lovely flavour, adored by French and usually dearer than sole – don't ask me why!); menu 40–89F; house wine 20F. Shut 20 Sept.–20 Oct.

Bar de la Criée, (98)92.02.40: second floor next to fish market at tip of harbour; lovely bay views; menu 40, 65F; wine from 15F.

Auberge du Kervéoch, 5 km on Quimper road, (98)92.07.58: delightful, quiet old farm, hidden in trees, 2 km from beaches; furnished

Douarnenez: historic fishing port, originally sardine boats, now mostly crayfish, langoustine; watersport centre; sailing schools; surfing; beaches 2 miles away. Superb scenery round bay enclosing legendary town of Ys, submerged by sea. Isle in estuary, le Tristan, was 16th-century HQ of brigand La Fontenelle – Ligeur who terrorized Brittany. Fish still auctioned at Rosmeur harbour; tourist sea fishing and boat trips leave from here in high summer. New fishing port in new harbour. Over river bridge is Tréboul, with narrow streets round little port; pleasure boat harbour; sailing centre.

Interesting and spectacular route. Road left leads to Réserve de Cap Sizun, bird sanctuary for sea birds in wild setting (auks, gulls, crested cormorants, guillemots). Guided visits 15 March–31 Aug. – binoculars help.

For Pointe-de-Van, park at Trouguer; path round headland little known.

in country style, old dark wood; big open fire; nice bedrooms; lovely place; you are expected to take dinner if booking room; menu 55–175F (restaurant shut Monday out of season); rooms 80–150F; half-board 150F per person.

Trépassés Bay (Bay of Dead because Druids were taken across for burial on Sein Island); tide race here frightening; great swell of sea rolls magnificently into this bay. Alas, like our Land's End, Raz point has become a tourist trap – car parks, souvenir shops, crêperies – but the walk round the point is spectacular and rewarding; do not attempt it if you hate heights. Use a guide and wear non-slip shoes; do not leave safety rope.

Ile de Sein men are fishermen who regarded even digging fields as women's work until recently. Once they lived by luring ships on to rocks and wrecking them. In June 1940, the entire male population, even 13-year-olds, sailed to England to join the Free French.

Lane off D784 leads to fishing hamlet of Bestrée; another to St Tugen (16th-century chapel).

Audierne: pretty fishing port on estuary of Goyen river – lobsters, crayfish, tunny, June–October; beach 1 mile away.

Pont-Croix, built on terraces up from river Goyen; photogenic; narrow streets between old houses to bridge; chapel with fine stained glass.

Quimper – Tour d'Auvergne, rue Reguaires, (98)95.08.70: charming, dignified old hotel, for long, social centre of Quimper. Restaurant now shut Saturday evening, Sunday from October–30 April; menu 55–130F; rooms 64–173F. Shut 18 Dec.–4 Jan.

Le Capucin Gourmand, rue Reguaires, (98)95.43.12: Luc Le Rhun, patron-chef, considered by locals to be one of best chefs around these parts; menu 88–180F. Shut Monday; part February.

Les Tritons, allée de Locmaria, (98)90.61.78: some unexpected dishes; good fresh produce; real potée Bretonne with meat and various cabbages and green vegetables; wines around 25F; menu 42, 60F; keeps open until 1 am. Shut Monday.

Despite traffic problems, Quimper is still one of my favourite towns. It is a happy place. Odet and Steir rivers meet here. Though dominated by huge Gothic cathedral with lacy spires, it is very much a market town and stalls spill out to line streets near to covered market. Splendid old streets, riverside roads; pottery (came from Nivernais in 1690). Quimper produces crêpes dentelles, crisp, lacy biscuits rolled like casing for cannelloni.

Worth taking drive round Odet river to Benodet and return (44 km). Boats on Odet to Benodet (1½ hours); tides rule sailing times.

At Vire-Court, river winds between high, wooded cliffs; narrowest point called 'Virgin's Leap'; inevitable story of girl leaping it to avoid rape. River bends so much that a Spanish fleet was too frightened to turn the bend and just sailed away.

Pont-l'Abbé – Tour d'Auvergne, pl Gambetta, (98)87.00.47: looks like hotel of same name in Quimper from outside. Traditional cooking with good local fish; excellent lobster à l'Armoricaine (80F); menu 45–85F; rooms 75–150F.

Pont-l'Abbé: 'capital' of Bigouden, country area where many women still wear the tall white coiffe on their heads at festivals. Bigouden museum in 14th-century castle, with costumes and furniture. Open 1 June–15 Sept.

Bretagne, pl République, (98)87.17.22: hotel, restaurant, crêperie; pleasant period furnishings; wide range of menus 38–185F; excellent fish and shellfish; try grilled lobster flambé in whisky (superb); crêperie open 15 June–15 Sept.; rooms 120–130F. Shut Monday out of season; 15 Oct.–9 Nov.

Château de Kernuz (2.5 km on D785), (98)87.01.59: magnificent, comfortable 16th-century château in large grounds; quiet, 5 km from sea; rooms 150F; repas (set meal) 60F; also carte; dinner, bed, breakfast 150F per person.

At Lesconil, little fishing port 9 km by D102 – La Plage, (98)58.10.10: pleasant France Accueil hotel; views of harbour; excellent choice of menus and dishes; good fish and shellfish; 80F menu fine value. Other menus 80–170F; rooms 90–120F. Restaurant open 1 March–31 Oct.; shut Monday except mid-summer.

Kerazan Manor (3 km on D2), castle left to French Institute by Joseph Astor who left money, too, to endow courses at the castle in embroidery and needlework for young Breton women. Fine collection of paintings and drawings from 15th century to today.

D785, D44
Bénodet
(11 km)

Many restaurants and hotels. Tourist office, 51 ave Plage, (98)91.00.14.

Le Minaret, Corniche de l'Estriatre, (98)91.03.13: superb views over attractive Odet estuary. Known for fresh fish even in a fish area; menu 50–120F; rooms 120–200F. Shut 1 Nov.–31 March.

Armoric, (98)91.04.03: my favourite here for good value meals, owner Xavier Palou was a *British* civil servant for 17 years, so speaks English fluently (in triplicate, of course!); beautiful shellfish, very good white fish, and splendid stew; attractive garden; 12 of 40 bedrooms have direct garden access to help handicapped or people of 'troisième âge' (nice French phrase for oldies like me, over 60). Menu 45–85F; rooms 110–178F. Open 20 May–20 Sept.

Poste, pl Poste, (98)91.01.09: modern but cosy, good value; tank ('vivier') for fresh shellfish; menu 49–75F; rooms 98–250F. Open all year; new hotel-restaurant planned.

New bridge (610 m/2000 ft long) over Odet opens up resort of Bénodet to west. Charming place, with fine beach, but taken over by campers in summer these days, so crowded; good yacht harbour; casino, lively high season. Boat trips to Quimper up river Odet (½ hour); also to Loctudy (pretty seaport – ½ hour) and Glénen Isles (famous sailing school; some isles uninhabited – kept as bird sanctuaries – 1¾ hrs).

D44 Fouesnant,
La Forêt-
Fousenant,
little road right
through
Kersicot to
Concarneau
(15 km)

At Beg Meil (6 km right on D45) – Thalamot, (98)94.97.38: my little old favourite Logis better known, more difficult to book, but as good as ever. Try lovely sea-trout, red mullet (rougets) in cream sauce; turbot; 30 m

Beg Meil, 6 km right on D45: my old hideout with nice beach backed by pines now gets terribly crowded mid-summer and summer weekends, with parked cars spoiling it a bit and car queues to reach it.

from beach; menu 57–125F; wines from 30F; rooms 65–151F. Open end March to end September.

Fouesnant – Armorique, rue de Cornouaille, (98)56.00.19: popular; old Breton inn with modern annexe in pleasant garden; known for its cider; wines from 16F; regional cooking; shellfish specialities; menu 50–100F; rooms 65–150F. Open 1 April–30 Sept.

La Forêt-Fouesnant – La Baie, (98)56.97.35: another old favourite of mine. Magnificent gourmand meal with lobster for 180F; other menus 55, 90F, fifty wines from 20–250F; rooms 89–155F. Hotel shut 1 Nov.–31 March. Restaurant open daily.

L'Espérance, (98)56.01.35: pleasant Logis with attractive dining room; menu 40–80F; rooms 67–150F. Shut 1 Oct.–31 March.

Auberge St Laurent, rte de Concarneau, (98)56.98.07: good restaurant near sea; menu 50, 100F. Opens 12.30 pm, 7.30 pm; Easter–30 Sept. and school holidays.

Hôtel du Port, (98)56.97.33: reasonably priced; simple but good value; menu 32–68F; rooms 47–90F; pension 111F.

Interesting little port, lobster boats, large sand beach with dunes.

Fouesnant: very pleasant little town among fruit orchards; produces best cider in Brittany.

La Forêt-Fouesnant: separate village, was hidden and quiet until Port-la-Forêt, huge port for yachtsmen and pleasure craft, opened in '72 – but separate from village – across estuary.

Concarneau
continued

Manoir du Stang (1.5 km N. on D783, private road), (98)56.97.37: lovely and absolutely charming 'gentleman's manor house' of 15th century with big estate right to the sea. Not cheap but good value; menu 100–150F; half board 225–290F; pension 255–325F. Open 1 May–30 Sept.

Concarneau – Grand Hôtel, ave Pierre Gueguen, (98)97.00.28: restaurant now closed, but convenient overnight hotel, facing port and Ville Close; rooms 90–200F. Shut 1 Oct.–1 May.

Bonne Auberge, Cabellon beach, (98)97.04.30: pleasant, fairly simple little hotel in nice position; traditional regional cooking; good local scallops, mussels; try tunny in cider; rooms 71–120F. Shut end September – spring.

La Douane, ave Alain-Le-Lay, (98)97.30.27: best meals I have tasted here; happy atmosphere; straightforward cooking of very fresh, good ingredients; menu 50F (excellent value); carte; well-chosen wine list. Shut Sunday; February.

Concarneau: Ville Close (14th-century walled town) surrounded by modern fishing harbour. Ville Close is totally surrounded by thick ramparts; despite many souvenir shops, crêperies and restaurants, still looks 'original' and impresses me after 20 visits; fishing museum in former arsenal (open Easter–30 Sept.); shellwork display centre shows artistic designs made of shells. Worth seeing inner harbour, where fishing boats unload (Concarneau is third biggest fishing port in France and has tunny fleet), and outer harbour with brightly coloured pleasure boats.

D783 Pont-Aven, Quimperlé (28 km)

Pont-Aven – Moulin de Rosmadec, (98)06.00.02: Pont-Aven once had more mills than houses. This 15th-century mill now comfortable gourmand restaurant. Pierre Sébilleau has light touch; gives heavy portions; menu 75, 145F; Shut Wednesday; part of Oct., Nov., Feb.

Pleasant resort where river Aven opens into tidal estuary. Made famous by Gauguin and his school of lesser artists in 1890s; they preached: 'Paint what you see, not what is there.' Artists not very popular with locals; he had punch-up with fishermen in Concarneau and

Quimperlé – at Hermitage (2 km on D49) – Manoir de Kerroch, (98)96.04.66: old manor in own grounds; heated pool; bedroom views to country or forest; riding stables ½ mile. Open 1 April–30 Oct.

Relais du Roch (tied to Manoir Kerroch above), (98)96.12.97: fine old-fashioned cooking, superb fresh seafood; lovely creamy, often alcoholic sauces. Happy service; menu 55–150F. Shut Monday out of season; mid December to mid-Jan. Recommended highly.

Auberge de Toulfoën (3 km on D49), (98)96.00.29: country inn with separate dining room for coach customers; near riding stable; pleasant; known for crêpes, sea food, roasts; wine from 16F; menu 60–130F; rooms 80–110F. Shut 25 Sept.–31 Oct.

Le Pouldu (14 km on D49) – Ster Laita, (98)96.94.98: old building on little port; superb sea food; try also quail with foie gras; menu 50–66F; rooms 93–165F.

broke a leg. None of his paintings in local museum, though sometimes he appears in temporary exhibitons. He moved to little port of Le Pouldu, at mouth of river Laita (14 km from Quimperlé on D49) where there is a statue to Gauguin next to chapel.

Quimperlé: beautiful old town where rivers Ellé and Isole join to form Lafta. Superb old houses, many with projecting upper storeys. Curious church of Ste Croix based on Church of Holy Sepulchre in Jerusalem. But 12th-century belfry collapsed on to it in 1862; rebuilt with separate belfry.

D22, D2 Plouay, D769, D110 through Valley of Scorff, skirting forest of Pont Calleck to Kernascléden (32 km)

Pont Calleck – Auberge du Pont Calleck, (97)32.08.75: right by bridge with own trout farm; menu 70–100F; odd opening times – check by phone.

Lovely run. On D110, ½ mile past Chapel of Ste. Anne-des-Bois, steep road takes you in ¼ mile to lake and children's home, once Pont-Calleck castle. Pleasant Kernascléden church, finished 1453, was officially built 30 years before Chapel

Kernascléden
continued

of St Fiacre at Le Faouet (15 km away), but every local child known they were built simultaneously, by the same workers, who were carried with their tools each night from one to the other by angels – ultimate in 'moonlighting'. Beautiful building – slender tower, rose-carvings, delicate tracery.

---

minor road south to Inguiniel, Bubry, D2 Pontivy, D764 Josselin (32 km)

Bubry – Moulin de Coët Diquel, (97)51.70.70: modern, in Breton traditional style; warm, solid furnishing; heated pool, terrace on to étang (small lake); fishing; all bedrooms different; family run. Open all year; menu 42–100F; rooms 65–180F. Good value.

Bubry has a big 'pardon' religious festival for St Hélèn (4th Sunday in July). Green, pretty area.

Pontivy has two towns – one of old houses and moated castle with 20 m (64 ft) ramparts (closed Nov., Dec.; Monday, Tuesday except June–Sept); and planned 'new' military town built by Napoleon. Pontivy is on river Blavet; Napoleon had trouble with our Royal Navy, especially moving ships from Nantes to Brest, decided to build canal between them. Pontivy was half-way, so he made it military centre. Blavet was canalized to improve communication with sea.

Josselin – Du Château, (97)22.20.11: alongside river, opposite castle walls; old favourite of mine, now popular; crowded high season. Fine view of castle from dining room. Reasonable prices for good quality; menu 42–110F;

Josselin is a charming little town in photogenic setting on the river Oust, near where it joins the Nantes–Brest canal which joins the river Blavet at Pontivy. Its riverside castle is like an illustration for a fairy-tale. Mostly built by Oliver de

wines from 15F; rooms 70–155F. Shut Sunday evening, Monday low season; February.

Clisson, who sided first with England, then with France (he became Constable of France), was called 'The Butcher' (his motto was ('I do as I please'). He married a widow of the great de Rohan family of Josselin, who still own the castle. ' Castle open daily 1 June–2 Sept.; Sundays, 19 March–31 May.

| D122 Ploërmel, N166 Vannes (46 km) | | |

At Toul Broch (10 km from Vannes on D101, before Baden) – La Gravinis, (97)57.00.01: not only good seafood but excellent pâtisseries; modern, with tasteful décor; pleasant garden; menu at 55F includes wine; other menus 75–130F; rooms 50–144F. Shut 15 Nov.–15 Jan.

Vannes – Marée Bleue, pl Bir-Makeim, (97)47.24.29: good value restaurant; menu 41.50F includes wine; other menus 42, 77.50, 161.50F; wines Gros Plant 25F; rooms 64–79F. Shut Sunday evening in winter; 18 Dec.–6 Jan.

Hôtel Marebaudière, rue A. Briand, (97)47.34.29: same owners as Marée Bleue above; use that restaurant; all rooms with bath or shower, WC 145–180F. Shut 18 Dec.–6 Jan.

Manche Océan, rue Lt-Col Maury, (97)47.26.46: comfortable hotel; no restaurant; rooms 80–180F.

Little D122 runs alongside canal to Ploërmel (old houses; Duc Lake, 2.5 km N, has beach, watersport centre). Road through moorlands of Lanvaux passes 1 km from Fortresse de Largoët (eleven towers) half-ruined castle where Henry Tudor was imprisoned when he fled after Wars of Roses; he became Henry VII of England.

Vannes: old market centre in Gulf of Morbihan, turning industrial. Old walled town grouped round cathedral is delightful.

Cathedral was built between 13th and 19th centuries and looks like it. Much mixture of styles. Medieval Parliament building (near cathedral) converted to interesting covered market, with craftsmen working in metal, leather; artists; crêperies. Oyster museum above tourist office (29 rue Thiers); Vannes is pretty town but so tourist-minded, it could become a 'museum' in old area.

Vannes
continued

Fine boat trips from Vannes into Gulf of Morbihan to Arz Island (3 km/2 miles long), Moines Isle (6 km/4 miles long) – quiet seaside resort where the women's beauty has aroused poets, and woods have such names as Wood of Love, Wood of Sighs, Wood of Regrets. Trips 2 hrs to whole day from Vannes.

N165, right on D780 along coast of Gulf of Morbihan, St Colombier, D20 Muzillac, N165 La Roche-Bernard (54 km)

Muzillac – Auberge de Pen-Mur, (97)41.67.58: six menus between 38F and 125F; my 60F menu included 9 oysters as first course choice; house wine 25F; rooms 60–75F. Closed 2–19 November.

On Gulf of Morbihan lived in first century BC the Veneti – powerful tribe of Gaul with fine fleet. Julius Caesar had to conquer them to hold Armor – Brittany. He built galleys at mouth of Loire. Gauls had 220 large sailing ships. Brutus, Caesar's Lieutenant, met them with flat galleys, rowed by oars. Alas for Gaul, the sea was calm and windless. Brutus had sickles tied to ropes which Romans threw into rigging of Gallic ships; mast and sails tumbled; Roman soldiers boarded the ships and killed crew.

La Roche-Bernard – Auberge des Deux Magots, (99)90.60.75: good traditional cooking; excellent value; in 50F menu, dozen oysters, langoustine mayonnaise salad, turbot ('fish of the day'), cheese or dessert; menus 38–110F; nice rooms

La Roche-Bernard: tiny town on tributary of Vilaine river near coast, overlooking river; in 17th century its shipyards were famous; now port for pleasure boats on Brittany's inland waterways. I took a cruiser from here to Dinan some years ago. Now you

120–250F. Shut Sunday evening, Monday out of season.

Auberge Bretonne, (99)90.60.28: bistro with modern 'light' cuisine, but very well done; menu 50–120F; rooms 50–130F. Shut mid-Nov. to mid-Dec.; Thursday out of season.

can hire one from a British company. But still a likeable little port, with a beautiful modern suspension bridge. In the Revolution, the Mayor was shot down by the King's soldiers for refusing to shout: 'Long live the King'. He kept shouting: 'Long Live the Republic'. The Tree of Liberty was set on fire and he was thrown in it, still alive. I feel that he won.

D774 La Baule (28 km) through the Brière Nature Park, D127 St André-des-Eaux, D47 St Lyphard, D51 La Chapelle-des-Marais, D50, D2 La Bretesche, Missillac (31 km)

See Route 1. Route from La Baule to Combourg almost follows Route 1 in reverse (See page 25.)

D126, D773 D164 Redon (30 km) D177 Rennes (64 km) N137 Hédé (22 km) D795 Combourg (14 km) D796, D83 Trans, D90, N176 Pontorson (28 km)

Pontorson – Bretagne, rue Couesnon, (33)60.10.55: a delight; 14th-century house with exposed wood frame, carefully renovated; beautifully finished, sympathetically furnished within; menu 40–85F; rooms 67–134F. Open 1 Feb.–1 Nov.; shut Monday.

Pontorson – you are in Normandy. Church founded by William the Conqueror in thanks for his army having been saved from Couesnon quicksands towards Le Mont-St-Michel. True Bretons believe they are now in foreign parts.

Pontorson *continued*	Du Chalet, pl Gare, (33)60.00.16: Logis de France; very reasonable, good value; excellent lamb; escalope Normande; seafood; good calamar in sharp Armoricaine sauce (if you like squid); menu 35–70F; wines from 15F; rooms 58–130F.

D976 Le Mont-St-Michel (9 km)

Du Guescelin, (33)60.14.10: famous Logis run by M. Nicolle, hotelier known all over France; shellfish, of course – local people once lived by selling cockles and the bay was full of oysters until disease wiped them out last century; try lamb; sheep thrive round here on salt-washed turf ('pré-salé'). Menu 55F and carte; rooms 58–150F. Shut Wednesday low season.

Du Mouton Blanc, (33)60.14.08: historic monument; serves historic and filling St Michel omelette as first course or sweet as dessert. Mine, as starter on 45F menu, nearly filled me before I tackled veal in cream sauce; menu 45–126F; rooms 64–150F. Shut 15 Nov.–20 Dec, Jan. to mid-Feb.

What new to say about 'La Première Site de France', the 'wonder of the Western World'? It *is* wonderful, this abbey on a hillock, protected by quicksands. Not surprising, since it was the Archangel Michael himself who, in the 8th century, told the Bishop of Avranches that he wanted a chapel built to him on the mound – and tapped the Cleric's head with his finger to stress the point. But you need to be reasonably fit to climb the 90 steps, once guarded by a fortified bridge, leading to the terrace – or in summer to push your way uphill from the car park through seething thousands, past souvenir shops, crêperies and restaurants, to reach the abbey. Only 6000 are allowed in at a time, so you might

Au Chapeau Rouge, (33)60.14.29: restaurant with family menu at 32F; 44F menu which includes six oysters. Specializes in cider.

La Digue, (33)60.14.02: modern, very comfortable hotel on edge of town; old style furnishings; panoramic views of abbey and bay from dining room; shellfish; mussels in cream; 'pré-salé lamb; good house pâtisseries; menu 42–150F; rooms 80–160F. Shut 15 Nov.–15 March.

have to wait. But the throng of pilgrims has been as great for centuries. In the 100 Years War, the English who held the approach area sold safe-conduct passes and tourists bought souvenirs of effigies of St Michael and lead caskets to fill with sand from the beach. Many drowned in quicksands. From the Revolution until the State started to restore it in 1874, it was a prison; prisoners made straw hats in the church. Church restored for worship in 1922.

Biggest crowds are often outside Hôtel de la Mère Poulard, watching them make omelettes in a long-handled copper pan over an open fire – so successfully that Mother Poulard's little café now has a Michelin star and menus from 115F to 230 F.

Prices mostly sky high in this place.

D976 return to
Pontorson,
N176 Dol-de-
Bretagne
(28 km)

Dol – Au Bon Accueil, rue Rennes, (99)48.06.14: happy, friendly little restaurant with remarkable 28F menu of starters, plat du jour, cheese, dessert. Carte also. Beubry family get many British customers and think them 'marvellous, with remarkable courtesy and amiability'. Shut Sunday.

De Bretagne, pl Chateaubriand, (99)48.02.03: very good value 40F menu with choice according to season (lamb, blanquette de veau or boeuf Bourguignon to follow house pâté or moules marinières when I was there). Try baked mackerel, grilled sardines; oysters; colin (hake); Muscadet-sur-lie 30F; 50 more wines; menu 40–70F; rooms 48–95F. Terrace for fine weather meals.

La Bresche-Arthur, bd Deminiac, (99)48.01.44: very good hotel with lively, friendly patron, Christian Faveau, who speaks English well. Five menus 30–125F. Try house duck foie gras; salmon escalope; duck with pineapple; particularly bar aux algues (seabass in a seaweed cooked like spinach – much better than it sounds); house wine 20F; neat rooms 85–138F; garden with children's play apparatus. Shut 15 Nov.–15 Dec.

Rich agricultural land reclaimed from sea and marsh, like Romney Marsh. Near Mont-St-Michel, Dutch name 'Polders' used; rest called Marais of Dol (marshland); was forest until 8th century, then sea poured in.

At Dol we are back in Brittany. Fine old town on a 20 m (64 ft) cliff. Bishopric of Dol founded around AD 530 by one of Brittany's 7847 saints – St Samson, a Welshman from monastery of Llantwit in Glamorgan and adept at killing dragons, witches and wizards, by telling them to drop dead. No longer a bishopric, but Dol's 13th-century cathedral is called St Samson's, with stained glass showing its history. Old houses in Grande-Rue-des-Stuarts.

Champ-Dolent Menhir (2 km – D795 for 600 yd, turn left into tarred road – leave car, walk): menirs were stones set up in prehistoric times at springs, near dolmens or in lines, probably as religious monuments in sun and moon worship; dolmens were burial chambers; the one here stands 9 m (30 ft) high.

Mont Dol (3 km NE): granite mound 65 m (208 ft) high; remains of prehistoric animals (mammoth, rhinoceros, elephant, reindeer) and flint tools unearthed from its slopes. Road round it; also narrow steep road with hairpin bend to top.

Tower (open Easter to All Saints' Day). Signal tower (1802), once part of semaphore chain for passing messages (Brest to Paris); now part of chapel. The Devil had a fight with St Michael on Mont Dol; now courting couples wrestle.

D155 to coast, follow it to D76 right to Cancale (23 km) D201 round Pointe du Grouin to Rothéneuf, St Malo (23 km)

Continental, (99)89.60.16: one of the superior restaurants among many near the port; bedrooms have views of port and sea; strong on lobster; good homard à l'Armoricaine (with that super tangy sauce); wines a bit pricey (Gros Plant sur-lie 45F); menu 73–132F, but I suggest meals à la carte in any of these super shellfish restaurants; rooms 65–240F. Personally, I pick an ordinary-looking restaurant here – open to the street, if possible, to carry away any over-riding smells of fish. Then I take a dozen oysters with Muscadet wine, and follow with mussels, stuffed clams, a plate of seafood, or, if feeling rich, a lobster, as the mood takes me – with more Muscadet, of course. But for something more elegant and restful with charming dining room looking to sea, a nice terrace and comfortable bedrooms, all with sea views, try:

Le Vivier-sur-Mer: oyster beds laid down quite recently, not yet a rival to Cancale.

Cancale: lobsters, clams, mussels, most fish; but above all – oysters; bred at sea, farmed in pounds down on the muddy sands; sold in thousands to wholesalers, in boxes to retailers, in dozens to travellers from quayside stalls, and in fiercely competitive restaurants beside quay. Not a pretty place, but one of the few from which I could not drive away because I was the worse for food – not wine! Take Muscadet or Gros Plant wines with your crustaceans.

St Malo
continued

Hôtel La Pointe du Grouin, at Pte de Grouin (4 km N), (99) 89.60.55: Yves Simon, patron, cooks his fresh fish and shellfish perfectly; simply a question of which to choose; menu 70–90F; rooms 85–175F. Shut 1 Oct.– 30 March.

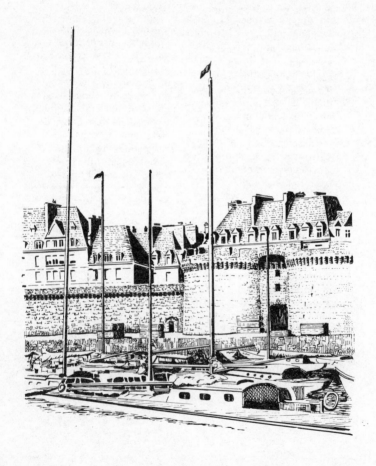

Route 6
Round the Loire Valley, Loir and Cher

The Loire is the longest river in France. The bit we regard as 'the Loire' is usually from Nantes to Nevers, especially from Angers to near Orléans, is mostly beautiful, surrounded by lovely châteaux and delightful towns, and very popular. The difficulty is to see these delightful places without being caught up with a mass of people in between. One trick is to follow the less popular bank of the river, as we have done from Angers to Tours. You could also skip Orléans, by taking small roads from Cléry to Sully.

Those beautiful Loire châteaux were mostly built for love, not war. The best are Montgeoffroi, Chenonceaux and Azay-le-Rideau, little towns of Beaugency and Sancerre (a delight with a bonus of its splendid wine), and take the route suggested from Nevers to Aubigny and back to the Loire on tiny roads through tiny places to get a taste of the countryside away from tourists.

Although I find the Loire food not quite in the class of the Dordogne and Périgord or of Brittany, you can eat very well on regional dishes, usually beautifully presented; try jambons de volaille (chicken legs boned, stuffed, cooked in wine, eaten cold): gogues (small vegetable and pork sausage); boudin blanc (wonderful soft creamy sausage of chicken and pork) and the gourmet boudin de volaille à la Richelieu (truffles, mushrooms and chicken creamed in a sausage). Plenty of game and duck. Beurre blanc, a rich, creamy sauce of butter, shallots and wine, is usually served with river fish (shad, pike, sandre).

Loire wines are easy to drink and appeal especially to people who drink wine rarely. Rosé wines of Anjou are too fragrant and sweet for me. Chinon red can be excellent but varies, Rabelais loved it. I like Bourgueil, dark red from north of the river, especially St Nicholas-de-Bourgueil (underestimated – don't advertise it or price will shoot up as with Sancerre and Cahors wines). Muscadet, the splendid very dry white wine, comes from Loire estuary. Flinty Pouilly-Fumé (made from different grape to Pouilly Fuissé of Burgundy) is now fashionable so pricey; so is the super Sancerre. Saumur's sparkling wine, made by full champagne method, is nearest to champagne I have tasted; a good still wine, too. Vouvray's still wine, slightly bubbling, is better than its famous sparkling mousseux. A tip – try Jasnières from the Loir for a fruity, delicate white wine.

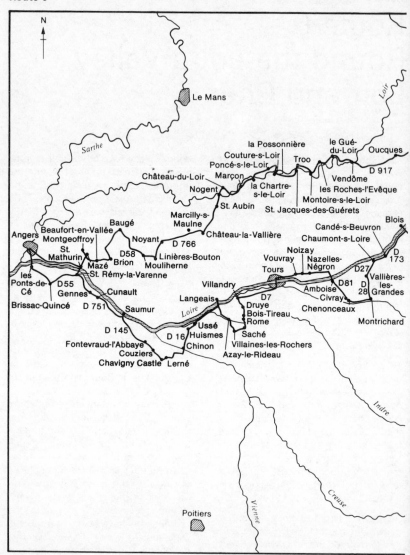

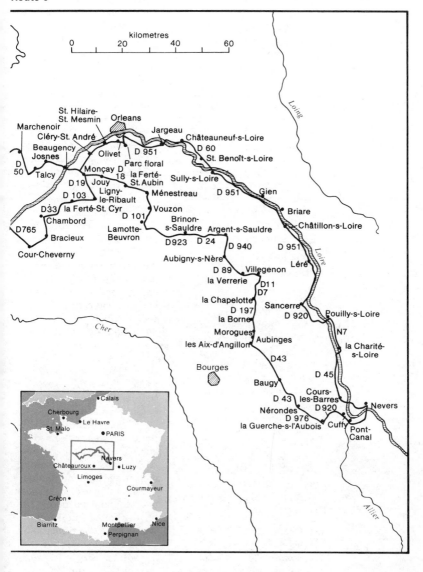

Angers

De France; Restaurant Les Plantagenets, pl Gare, (41)88.49.42: grand old hotel of sort too many towns have knocked down, which they will regret later. Run by Bouyer family since built in 1890 and has fin de siècle décor and furniture. Prices fairly down to earth. Good 52F menu – 4 courses, no choice; reasonable carte prices with very good choice. Good choice too of Loire wines from 25F. 'Le Pub' snack bar; rooms mostly big; 40 with bath or shower: 150–200F. Shut 19 Dec.-23 Jan.

Saint-Jacques, rue Saint-Jacques, (41)48.51.05: good value; regional dishes and wine; pike or sandre (perch-pike with more delicate flavour) from local rivers in beurre blanc (butter whipped with stock of shallot and Muscadet wine); chicken in Cabernet red wine of Anjou (in coq au vin dishes it makes a great difference which wine is used – I don't like coq au battery acid!); menu 35, 65, 120F; Loire and Anjou wines 30–50F; rooms 70–159F; in narrow street with traffic. Restaurant shut 16 Aug.–18 Sept. Hotel open all year.

Le Quéré, pl Ralliement, (41)87.64.98: highly recommended to me as a shrine by devoted disciples of Nouvelle Cuisine. I have not been there yet. Some dishes I saw on menus look daunting – gâteau of young rabbit in sorbet of fresh mint;

Former capital of Anjou, on banks of river Maine, 8 km before it joins the Loire. Centre for Anjou wines, liqueurs, fruit, vegetables. Once belonged to England under Henry II. King John lost it. Old city (13th-century castle, 12th-century cathedral) plus modern city (electronic, farm machinery factories); many parks; old ramparts now tree-lined boulevards. City of tapestries – Apocalypse tapestry, displayed in special gallery in castle, is longest woven in France. Originally 164 m (540 ft) long, it was thrown into the street during the Revolution and citizens cut bits off for carpets, horse blankets and cart covers! In 1843 the Bishop rescued two-thirds of it. About 100 m (320 ft) on show; woven from 1373–80 for Louis I in Paris. More tapestries in castle's Logis Royal (15th-century Flemish, of the Passion) and Logis du Gouverneur (lives of saints). But other great work is in St John's old hospital – 78 m (258 ft) masterpiece of ten tapestries 'Chant du Monde' (Song of the World). Its black background exploding in intense colours, purity of line, scintillating design by Jean Lurçat, greatest of modern tapestry artists, who died in 1966 when planning another seven hangings for this series. Those shown took nine years to weave. They were Lurçat's Humanist reply to religious

artichokes and avocados in mussels and sherry. But I like the sound of boudin de poissons de la Loire and sole in sweet Chaumes wine with chopped leeks. Must be some cook, this Paul le Quéré. Menu 70F; special recommended meal 160F. Shut Tuesday evening, Wednesday; part February.

despair of Apocalypse. He wrote a commentary himself; on sale (in English translation) at the museum.

N160 les Ponts-de-Cé, D748 Brissac-Quincé, D55, 56 St Rémy-la-Varenne, D132 beside river to Gennes (39 km)

Gennes – Hostellerie de Loire, (41)51.81.03: attractive, beamed, tastefully decorated; terrace with flowers overlooking Loire; Loire river fish excellent (salmon, sandre, friture of small fish); good guinea-fowl and quail; traditional cooking. Known as far as Paris for good value. Menu 48–90F; wines – Loire (cheap), Bordeaux, Burgundy; rooms 66–158F. Shut Monday evening, Tuesday except July, August.

Les Rosiers – Val de Loire, (41)51.80.30: informal, rustic, fun. Good value meals; good desserts; menu 38–76F; rooms 62–140F. Shut Monday; October.

Loire divides into three arms at les Ponts de Cé; bridge crosses all three. Isles between have octagonal tower from castle, scene of bloody battle in 1793, and a church.

Brissac is most impressive from outside and within; in lovely park with river Aubance running through.

Second Duke of Cossé-Brissac, made Marshal of France for handing over Paris to Henry IV, started it between 1610 and 1620 (perfect example of its time). He had to leave two towers of medieval castle – he could not blow them up! Damaged in Revolution; restored from mid 19th century. Present Duke lives there. Intricate painted ceilings, rich tapestries, fine period furniture. (Open daily except Tuesday.)

Moulin de Bablut (restored windmill) alongside vineyards on D748, open for wine tastings. Red wine from Gamay grape is strong, full of flavour.

St Rémy-la-Varenne: nice village among trees; 10th-century church.

Jeanne de Laval, (41)51.80.17: Albert Augerau's lovely old inn and manor house annexe were chosen by the Queen Mother for her 1981 stay. I don't blame her. Really splendid cooking – well worth the prices; magnificent foie gras of duck; menu 110–180F; rooms 130–250F. Shut Monday, Tuesday lunch.

Boumois Castle (7 km on D952 – also 8 km from Saumur (below) by bridge over Loire, left on D952): fairy-tale castle from road; Gothic primness from rear; round towers with conical 'hats'; 15th–16th century. Here lived Aristide-Aubert Dupetit-Thouars, French admiral who, when Nelson was sinking Napoleon's fleet at Aboukir, Egypt, in 1798, lost a leg, had both arms shattered, had his men put him upright in a barrel of bran to continue his command. Died ordering his colours to be nailed to the mast. Nelson's descendants pay tribute by visiting the château. In grounds are huge dovecotes with 1800 nesting holes. Only the Lord could keep doves; used for shooting practice and food and allowed to feed, protected, on peasants' land – one reason why downtrodden peasants joined the Revolution.

D751 Cunault, Chênehutte-les-Tuffeaux, Saumur (15 km)

Chênehutte – Le Prieuré, (41)50.15.31: Château Hôtel de France (Relais de Campagne); in old priory, made into pretty Renaissance manor house, now hotel in park – magnificent position overlooking Loire. Some simpler bedrooms in bungalows in grounds. Absolute peace – at a price; menu 90–200F; rooms 160–425F (suites). Shut January, February.

Saumur – Gambetta, rue Gambetta, (41)51.11.13: best value meals in Saumur; local wines include red Champigny; menu 45, 80, 110F. Shut Sunday evening, Monday.

Hôtel de la Gare, facing station, (41)50.34.24: something for everyone: dish of the day 18F; menu 35–110F; rooms 50–170F. Views of Loire and castle. Open April-end October.

At St Hilaire–St Florent, a Saumur suburb where rivers meet, taste the fruity white wine of Saumur at the firm of Ackerman. Laurence Ackerman, an Alsatian, taught the locals to put in the sparkle by the champagne method in 1811 and it is a pleasant drink, brut or demi-sec, though no substitute for champagne. The still wine, a fine apéritif, is being made more extensively now and I like it. (Visits 9.30–11.30 am, 3–5 pm, 1 May–30 Sept.)

Huguenot stronghold, Saumur is now known for wine, religious medals and its cavalry school. The spectacular Louis X 14th-century castle on a sheer cliff, with lovely views, has a remarkable ceramic museum and museum of the horse. The Cavalry and Armoured School was started in 1763 when the best horsemen in

Saumur
continued

Budan, quai Carnot, (41)51.28.76: comfort overlooking Loire. Solid meals. I have never eaten badly here. Good wine list. Try fried ablette (small river fish), river fish terrine, wood-grilled local salmon; menu 70F; rooms 180–228F. Shut 1 Nov.–31 March.

France were sent there. The 'Black Squadron' still gives horse and tank displays. Fine tapestries in Notre Dame church, better ones in Hospices Jeanne Delanoue. Jardin des Plantes – a series of flowered terraces down the castle slope, garlanded with vines, is delightful.

D145
Fontevraud-
l'Abbaye, small
road (V3)
Couziers, left,
then quickly
right to reach
D117, left on
D117 to
Chavigny
Castle, Lerné,
La Devinière,
left on D759,
right on D751,
left on D749
over river
Vienne to
Chinon (31 km)

At Montsoreau – Restaurant
Diane de Méridor,
(45)51.70.18: view of castle
and Loire; simple; attractive
period furniture; rightly
proud of its Loire fish dishes;
menu 51–85F; rooms 48–
170F. Shut Tuesday.

Fontevraud Abbey, built in
1099, had an abbess in
charge, which annoyed some
male chauvinist monks. The
fine church (1119) contains
the tombs of Plantagenets,
including our Henry II, his
wife Eleanor, their son
Richard Coeur de Lion, and
King John's wife Isabelle.

D417 N, 4.5 km – Château of
Montsoreau, pretty and
impressive, built by Charles
VII's steward in 15th century,
Gothic to Renaissance style.
A Moroccan museum inside.
Napoleon made it a prison
and it remained so until
1963.

After La Devinière on D759
at La Roche-Clermault –
Auberge du Haut-Clos,
(47)95.94.50: rustic Logis,
modern annexe; good views;
attractive; cooking over huge
log fire; menu 39–93F; cheap
red house wine; rooms 45–
140F. Shut Friday off-season;
Jan., Feb.

La Devinière: a manor house
where Rabelais, great satirist,
also priest and eminent
physician, spent his
childhood and was possibly
born (around 1494) despite
plaque in Chinon claiming to
be his birthplace.

Chinon – Auberge St Jean,
rue St Jean, (47)93.09.29:
Auberge Rurale, specializes
in cooking with Chinon wine
(meat, fish, dessert); menu
35–90F. Small cheap hotel
opposite.

Hostellerie Gargantua, rue
Haute St Maurice,
(47)93.04.71: in turreted 15th-
century palace. Try Loire fish
and eels; locals praise
cooking. Wide choice of
wines includes local
Bourgueil. Named after

Chinon: a near surfeit of
history in this delightful town
on river Vienne. Richelieu
owned it, our Henry II died in
the castle, then called Castle
of St George. His son,
Richard Lionheart, held it, but
King John lost it to the
French. Charles VII moved
the French court here,
listened to Joan of Arc's
strange story, believed her
and gave her an army. The
château, partly ruined, is still
magnificent (Joan of Arc
museum).

Chinon
continued

Rabelais' hero, Gargantua, loud-mouthed, voracious giant. Menu 79–105F; rooms 90–200F. Shut February.

Grand Hôtel, Restaurant Boule d'Or, quai Jeanne d'Arc, (47)93.03.13: matelote d'anguille au Chinon blanc (very good, and sounds better in French than 'river eels in white Chinon wine'); tournedos; coq au vin; 'cigare' (grey mullet); menu 42–120F; rooms 65–110F.

Château de Marcay (7 km on D749, D116, (47)93.03.47: in magnificent château; very pricey. Imaginative cuisine, à la carte only: 120–160F. Try duck pie, cold bouillabaisse 'en gelée'. Rooms 230–530F. Heated pool. Shut January, February.

Old town of alleys and turreted houses – rue Voltaire and Grand Carroi outstanding.

Chinon red wines, made from Cabernet Franc grapes, rate with those of Bourgueil, just across Loire river, as best of Loire; fruity, crisp, like best Beaujolais; young wine drunk cold, like Beaujolais. Chinon softer than Bourgueil.

D16 north, D9
Huismes, D7
Rigny, Ussé
(14 km)

Ussé castle inspired Perrault to write *The Sleeping Beauty*, though now surrounded by lawns and flowers, not bushes and brambles. Overlooks Indre river; in white stone, its towers, dormer windows, chimneys give it a poetic appearance. Belongs now to Marquis de Blacas; 16th-century, pure Renaissance chapel in park.

local road (C12)
across Indre
river to Ile St
Martin, right on
D16 to bridge
leading over
Loire to

Langeais, right
on D57 to
Azay-le-Rideau
(9 km)

Azay-le-Rideau – Le Grand Monarque, pl République, (47)43.30.08: Jacquet family has run this splendid hotel since 1900 and it has supporters world-wide, but especially in Britain. Patron Serge Jacquet is an artist; his pictures decorate walls. Restaurant not cheap but worth every franc. Last time we had super soup, shad (a fine fish) in sorrel sauce; Charolais steak Bordelaise with creamed celery, cheese, pâtisserie – all for 105F; without second course (fish or soufflé) price is 75F; superb gastronomic meal for 180F; over 120 wines, mostly Loire; rooms 65–216F. Shut 1 Dec.–1 Mar.

Les 3 Lys, rue Château, (47)43.24.36: useful little hotel; good rooms, all with bath or shower; cheap menus 47, 57F; try rillons de Tournai (tasty pork dish); ham in Madeira sauce. Rooms 150F.

Langeais château (across Loire) remarkable because it is unaltered since built in five years from 1465 for Louis XI as defence against Bretons. Charles VIII and Anne of Brittany married here.

Azay-le-Rideau château is not *quite* so lovely as Chenonceaux but second best. Renaissance gem of grace and strength, white walls and blue-grey slate reflected in ornamental lake and river Indre, from whose bed the castle rises on one side. Built from 1518 to 1527 by Gilles Berthelot, Treasurer-General of France – related to Catherine Briconnet who built Chenonceaux and Jacques de Semblencay, the King's Treasurer. Semblancay was accused by King Francis I of corruption and beheaded; Berthelot fled to Italy, his books were examined and he was found guilty of fiddling the nation's accounts. The King grabbed his château as he had done Chenonceaux. Interior is Renaissance showpiece with fine furniture. (Closed Sunday.)

across Indre river on D57 to Villaine-les-Rochers, NE on D127, right on D17 to Saché; recross Indre river on small road (C7) to Rome, Bois-Tireau, Druye, left on D121, then right past La Racaudière signposted to Villandry (25 km)

At Savonnières (2 km past Villandry on D7) – Hôtel des Cèdres, (47)53.00.28: pleasant building; swimming pool; Relais du Silence; bedrooms with bath or shower, WC, 165–240F. Restaurant alongside – separate management.

Restaurant des Cèdres, (47)53.37.58: good river fish; chicken in crayfish sauce; good trolleys of cheese (35 varieties) and desserts; menu 70–130F. Shut Friday.

Villandry – Cheval Rouge, (47)50.02.07: at exit of château gardens; reasonable number of dishes freshly prepared; right balance between choice and care in preparation; menu 67–155F; rooms 127–190F. Shut Monday; January; open weekends only Nov., Dec., Feb.

Villaine-les-Rochers: famous for wickerwork baskets; green rushes and black and yellow osiers cut in winter, soaked in water until May. Village priest found craft dying, so formed cooperative in 1849. Still going – prototype of French peasant coops of which there are tens of thousands. To see basket-makers at work apply at La Vannerie in village. On Azay road is troglodyte village; local people once lived there; believed to be gypsies who brought traditional art of wickerwork with them. Caves still used for work. Also a ferronnerie (iron foundry) making beautiful items in iron.

Saché has château where French writer Balzac wrote much of his best work, and went to escape his creditors.

Château de Villandry: known for its gardens; formal, geometric French gardens were cleared in 18th century for making English landscaped park-like gardens. Even paths are raked into formal designs. (Open 8 am to sunset, 15 March–15 Nov.)

D7 Tours (15 km)

Restaurant La Petite Marmite, 103 ave la Tranchée, (47) 54.03.85: in busy road N10 north of river; the 'people's' version of the great Charles Barrier restaurant (see Restaurant Barrier below); very good modern restaurant. Sound, straightforward cooking of

Has become very industrial, filling four-mile gap between Loire and Cher. Old centre still most attractive; cathedral started in 13th century, finished in 16th, is classic Gothic building incorporating all styles; rich Flamboyant decoration makes it awe-inspiring; alas, limestone

fresh food. Menu 47, 80F; wines a little pricey. Shut Wednesday, Sunday evening; part July, Feb.

Restaurant La Ruche, 105 rue Colbert, (47)66.69.83: charming little bistro; menu 42F; carte; only serves fresh produce according to season. Shut Sunday, Monday lunch.

La Renaissance, 64 rue Colbert, (47)66.63.25: Jacques Barthès and his wife offer good quality at low prices; honest dishes like coq au vin, escalope, entrecôte Marchand-de-Vin; pot-roasted chicken (cocotte); family run, very French. Menu at 31F includes drinks; also menus at 45, 70F; wines – 180 from 20F; visit the cellars. Shut Monday.

Barrier, 101 ave Tranchée, (47)54.20.39: a chance to tell your grandchildren 'I ate a meal by Charles Barrier.' Like me, he gets no younger, but *he* still achieves near perfection. Classic French cooking at its best; menu 230, 280F. Shut Sunday evening, Wednesday; February.

crumbling and remedy not found; superb stained-glass windows 13th–16th century. Many museums, from Gemmail (rue du Murier) on stained glass to Wine Museum (16 rue Nationale).

Good daily market in Les Halles (food and veg.); famous flower market Wednesday, Saturday.

---

cross Loire on to N152 Rochecorbon, Vouvray, D46 Vernou, D1 Noizay, Bardouillière, Nazelles – Négron, right into Amboise (28 km)

Rochecorbon (3 km from Tours) – Les Fontaines, (47)52.52.86: charming little hotel in garden; neatly, pleasantly furnished; some four-posters; no restaurant; rooms 90–180F.

Rochecorbon: just off N152; troglodyte (cave) dwellings built into cliff-face.

Vouvray: some troglodyte houses; centre of Vouvray wine district; visitors to caves very welcome. Cave Bonne Dame is vast cellar dug out of rock.

Vouvray
continued

Hostellerie Lanterne (4 km from Tours), (47)52.50.02: very good 50F menu with reasonable choice (ours included boudin noir – that splendid French black pudding; creamed escalope or kidneys in red wine); wines from 26.50F. Shut Monday, Sunday evening low season; part Jan., Feb.

Vouvray – Val Joli (on N152 just after D46 turn off), (47)52.70.18: overlooks Loire; nice garden; wine tastings; good river fish; coq au vin de Chinon; appellation contrôllée (A.C.) wines from 35F; menu 40, 54, 85, 100F. Shut Wednesday.

Grand Vatel, rue Brûlé, (47)52.70.32: Rabelaisian murals help you enjoy generous portions of tasteful dishes; menu 60–130F; rooms 95–150F. Shut Monday; December.

Wine route is marked along D1 from Vernou, left after Bardouillière on D79 towards Reugny, left on D46; right to Vaugondy and Valley of Cocotte to visit Cooperative cellars. Back to Vouvray (about 35 km). Chalk soil produces from Chenin Blanc grape a still white wine underestimated outside the Loire; it matures in bottles – unusual for a delicate white wine; some dry, better ones semi-sweet or honey-sweet. When vintage is not the best, it is made into very good sparkling wine (it tends to referment in bottle, anyway). So do make sure which wine you are ordering – still, pétillant (slightly sparkling), or full sparkling; dry, semi-sweet or sweet.

D81 through Amboise Forest to Civray, left on D40 Chenonceaux (10 km) N76 along Cher river bank to Montrichard (8 km)

Amboise – see Route 2 (page 61).

Chenonceaux – see Route 2 (page 63).

Montrichard – see Route 2 (page 64).

At Monthou-sur-Cher (9 km from Montrichard by N76, left on D21) – Château du Gué Péan, one of the greatest Renaissance châteaux in France; white, blue roof; round courtyard with pool; superb round towers at each corner.

Magnificent Louis XV and
XVI furnishings; monumental
white fireplace; paintings by
Fragonard, Gérard, David.
Wonderful library with
autograph collection of
famous people.

D28 Vallières-
les-Grandes,
D27 Chaumont-
sur-Loire
(18 km)

At Rilly-sur-Loire (W of
Chaumont on D751 – 4 km) –
Château Haute-Borde,
(54)46.98.09: superb country
house in own park; our
bedroom led direct to terrace
overlooking grounds; very
quiet; good trout; duck (à
l'orange); very good value;
menu 48–100F; wines from
25F (Gamay), Sauvignon 26F;
rooms 70–140F. Shut
Monday; 15 Nov.–15 March.

Auberge des Voyageurs,
(54)79.88.85: charming Logis
with beamed front; very
French bistro-style dining
room; small bedrooms
(basin, bidet); menu 33–75F;
rooms 48F.

Chaumont – Hostellerie du
Château, (54)46.98.04: very
attractive; fine garden;
beautifully furnished; pretty

Château de Chaumont: looks
fearsome beside most
elegant Loire châteaux; fine
views over valley. Guides say
Catherine de Medici lived
here when Henry II, her
husband, was killed
accidentally in a joust and
she became Regent, and one
room is said to have been
given to the astrologer in
whom she believed,
Ruggieri. But evidence is
slight. More likely she
bought it to swop for
Chenonceaux with her
husband's mistress Diane de
Poitiers, who didn't like it
and left it immediately.
Madame de Staël, the great
writer, lived here during her
banishment from Paris by
Napoleon – and didn't like it.
The stables are most elegant
– lined with velvet.

Chaumont-sur-Loire *continued*	bedrooms, all with bath, WC; swimming pool; good cooking; menu 80F (weekdays), 120F; rooms 205–328F. Shut 15 Dec.– 15 Feb.	

D751 Candé-sur-Beuvron, D173 Blois (18 km)

Candé – Relais de Bacchus, (54)44.03.86: changed hands 1982; typical wayside inn; excellent noisette of fillet steak; good sole, scallops; prices very reasonable; menu 45–85F; rooms (basin, shower) 45F.

Lion d'Or (54)44.04.66: friendly; good cooking; very good value; try home-made rillettes, quail pâté in port; game; peppered tournedos; private river-bank with fishing. Menu 30–78F; rooms 55–135F. Shut December.

Hostellerie de la Caillère, rte Montils, (54)44.03.08: well known, pricey; very good. Beautiful old house, nicely furnished; friendly, good service; very good cooking; good desserts; menu 90–160F.

Blois – Le Vendôme, Restaurant Noë, ave Vendôme, (54)74.16.66: comfortable; restaurant well known and respected; daily purchase of best fresh ingredients for meals; menu 60F and carte; rooms 65–125F.

Blois: centre of big farming area – strawberries and bulbs to vegetables and wine. Château played big part in French history. In 16th century, Louis XII and his wife, Anne of Brittany, made it centre of Court life (like Versailles later). States General (Parliament) met here twice, once to suppress Protestant Church (1576); in 1688 Henri de Guise, head of violent Catholic 'League' and most powerful man in land, called States General here with intention of deposing Henry III and making Guise King. Henry guessed the plot, murdered Guise in the Château. Henry was murdered eight months later. In 1662 Louis XIII banished his brother, Gaston d'Orléans, a perpetual conspirator, to Blois, gave him money to rebuild the château to keep him quiet. Gaston hired great architect Mansart. 'Son et Lumière' most nights 26 March–19 Sept. (not Thursdays except in July, August) – show in French, followed by one in English (starts 10 pm to 11.15 pm midsummer). No booking. Tickets at entrance.

Au Grand Cerf, ave Wilson, (54)78.02.16: widest range of menus, between 40F and 155F; Périgordine cooking, so try duck, goose; truffled omelette; confit aux cèpes. Wines: Sauvignon white 28F; Gamay red 31F. Rooms 84–105F.

Château Beauregard (just off D765 on way to Cheverny): delightful; one of prettiest in Loire. Built 1550 as 'hunting lodge' for extravagant Francis I. Remarkable gallery with 363 portraits of important people, and Delft-tiled floor showing army of Louis XIII. Still lived in.

D765 Cour-Cheverny, D102 Bracieux, D112 Chambord (33 km)

Cour-Cheverny – St Hubert, (54)79.96.60: famous for its game, in season; cosy, friendly; wines from 25F; menu 55F (weekdays), 85F; rooms 69–159F (some for 3 people). Shut Wednesday (low season); 5 Dec.-15 Jan.

Taverne Berrichonne, (54)79.96.49: ordinary bistro; simple; good value; locals use it; menu 32–68F; snacks – good omelette 10F; rooms 35–50F.

Chambord – Hôtel St Michel, (54)46.31.31: opposite château; game in season; good goat's cheese; front row seat for castle's 'Son et Lumière'! Restful; big open fire; décor of woodland and hunting scenes; menu 65F and carte; local Cheverny white wine 18F; red Gamay 38F. Rooms 80–180F.

Château de Cheverny: one of nicest; white, 'fat and friendly'; still has its 17th-century furnishings and lavish decorations. Some rooms almost overpowering. Fine park, with long drive; 18th-century Orangerie converted for receptions. Château built 1634; previous château now part of outbuildings; present owner, Marquis of Vibraye, descendant of Huraults family who built it. Open to public. I prefer it to Blois or Chambord – not so stark nor like museum.

Château Chambord must be one of the most uncomfortably ostentatious houses ever built. Its park surrounded by walls 20 miles long; 365 chimneys; 440 rooms separated by 80 staircases; Francis I ('always hunting stags or women') built it as a hunting lodge. Possibly he needed the rooms – whole Court always travelled with him; 12,000 horses carried them, their servants, furniture, crockery,

Chambord
continued

baggage. Francis loved show and was determined to outshine Henry VIII of England and Charles V of Spain. But he stayed at Chambord a total of 40 days. Now château belongs to the State, is open most days except Tuesdays, but most of park is a National Hunting Reserve for a privileged few, such as members of the Government and friends.

Castle 'Son et Lumière' shows in evenings 1 May-30 Sept.

D33, D103 La Ferté-St Cyr, D103, D61 Ligny-le-Ribault, D19 past Monçay, les Gachetières to D951 Cléry-St André, St Hilaire-St Mesmin, right on D14 Olivet, D14 Parc Floral, Orléans (62 km)

La Ferté – Commerce, (54) 27.90.14: creeper-clad Logis on roadside; menus 35, 55, 73 and 90F with local specialities; wines from 13F; rooms 67–95F. Shut 1–15 Aug.

Robin des Bois, (54)81.90.20: real old country inn with small, simple bedrooms; good traditional dishes; try pièce de boeuf (top rump) in Roquefort sauce; wild boar; menu 58–85F; house wine 28F; rooms 53F. Shut mid-Jan. to mid-Feb.

Saint Cyr Hôtel, (54)81.90.51: modern, family run, homely atmosphere; open fire; very nice bedrooms (all with bath, some WC); small dining room; traditional cooking; menu 42, 50F; wines from 22 and 30F; rooms 110, 135F.

La Ferté-St Cyr: centre for fishing in étangs (small lakes) and streams, and woodland walks. Pheasants are reared round here.

Beaugency (straight on at crossroads of D19 and D951 – 5 km: beautiful old town across the Loire; see this route on return journey. Return route crosses this outward route near Monçay.

At Cléry-St André, left on D18 across Loire river is Meung-sur-Loire, attractive small town; walks under lime trees along river Mauves, tributary of Loire, rich in fish. Château was English headquarters of General Talbot and Earl of Salisbury in final days of 100 Years War. Talbot lost to Joan of Arc; Salisbury had his head blown off at Siege of Orléans. Bishops of Orléans mostly held it 1200–1789.

Les Salstices, tiny local restaurant with 22F and 35F menus, plus evening menu 65F with apéritif; help yourself to choice of 25 terrines; plate of vegetables (choice); meat or fish grilled over wood fire; salad; cheese; unlimited wine.

Cléry-St André – Hôtel Notre Dame, (38)45.70.22: typical corner Logis in small town; used by local people; friendly; menu 53–85F; wines from 21F; rooms 58–105F.

St Hilaire-St Mesmin – L'Escale du Port-Arthur, 205 rue de l'Eglise, (38)80.30.36: very quiet on banks of Loiret near where it joins Loire. Modern, superb position overlooking river; comfortable bedrooms, mostly with bath or shower and river views; pleasant dining room; try tasty feuilleté of scallops; salmon in grain-mustard sauce (super); chicken in crayfish sauce; hot salad of crottin (smelly goats' milk cheese with unpleasant name – goat's dung – and gorgeous taste); menu 60–125F; wines 30–380F; rooms 60–110F.

Olivet – Le Rivage, (38)66.02.93: my favourite of yesteryear; famous now, but still most pleasant; alongside river Loiret; riverside terrace for good-weather eating; boats tied up below it for rowing, fishing. True Loire dishes – friture of small fish;

Beautifully furnished. Only château hereabouts with dungeons underground.

François Villon was held here – great 15th-century poet who was also a tramp and a burglar. Open Easter-November.

Olivet: I would pick quiet little St Hilaire or Olivet on Loiret river for staying overnight rather than modern Orléans. Olivet in charming setting on river banks, where Orléans people have always gone for fishing, boating, picnics; river banks lined with fine old houses and watermills; riverside paths, cafés, restaurants; like a modernized scene from Renoir. Market gardens; fields of flowers, nurseries.

New town of Orléans with new university campus has been built south of Floral Park. Park covers 86 acres – superb from April to November. Old trees, fountains, modern sculptures surrounded by massed blooms – tulips, iris, dahlias, chrysanthemums, 200,000 rose bushes. Still attractive in winter, when it is open only afternoons. In centre is remarkable 'source' of Loiret. True source at St Benoit, but river re-emerges here, with water bubbling out at 1400 cu. ft a minute, temperature 12–15°C (54–59°F), which helps flower cultivation. Also,

Orléans
continued

river eel in feuilleté of puff pastry (eel is surprisingly tasty, more like meat than fish); sandre; crayfish. Good traditional French cooking; menu 70, 90, 135F; rooms (bath or shower – many with river views) 111–140F.

Hôtel-Restaurant Paul Forêt, 138 allée Grande Coteaux, (38)63.56.46: big old house of character in lovely position overlooking Loiret; showing its age a bit (like me) but attractively different (like me?); nice rooms; restaurant very popular; Michel Forêt cooks well; good value; try trout; poussin (tiny chicken) vigneron flambé; menu 30–70F; good choice of wines from 26F; rooms 60–80F.

flamingoes, many ducks and other web-footed friends winter here. Little train runs through park. Restaurant, rather like eating in greenhouse (rubber plants and tree décor).

Orléans: nice modern city, rebuilt after wartime destruction but little left for Joan of Arc fans. Statue of her in pl Martroi by Foyatier (1855) with bas-reliefs on pedestal in Renaissance-style by Vital-Dubray. When Joan arrived with her troops in 1429, French defenders were tired and dispirited, English attackers down to 2000 tired men, the rest had been withdrawn. She breathed new spirit into the French; English thought she was a witch. Her courage and morale saved Orléans. In cathedral at top of splendid modern shopping street, rue

Orléans
continued

Le Manderley, 117 Sentier des Près, (38)66.19.85: restaurant only, lovely riverside terrace; good river fish; duck; quail; menu 60–121F; in garden – Le Semainier – quick service grill. Shut Monday evening, Tuesday.

Orléans – Restaurant Jeanne, rue Ste Catherine near Joan's statue in pl Martroi, (38)53.40.87: nice bistro; good value meals; menu 42–83F. Shut Sunday.

Etoile d'Or, pl Vieux Marché, (38)53.49.20: big fin de siècle restaurant with good choice and value; on 46F menu, 20 choices on main course including steak fauxfilet, duck cassoulet, trout; menu 41–75F; wine from 16F litre; rooms 46–102F. Shut Sunday; August.

Jeanne d'Arc, is statue of Cardinal Touchet (died 1926) whose life's work was to propagate the cult of the Maid and get her made a saint by the Pope; succeeded in 1920; made patron saint of France. Statue of her in town hall by Princess Marie of Orléans, daughter of King Louis-Philippe.

D951 Jargeau; over Loire on to N152, Châteauneuf-sur-Loire, D60 St Benoît-sur-Loire (17 km)

Châteauneuf – La Capitainerie, Grande rue, (38)58.42.16: most pleasant inn with charming terrace alongside park. Seasonal dishes; menu 65–115F; rooms 60–170F. Shut 1 Jan.-15 Feb.

Châteauneuf: likeable market town; lovely riverside walks; waterfowl; wild park with rare trees, shrubs, red squirrels; wild rhododendrons in June; huge magnolias; big carp in moat. Domed rotunda of old castle now town hall. Castle rebuilt in 17th century as miniature Versailles. Little left except park.

Church of St Benoît (St Benedict) one of finest Romanesque buildings in Europe (started 1026 – mostly 11th century).

St Benoît-
sur-Loire
continued

Benedictine abbey here in
7th century. Abbot stole
remains of St Benoît from
Monte Casino monastery in
Italy in a raid! Under
Charlemagne became one of
Europe's leading educational
centres, with 20,000 pupils.
Renowned for Gregorian
Chant.

D60 Sully-sur-
Loire (8 km)
D951 Gien,
Briare (road
crosses Loire
bridge),
Châtillon,
Léré, D751,
D955 Sancerre
(67 km)

See Route 3.

D920, then
over Loire on
D59 Pouilly-
sur-Loire
(24 km)

Relais Fleurie et Restaurant
Le Coq Hardi, ave de la
Tuilerie, (86)39.12.99: flower
gardens, river view; excellent
cooking by chef-patron Jean-
Claude Astruc: duck; chicken
in local wine; river fish
(salmon, sandre; try salmon
à l'orange) good value;
menu 41, 69F (excellent), 90,
175F; good wine list.

La Vieille Auberge,
(86)39.17.98: a nice
discovery; good value meals;
sensible wine list; menu 70–
130F. Shut Wednesday.

Château de la Grange (on
D920): built in reign of Henry
IV; curious, many-sided
dome.

Home of Pouilly-Fumé, the
flinty dry white wine (not to
be confused with Pouilly-
Fuissé from Burgundy).
Made from Sauvignon
grapes, its recent popularity
has made it rather dear. The
litre-lappers' cheaper
substitute, Pouilly-sur-Loire
wine is made from
Chasselas, grown originally
for Kings at Fontainebleau,
but not so fruity as Fumé.

Do not judge this town from
what you see on N7; go
down to the Loire and savour
its river views (and wines)
from Relais Fleurie (see
restaurants).

N7 La Charité-sur-Loire (13 km) over river Loire to D45, left to Cours-les-Barres, D12, then left over Loire to Nevers (20 km)	See Route 3. Nevers – see Route 3.	More interesting route than N7, avoids lorries. Marseilles-les-Aubigny is working canal port; barges may have come from Germany, Holland, Switzerland or distant parts of France.
south on N7 3.5 km, then right D970 Pont Canal; soon, little road right D45N to Cuffy, left on D50e through Bois des Ribaudières to D920, turn left to St Guerche-sur-l'Aubois, D976 right to Nérondes, 2 km past Nérondes right on D43 Baugy, les Aix d'Anguillon, at far end of village take D185 (not D46) to Aubinges, Morogues (67 km)		Just before Pont Canal at Guetin, Canal Latéral crosses river Allier by aqueduct; barges mount a stairway of three locks, descend a similar flight. Morogues: Château de Maupas; private house of Marquis de Maupas; much restored 15th-century château amid formal French gardens; beautifully furnished; mementoes of amusing and liberated Duchess of Berry, a Neopolitan princess who married French duke of royal blood, and who started fashion for sea-bathing at Dieppe, and for climbing the Pyrenees, horrifying French society.
D46 La Borne, D197 through Bois d'Henriche-mont to la Chapelotte, D7, D11 Villegenon, D89 La Verrerie,	Aubigny – La Chaumière, (48)58.04.01: much more comfortable and inviting than it looks; very good cooking; menu 50, 80, 140F; a peep inside Daniel Brunneval's kitchen is a joy – row on row of different sized copper pans as décor; tables laden with	La Borne: small village in woods; pottery produced for 300 years from local clay; craft being replaced. La Verrerie: summer château of Scottish Stuarts. Darnley settled here when fighting English in 15th century.

Aubigny-sur-Nère (42 km)

salmon, trout, lobster, huge joints, pretty desserts; rooms 50–130F.

Louis XIV took back town when last Stuart male heir died, gave it to Louise de Keroualle (Duchess of Portsmouth and mistress to another Stuart – Charles II). Her descendants are Dukes of Richmond; sold château in 1834. Marquis de Vogué bought it – descendants still own it. Stands reflected in lake – a Renaissance 'fairy' castle. Elegant and beautiful; fine furniture, tapestries; superb little chapel; 16th-century wall paintings. (Open Feb.–mid Nov. except Tuesday.)

In Aubigny, the Stuart château is now the town hall. This was given to Duchess of Portsmouth, too.

D940 Argent-sur-Sauldre, D24, D923 Brinon-sur-Sauldre, Lamotte-Beuvron (35 km)

Argent – Relais de la Poste, (48)73.60.25: just off main road; pleasant; known for good cooking; menu 50–160F; rooms 55–140F. Shut Monday except high season; February.

Lamotte-Beuvron – Hostellerie de la Cloche, ave République, (54)88.02.20: friendly, cosy, run by family with young, enthusiastic team; on noisy N20, but back is quiet; good value; old regional recipes and original dishes by careful, enthusiastic chef. Game in season; river fish; home-made terrines; menu 42–85F; wines from 19F; rooms (6) 47–73.50F. Shut Tuesday.

Argent: makes lingerie and hoisting machinery; 15th-century château with terrace overlooking Sauldre river.

Pleasant route through forests, farms of Sologne (swamps area drained by Napoleon III, now fertile) and small lakes; misses busy N20 except when crossing it.

D101 Vouzon,
D129, D108
Ménestreau,
D17 La Ferté-
St Aubin, D18
Jouy, D103 to
near Monçay,
D19 over Loire
Beaugency
(54 km)

La Ferté – Du Perron, rue Général Leclerc, (38)91.53.36: old-style hunting inn; beams, brick, open fire; local dishes – wild boar, ham, carp, other game, river fish; menu 58, 94F; rooms 63–159F. Shut January.

Beaugency – Ecu de Bretagne, pl Martroi, (38)44.67.60: big auberge with flowered surrounds; name existed as inn since Joan of Arc. Mostly traditional and regional dishes – we had good crayfish omelette, then quail; original dishes include honey-roast rabbit (delicious); terrine of sole in red wine; pike cutlets in nuts; game fondu; menu 65–110F; good-sized rooms 69–159F.

Relais des Templiers, rue Pont, (38)44.53.78: comfortable; bed and breakfast; rooms 90–180F.

Ménestreau: among small woodland lakes; village of flowers.

La Ferté-St Aubin: Ferté means small fortress. River Cosson flows through castle moats, lined by elegant 17th-century balustrades; large park.

At Monçay outward route crosses this one.

Beaugency: lovely old town, excellent for a rest while exploring châteaux; quieter, more charming than Blois. But beware – the Devil still lives in Tour du Diable, next door to old abbey which became a hotel. The splendid Loire bridge (440 m/1444 ft long, 22 arches) made Beaugency a war target through history – as a river crossing. French themselves blew up part in 1940 to delay Nazis. Replaced perfectly; central arches are original. English took town four times in 100 Years War.

Beach for river swimming; good fishing. 15th-century castle with interesting museum of historic dress, coiffe head-dresses, furniture.

D917 Josnes,
then left D70A
Talcy, D70
Mauvoy, right
on D50
Marchenoir,
D917 Oucques,
Vendôme
(54 km)

Oucques – Commerce, rue Beaugency, (54)23.20.41: typical, small town hotel with some of best cooking we have found in the Loire; perfect canard bigarade (bitter orange sauce); excellent terrine with chopped avocados and

Château de Talcy: Renaissance; built 1520 by Italian cousin of Catherine de Médici; Ronsard, the poet, wrote love sonnets to owner's blonde daughter Cassandre; granddaughter Diana inspired love poems from Agrippa d'Aubigné.

langoustine tails; very good chicken in cream and leek sauce; trout in leek purée; menu 55–155F; wines from 20F; rooms 70–148F. Restaurant shut Sunday, Monday evening.

Auberge Bon Laboureur, Grande rue, (54)23.20.22: bistro, pleasant inside, good value; menu 48F (also 34F weekday lunch), carte. Shut Tuesday evening, Wednesday.

Vendôme – see Route 2 (page 59).

Small wonder that a descendant was Alfred de Musset, one of France's greatest poets. Defence-keeps added later give outside a fortress look, but inside a lovely arcaded gallery, and rooms are exquisitely furnished. I could live here – especially as the 400-year-old winepress still works, giving 10 barrels of juice at one pressing.

D5 Le Guéle
Loire,
Bonaventure,
D24 Les Zoules
L'Eveque, D917
Montoire
(19 km)

Montoire – see Route 2.

Villiers: clings to hillside above vineyards, looking across to Château Rochambeau; church has 16th-century murals of St Christopher, patron saint of travellers. Also 15th-century choir stalls.

Le Gué-du-Loir: at meeting of Loir and Boulon rivers; lush meadows. Renaissance Bonaventure Manor, now in ruins, belonged to a Bourbon – father of Henry IV and ancestor of poet Alfred Musset.

Les Roches l'Evêque: troglodyte houses, some with wistaria round entrance. Near by is troglodyte chapel.

D917 Troo,
across river
Loir to St
Jacques-des-
Guérets, D8
(for 3 km) right
on D10 to La
Possonière,
D57 Couture-
sur-le-Loir,
D305 La
Chartre-sur-le-
Loir (28 km)

Couture-sur-le-Loir – La Grand St Vincent, (54)85.92.02: simple, cheap local Relais; menu 35F (4 courses, no choice), 55F (4 courses, 3 choices); rooms 45F (2 people), 55F (for 3).

Auberge de l'Etang Ronsard, (54)85.90.16: lakeside fisherman's auberge, away from village; you wouldn't look twice; inside cosy dining room with open fire; good value, cheap meals; menu 32, 42F (fair choice includes roast pork or beef), 65F (good – 5 courses; fine quenelles of crayfish).

La Chartre – De France, pl République, (43)44.40.16: Aston Martin and Lagonda teams used to stay here for

Troo: odd town on steep slope, still with troglodyte houses cut into hillside (Rue Haute); town built in tiers, linked by narrow alleys, passageways, stairways. Underground is labyrinth of galleries used as refuge in old wars. Remains of 11th-century fortifications.

St Jacques-des-Guérets: church with mural paintings from 12th century.

La Possonière: manor birthplace of poet Pierre de Ronsard (1524); visits only with written permission from owner.

At Poncé-sur-le-Loir (3½ km past Couture-sur-Loir, across Loir on D57, left 1 km on D305): attractive château

La Chartre-sur-le-Loir *continued*

Le Mans 24-hour race in Stirling Moss's day – when we used to win! Very French-looking, with pavement tables, umbrellas, tubs of flowers; old-style comfort inside; lovely garden with terrace, flower beds; excellent value meals; traditional cooking; menu 45, 70, 105F. Rooms 77–125F; vary; all fair; ours at 117F with bathroom excellent. We recommend this hotel thoroughly. Shut 20 Nov.-20 Dec.

(open daily; afternoon only on Sunday); remarkable Renaissance staircase with superb sculptured ceilings (well worth seeing); huge dovecote with 1800 holes; museum of local crafts; church has murals of crusades; craftsmen in outbuildings (iron-forging; glass-blowing; Grès du Loir pottery; weaving; carpentry).

La Chartre-sur-le-Loir: a fair sweet white wine produced here.

D305 Marçon on to join N138 right to Château-du-Loir (16 km)
D10 over Loir at Nogent, St Aubin, D38 Château-la-Vallière, D766 Marcilly-sur-Maulne, Noyant, D767 Linières-Bouton, right on D62 Mouliherne, D58 NW through forest of Chandelais to Baugé (67 km)

Noyant – Hostellerie St Martin, (41)89.60.44: simple Relais; our simple room, rather bare, clean 60F (for 2); menu 45F.

Mouliherne – Cheval Blanc, (41)51.52.13: very cheap; basic, simple bedrooms; good value meals; menu 28F; rooms 35F.

Baugé – Boule d'Or, rue Cygne, (41)89.82.12: good fresh river fish (including salmon); local duck; menu 38–100F; rooms 60–130F.

Marçon white wines deserve to be better known. Not in Vouvray or Sancerre class but good for quaffing in litres.

Baugé: interesting and delightful little town in very heart of Anjou, among forests, heaths; market town; old part has lovely big houses. Château much restored (now town hall, fine museum of old weapons; open to public 1 June-15 Sept. a favourite residence of Good King René in 15th century, Duke of Anjou who inherited the Kingdom of Sicily, and Anjou and Sicily were joined into an unlikely alliance. Anjou was annexed by France in 1484.

St Joseph Hospital, founded 1643, has remarkable historical dispensary.

Baugé
continued

La Camusière (pl Camusière just north, roundabout where D938 meets D766), (41)89.29.11: Relais Routiers; meals 8 a.m.–9 p.m. in snack-brasserie; specialities – cassoulet; tripes Lyonnaises flambées in brandy; special sauerkraut dish; frogs' legs in cream. Steak and other dishes, too. Breton crêpes (pancakes). Menu 30–78F. Shut Saturday evening.

D60 left on D211 to Brion, D7 Beaufort-en-Vallée, N138, D74 Montgeoffroy, 2 km further on D74 to Mazé, D55 to St Mathurin, D952 by river Loire into Angers (43 km)

Beaufort-en-Vallée: fine views from hilltop, with castle ruins. Surrounded by rich plains.

Château Montgeoffroy: a masterpiece; probably most interesting château in France. Built, decorated and furnished in 1772 for Marshal of Contades by greatest craftsmen of the time, it remains totally unchanged and unmodernized. You can see exactly how noblemen of late 18th century lived. Open Easter – All Saints' Day. Don't miss this château!

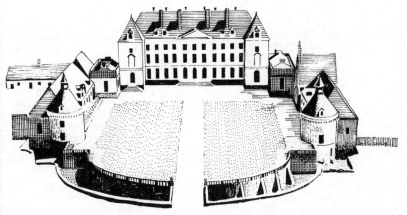

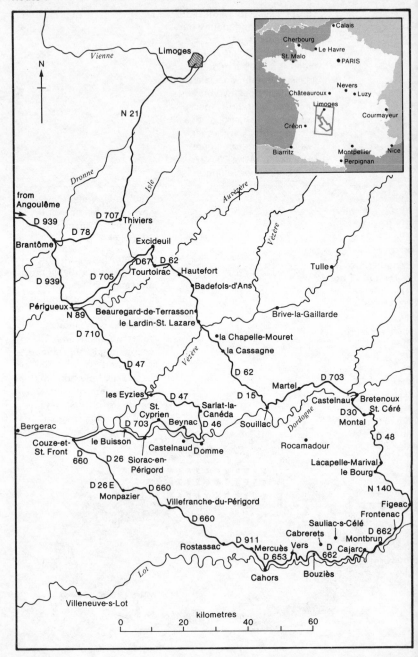

Route 7
Round north Dordogne, Lot and Quercy

The wonderland that we call the Dordogne but which is really Périgord, parts of Limousin and Quercy, is the tourist discovery of the last twenty years. But it is still almost empty most of the year, and even in July and August whole areas of it are still and silent. It has so many hideaway villages, valleys, wooded hillsides and tiny roads that you could hide armies there. I sat by a roadside in summer for a whole morning, a mile from where tourists were arriving in hundreds to see a famous château, and only one person passed me. As for the Lot, though Cahors attracts many people (and deserves to, for its medieval bridge alone), this more rugged, rockier country has not pulled in sightseers in the same way as the Dordogne, though the river Lot is most attractive and you will find the route alongside it from Cahors a revelation.

It is easier to see the highlights of the Dordogne and still find some privacy between than it is in the Loire valley, which is so near Paris. Dordogne and Lot châteaux were for defence – the front line in big wars. Even a sketchy knowledge of history makes the whole tour much more interesting: especially the story of the 100 Years War between England and France, of the Plantagenet kings of England and Aquitaine, such as Henry II and Richard Lionheart, and their very bold, and often very bad, barons. The river Dordogne was often the frontline, with the English, who once ruled Guyenne (Périgord, Quercy Rouerge) to the south, the French to the north. South and north, I have taken you through areas which few Frenchmen know.

The truffle, the walnut, the goose, the duck, superb river fish, with fresh vegetables, are used here to make some of the best dishes in the world. Making a sauce Périgueux, with white wine scented with shallots and truffles, mixed with the juice of the meat or poultry it is to accompany, is a great art. Bleue de Causses (or de Quercy) is a blue-veined cheese matured in caves naturally, like Roquefort, but made from skimmed cow's milk, not ewe's milk.

Bergerac red, white or rosé wines are pleasant. Pécharmant of Dordogne is light red for lunch drinking. Cahors has a splendid deep, strong, fruity red which could surprise a Burgundy addict.

Thiviers (join
here from
Limoges)

Busy little town; market for
foie gras, poultry, truffles
(little black magical fungus –
grows underground beneath
oaks; snuffed out by trained
pigs or dogs); Périgord is
main source; brings out
delicate flavour in other
ingredients – pâté, terrine,
etc.; now incredibly
expensive. Small goats'
cheese made here. Sold at
famous fairs.

D707, D78
Brantôme
(26 km) (join
here from
Angoulême)

Auberge du Soir, rue
Georges Saumande,
(53)05.82.93: attractive
simple Auberge Rurale; good
value, cheap menu, good
gastronomic; menu 38–120F;
rooms 80F. Shut January.

Moulin de l'Abbaye,
(53)05.80.20: superb
conversion by Regis and
Catherine Bulot-Benoist of
old picturesque riverside mill
into 4-star hotel. Romantic,
beautifully furnished;
inevitably expensive; mostly
Périgordian cooking; menu
75–165F; rooms 240–350F.
Open mid-May to mid-Oct.

Chabrol, rue Gambetta,
(53)05.70.15: sorry, another
pricey hotel in lovely
riverside position. Jean-
Claude Charbonnel deserves
his Michelin star. Superb
salmon pâté; succulent
chicken in truffled sauce;
meals 80–200F; rooms 140–
180F. Check winter closing.

Delightful old town beside
river Dronne in Périgord,
rich in old buildings,
including riverside houses
with flowered balconies and
vines, and riverside gardens
with willows. You enter by a
16th-century elbow bridge
leading to the old abbey
church, with 12th-century
belfry and a fountain garden
with a bust of the scandalous
16th-century abbot, diplomat
and witty, cynical chronicler
of Court life known as
'Brantôme' (Pierre de
Bourdeilles). Superb riverside
strolls. Monastery buildings
now town hall, schools and
Bernard Desmoulin museum
which includes works by this
artist, painted, they say,
when under the influence of
a medium. He died in 1914.

7 km on D18: Bourdeilles
castle, over which the
Plantagenets and French
squabbled for years; set
spectacularly up a cliffside

At Bourdeilles (10 km on D78) – Griffons, (53)05.75.61: 16th-century house by river bridge, converted by patronne-chef Denise Deborde. Good cooking; menu 75–150F; rooms 185F. Open 1 April–1 Oct.

above the river, village and medieval mill. Superb! Brantôme's family built a Renaissance palace on to it.

D939
Périgueux (27 km)

Restaurants in Périgueux inevitably charge a lot for pâté de foie gras and truffles – most costly items. Truffles appear in many dishes, too. To really *taste* them, you must try them 'sous les cendres' –

The white domes of the cathedral, as you enter the capital of Périgourdine food, also promise an architectural feast; alas, many old buildings have been destroyed. The curious 12th-century cathedral, St Front,

Périgueux
continued

moistened with spirits, wrapped in sheet of fat bacon and cooked in ashes.

Léon, cours Tourny, (53)53.41.93: Henri Raynaud, truly great chef, has had his restaurant's austere front brightened and added a few 'nouvelles' dishes with light sauces – great concession. I shall stick to his superb Périgordian sauces. All great from simple 40F menu to regional 48F and gastronomic 110F. Try all Périgordian dishes; also salmon-trout with chives, duck stuffed with cèpes, snails in garlic sauce. Excellent wines and service. Shut Monday.

owes its flamboyance to the 19th-century architect Abbadie (called 'the Wrecker') who, when 'restoring', added seventeen turrets. Medieval houses can be seen from Barris bridge and in the old town.

Périgueux changed sides between France and England twice during the 100 Years War, finally opting for France.

Pleasant drive to two ancient abbey churches, Chancelade and Marlande in Feytaud forest. (Back along D939, D710 for very short distance; right on D1, then D2.)

Du Périgord, rue Victor Hugo, (53)53.33.63: a favourite for years, now highly recommended by readers. Warm welcome, pleasant rooms, pretty courtyard and garden with tables; excellent cooking; try beef fillet in Périgueux sauce; menu 42–95F (good value); wines from 22F; rooms 60–140F.

Hostellerie du Moulin et du Château de Rognac (8 km by D5 near Bassillac), (53)54.40.78: superb old building; courageously converted from a ruin 20 years ago by Madame Daudrix; a joy to stay in. Expensive menu is fine; cheaper menus not so good; too ambitious, I think. Menu 60, 78, 145F; rooms 115–190F. Shut 1 Nov.-30 March.

Domino, pl Francheville, (53)08.25.80: old style, warm charm, pretty garden with restaurant; genuine local dishes; excellent wine cave; menu 55–180F; rooms 80–250F.

N89, D710, D47 Les Eyzies (43 km)	Le Centre, pl Mairie, (53)06.97.13: in shady, quiet square, pretty dining room with pretty patronne, blonde Mme Brun; husband Gérard cooks in pure Périgourdine style, with confit, cèpes; local duck, goose, chickens; excellent cooking and value.	Prehistoric man, who came south to these caves for warmth in second Ice Age would get a shock if he saw tens of thousands of travellers in cars and coaches who come so far to see his humble cave home. Even if cavemen leave you cold, you

Les Eyzies
continued

Remarkable 75F 4-course menu; we had delicious jugged hare with fresh cèpes (gorgeous fungi). Charmingly furnished; garden by river Vezère. Menu 55–150F; wine from 12F; rooms 100–160F. Shut 15 Nov.–7 Feb.

De France, (53)06.97.23: comfortable, traditional old hotel; five menus from 3-course at 40F (choice steak, trout, chicken) to magnificent Périgordine gastronomic menu at 150F; others at 50, 65, 90F; wines from 15F; rooms 53–133F.

Du Centenaire, (53)06.97.18: superb cooking, inevitably expensive, though 4-course 80F menu very palatable; 150F menu to my taste for traditional cooking; rich and beautiful gastronomic menu at 240F (8 courses); superb wine list rated in top 25 for France by l'Académie des Vins; nice garden; attractive bedrooms in quiet annexe half-mile away, 140–200F.

will surely be interested. Men lived here in caves for tens of thousands of years, leaving behind bones, tools, weapons, pottery, jewellery; they left the caves for sunny slopes when world grew warmer. Archaeologists started to uncover flints, carved bones and ivory, skeletons coloured with ochre. Font-de-Gaume cave has prehistoric wall paintings of horses, bison, mammoths, reindeer; visitors have come since 18th century and left their graffiti. Grand Roc Cave (good view from stairs up to it) unusual show of stalactites, stalagmites, other formations. Cro-Magnon Cave discovered when railway was laid (1868); three skeletons of great importance to historians. See Museum of Prehistory in 11th-century castle of barons of Beynac, beneath overhanging rocks; books and pamphlets available (shut Tuesdays).

D47 Sarlat
(21 km)

Saint-Albert, (53)59.01.09: happy memories of many evenings eating, drinking, laughing with local people here. Modernized nowadays; posher bedrooms in an annexe opposite; but same friendly, informal atmosphere, willing service. More tourists, but locals still use it. 62F menu good value, good choice; 82F menu excellent. Magnificent 160F

I loved Sarlat when it was a half-forgotten, crumbling town with medieval and Renaissance houses; tourists were few, little happened there. That was before 1966 when Société d'Economie Mixte started rehabilitating mansions, cleaning lovely honey-coloured stone, putting plumbing into grateful citizens' houses. Now, in summer especially,

gastronomic menu (8 courses, including truffled omelette, confit of duck). Arrive hungry – generous portions; Menu 52–160F; rooms 80–140F

Salamandre, rue Abbe Surguer, (53)59.35.98: 3-star hotel owned by family of Saint-Albert (above); bed and breakfast, attractively furnished; quiet; all bedrooms with bath or shower, WC; rooms 140–200F, apartments for 4, 250F. Shut March.

Rossignol, bd Henri Arlet, (53)59.03.20: restaurant with Périgourdine dishes – confit of goose; neck of goose; stuffed trout; truffled omelette; menu 40–100F. Shut 1–15 May; 15 Nov–1 Dec.

you must climb steep narrow side roads and alleys to miss tourist crowds. But still delightful, with big market where, in last weeks of July, first of August, classical drama arrives with players from Comédie Française. Also goose market in Place des Oies Saturday morning. In 100 Years War, an English garrison town for 10 years from 1360; in 1970, 350 coins found bearing effigy of Black Prince.

A local lad who became Pope made town a bishopric in 1316; remained so until 1790.

D46 to near Domme, D703 Beynac, St Cyprien (31 km)

Domme – Esplanade, (53)28.31.41: superb views over Dordogne valley (150 m/492 ft below) to Sarlat from terrace where you can eat; nice little country-style hotel; menu 70–125F; rooms 140–215F.

Domme: across river bridge on rocky crag overlooking lovely Dordogne valley countryside; with 14th-century medieval buildings. From Belvedere de la Barre one of the best panoramic views in Dordogne – caves where local people hid in 100 Years War and Wars of Religion, open to visitors (Palm Sunday to 31 October).

La Roque-Gageac – Belle Etoile, (53)29.51.44: perfect vine-shaded terrace for meals on hot days; menu 42–85F; rooms 80–140F. Open 15 Mar.–15 Oct.

La Roque-Gageac: another castle (Malartie) with superb riverside site under cliffs; village streets just alleys; Tarde Manor with round turret was home of 16th-century humanist, Canon Tarde.

Beynac
continued

Beynac – Bonnet,
(53)29.50.01: I stayed here
first in the '50s to walk, eat,
drink, sleep and to fish in
Dordogne river across the
road. Hardly a car passed.
Still quiet, right below cliff
where castle is perched.
Walk down towpath of river
and you are alone. Terrace
overlooking river. Old-style
Logis, run by Mlle Renée
Bonnet in tradition of her
family. Little altered except
better plumbing; friendly,
good food, restful. I love it.
Menu 65–120F; rooms 125–
150F. Shut 15 Oct.–1 April.

Beynac castle has splendid
views over Dordogne. In 12th
century Richard Lionheart's
frontline against French. De
Montfort partly dismantled it
in 1214 but rebuilt soon after.
Now being restored by
department of Beaux Arts.
Well worth seeing (open 1
March–5 Nov.).

Over river bridge just before
Beynac, then right, are ruins
of Castelnaud – built by
French as defence against
English at Beynac.
Impressive 12th-century ruins
tower over valley. Changed
hands between French and
English, and also centre of
cunning family feuding in
16th century when Anne de
Caumont, whose father had
been poisoned, became
France's richest heiress;
kidnapped and forcibly
married at 7; widowed at 12;
kidnapped and married to a
boy of 9; marriage annulled;
kidnapped again at 18 and
married to Comte de St Pol,
of royal blood. She left him;
her son killed in battle as
page to Louis XIII, she took
to a convent, was
disinherited! Alexandre
Dumas could not have made
a better plot! Castelnaud
being restored.

St Cyprien – L'Abbaye, (53)29.20.48: modern hotel; good; rather pricey; menu 40–145F; rooms 125–210F. Open 15 Mar.–15 Sept.

St Cyprien clings to hillside above river; massive 12th–14th-century church; ruined Château de Fages (Renaissance – interior restoration of painted walls, ceilings in progress).

D703, bridge over Dordogne on left to Siorac-en-Périgord, D25 Le Buisson, D29 Badefols-sur-Dordogne, D29, then over river at Lalinde on to D703, back over river shortly to Couze-et-St-Front, D660, after 8 km take small left D26 beside river Couze, then right on D26F to Monpazier (41 km)

Siorac – Scholly, pl Poste, (53)28.60.02: classic French cooking with super rich sauces in hotel-restaurant away from traffic with delightful shady terrace; peace, excellent food; Dordogne river for swimming, fishing, boating. Do try trout soufflé in Riesling; quail stuffed with foie gras; stuffed goose neck (like a jumbo sausage). Mixture of Périgourdine and Alsatian cooking; menu 75–180F; fine wine cellar but starts at 48F; good rooms 90–180F.

L'Escale, (53)28.60.23: modern hotel in old style right on banks of river; terrace overlooks water; quiet, peaceful; very reasonable prices for ambience, position and quality; plats du jour 35F; menus 35, 58, 65, 80, 110F; all Périgordian specialities; also try local crayfish in rich, sharp Armoricaine sauce. Rooms 80–105F.

Monpazier – De France, rue St Jacques, (53)61.60.06: 13th-century building; former annexe of Château de Brion; pleasant inside; nice atmosphere; splendid value.

Winding route beside fields and woods.

Siorac: massive 17th-century château; town hall is in one wing.

Badefols – 15th-16th-century château destroyed in Revolution; ruins used later by river-pirates preying on Dordogne barges. Dordogne was main route to Bordeaux; wine was taken on flat-bottomed barges (called 'garbares'), poled down fast flowing river.

Lalinde: built as fortress town by ford across Dordogne by Edward III of England in 1270. Still has three castles – one ruined.

Couze-et-St-Front: busy little town; nice Romanesque church now a warehouse. Some troglodyte houses; mushrooms grown here.

Monpazier: fortified town built by Edward I of England in 1285; lovely old squares with alleys between old buildings; arcaded central square is delightful. Scene of peasant revolt in 1594 with 8000 teaming through countryside plundering castles. Away from tourist routes.

Monpazier
continued

40F menu was cheese soup and hors d'oeuvres including melon, ham, charcuterie and pâté (help yourself); trout or pork chop; cheese or mousse; plus ¼ litre of wine and coffee. 55F menu – soup and hors d'oeuvres; crayfish à l'Armoricaine, guinea-fowl, trout in almonds or roast ribs of mutton; cheese and dessert. True gastronomic Périgordine menu 120F. Off the tourist routes! Other menus 65, 95F; wines from 20F; neat bedrooms 53F.

D660
Villefranche-du-
Périgord
(20 km)

Commerce, (53)20.90.11: charming honey-coloured stone building with outside arcade making terrace, views across countryside; open fire in dining room; bar used by locals; family atmosphere; good value meals; six menus 38–120F; wines from 17F; plats du jour 28F; rooms (all WC, bath or shower) 90–120F. Shut 15 Dec.–1 Mar.

Almost at meeting of Dordogne area, Lot and Lot-et-Garonne. Winding route, lined with trees (walnuts, silver birch, firs). Another bastide (fortified town) – 13th century; ancient vast market hall; surrounding forests of oaks, pines, chestnuts; truffle-hunting country; peaceful; clear, clean streams.

D660
Rostassac,
D911 Mercuès,
Cahors (43 km)

Almost gourmand country, with temptation to over-eat. The vineyards produce a good strong red Cahors wine (alas, recenty discovered by Parisians) and Blanc de Lot.

La Taverne, rue J-B-Delpech, (65)35.28.66: Pierre Escorbiac has gone! Another of the old school of superb sauces and man-size meals has left us. But good news! Spies tell me that young Patrick Lannes, Paul Bocuse chef, has altered neither the eccentric decor, the splendid old-fashioned classic cuisine nor the splendidly filled wine cellar. He has added his own 'plats du marché' of fresh seasonal dishes. Menu 50–150F. Shut November.

Restaurant Le Fénélon, pl Emilion-Imbert, (65)35.32.38: good value; good 40F meal, excellent 65F; real Quercy 108F menu. Happy atmosphere. 1900 décor. Wines reasonable.

Cahors: a lovely old town in a superb position in and around a horseshoe of the river Lot, with vine-covered hills behind. The fortified medieval bridge with three slim towers, Valentré, is one of the most beautiful in the world. Legend claims that the Devil himself helped to finish it on time, then was tricked out of payment. St Etienne's cathedral, also fortified, founded 1119 and altered until 1500, has medieval paintings and a supremely lovely medieval door. The town is rich in old buildings and surrounding country reminds me of the Dordogne twenty-five years ago before the main stream of travellers found it.

Magnificent view of town and river from Mont St Cyr, but reached on foot by steep path from near Louis-Philippe Bridge (1½ hrs).

D653 Vers,
D662 alongside
river Lot to
Bouziès
(29 km)

At Laroque des Arcs (5 km on D653) – Hostellerie Beau Rivage, (65)35.30.58: nice building over-looking Lot river; beautiful situation; river views from most bedrooms; own stretch of fishing; naturally serves excellent trout; also good crayfish, superb confit of duck with cèpes; menu 40–120F; rooms 100–130F. Hotel shut 2 Nov.–15 March. Restaurant shut 15 Feb.–15 March.

Vers – Hôtel des Châlets, (65)31.41.53: attractive; in strange position between roads; pretty tiny waterfall just below; local ingredients, good trout; menu 45, 85F; rooms 70–120F.

St Cirq-LaPopie – Auberge du Sombral, Aux Bonnes Choses, (65)31.26.08: beautifully restored old building; popular around whole Cahors area; good value; 4 courses 48F; 5 courses 75F; gourmand meal 160F; rooms (all with WC, bath or shower) 85–120F. Shut 15 Nov.–15 Feb.

Cabrerets – Auberge de la Sagne (65)31.26.62: charming old inn, in quiet spot, own grounds; very good value; specialities – cassoulet and confit; menu 41, 58F; rooms 70–124F. Shut mid-November to Palm Sunday.

Route follows Lot river; good views, particularly just before Vers; past fields of sunflowers, sweetcorn.

Bouziès: high cliff riddled with caves; some were home to prehistoric families; biggest fortified at entrance, with a castellated wall, by English in 100 Years War; called 'Château des Anglais'.

Two ways to go for explorers from Bouziès:
(a) St Cirq-LaPopie by D40 (5 km) on south of Lot river: village perched on rock above river; beautiful old houses; narrow streets; artisan shops; remains of 13th-century château: magnificent view as D40 winds through rocky hills; also from village, one of those called 'most beautiful village in France'. Fortified 15th-century church, with tower castle; museum contains Ming period Chinese treasures.

b) from just past Bouziès at Conduché, take D41 to Cabrerets (5 km) – caves Pech-Merle have good prehistoric wall drawings, of mammoths, bison, deer, horses, human hands, female bodies; also bones of cavebears. Two 14-year-old boys rediscovered caves in 1922; had been used as hiding-place in Revolution, open Palm Sunday – 30 Sept., Oct. (weekdays only);

La Pescaline, (65)31.22.55: gorgeous old country house of honey stone with red brown roof, towers and turrets; built 12th–17th century; beautiful garden; superb old furniture, even genuine 18th-century kitchen still used; interesting, comfortable bedrooms with beams and old furniture; all in perfect taste. Run by two surgeons; one still works at Cahors hospital, other one cooks. Not cheap; worth every franc. Trout fresh from own millstream. Menu 110–140F; rooms 200–350F. Shut 1 Nov.–1 April.

Des Grottes, (65)31.27.02: on river banks; quiet; swimming pool; real Périgourdine cooking; good value menus 41, 62, 76F; à la carte dishes include goose confit, truffled omelette, beef fillet in Périgueux sauces, jugged hare; wine from 9F! Rooms 67–120F. Shut 1 Nov. to Palm Sunday.

museum all year. Cabrerets is in dip at meeting of Célé and Sagné rivers in fairly wild country. Romantic-looking ruins of Devil's Castle (Château du Diable) cling to chilling Rochecourbe cliff; an English eyrie from 100 Years War from which they could rule countryside.

Pescalerie Fountain sprouts from rock wall beside road – underground river surfacing; ivy-covered mill alongside. After Cabrerets road crosses face of high stone cliffs; tunnel through them, then they overhang river Célé's right bank.

Sauliac (6 km further on D41): hamlet clinging to fearsome cliff of odd coloured rocks, with openings to fortified caves used as war refuges; the fit climbed ropes, others hoisted in baskets.

Return by D41 to Conduché to pick up route on D662.

---

from Bouziès D662 Cajarc, Montbrun, Frontenac, Figeac (49 km)

At Larnegal (turn left (sign) for 4 km hilly, rough road) – Mas de Cariteau, (65)31.28.77: whole hamlet restored and converted into hotel; local dishes, especially duck, river fish; bedrooms spread round village, all with WC, bath or shower; meals most reasonable; menu at 47F, 5 courses with good choice; I had charcuterie, grilled sardines, brochette of beef with vegetables (local trout in choice), cheese,

Away from main tourist routes. Quiet, sometimes deserted countryside, especially on side roads. Road follows river through rocky cliffs to Montbrun: village rises in tiers on jutting rock by steep cliffs; looks down on Lot. Ruined castle above. Road climbs steeply after Frontenac – lovely views on right across Lot valley and of Faycelles, hillside village.

dessert; very good 82F menu; wine from 18F; rooms 140–185F; swimming pool. Shut October–May.

Cajarc – Du Pont, (65)40.67.84: by river; simple, clean rooms; cheap; good cooking; menu 35–50F; house wine 8.50F a litre; rooms 35–50F. Shut Saturday low season. Parking not easy.

La Promenade, (65)40.61.21: useful bar-restaurant in main square; menus 32, 60F – both include wine; rooms (15 June–15 Sept) 40–55F.

Figeac – Des Carmes, (65)34.20.78: outstanding cooking in box-like modern hotel not quite my style; Quercy dishes with individual touches; superb duck confit 'grandmère' with sweet-sour onions; scrambled eggs (brouillard) with truffles (delicious); delicious Causse lamb; menu 65–165F; comfortable rooms 95–225F; swimming pool, garden. Shut Saturday (October – Easter); 15 Dec–15 Jan.

Terminus – St Jacques, ave Clemenceau, (65)34.00.43: old-style cheaper hotel by station; pleasant; good value; good modern paintings; menu 40–85F; rooms 50–110F (many with baths).

At La Madeleine (7 km on D922) – Belle Rive, (65)67.62.14: outstanding value; very good cooking in

Figeac: along bank of Célé; Auvergne begins here; Needles, 12th-century obelisks, 15 m (50 ft) tall, marked boundaries of Benedictine abbey land. You could not pursue an enemy within boundaries. Old houses, half timbered, with decorated boundaries, beside 'oustal dé lo Mounéds' (the Mint), fine old building. Old houses round pl Sully; in alleys such as Trou de la Belle, vagrants and thieves lived until 1945; oldest street, rue Emile Zola, now has artisan shops again, as in ancient times.

32F menu; 50F menu excellent (4 courses); good trout soufflé in vermouth; menu 32–85F; dining room overlooks river; comfortable rooms 65–110F. Shut 1–15 March.

N140 Le Bourg, D940 Lacapelle-Marival (21 km)

Cardaillac – Chez Marcel, (65)34.13.16: charming old inn; very good value indeed; 4-course 38F menu includes cèpes omelette as entrée, steak, escalope or roast main course; in 65F menu you could choose delicious country soup *and* hors d'ouvres, a dozen snails (or other dish), cèpes, succulent Causse lamb, cheese and Tatin (apple) tart; menu 38–100F; house wine 12.50F litre; rooms 52–55F. Shut Mondays; part October.

Lacapelle-Marival – Terrasse, opposite château, (65)40.80.07: pretty garden; new bedrooms with bathrooms added; menu 45–140F; rooms 80–150F. Shut 20 Dec.–1 April.

7 km from Figeac on N140, turn right on D18 for 2 km to Cardaillac – old part around fort on rocky spur above town. 12th-century tower; lovely views from top of spiral staircase.

Lacapelle-Marival: castle (13th century) with round watch-towers, church, old gateway to town and covered market on stone piles make photogenic scene. Watch-towers 'stuck on' to four corners of huge square keep. Built by Cardaillac family, married into Plantagenets, Kings of England.

D48 St Céré D673 Montal (30 km)

Hôtel de Paris et du Coq Arlequin, bd Dr Roux, (65)38.02.13: delightful; in Bizat family 100 years. Charming furnishings; Lurçat tapestry in dining room, restaurant named after it; also paintings by Gérard Bizat, owner. Fine cooking; try scallop mousse with avocado sauce; local dish – chicken and sweetbreads in super sauce covered with lightest flake pastry; cassis sorbet; menu 58–140F;

St Céré is splendid – a smiling little town with the river Bavé running through its streets and flower-decked riverside houses. St Laurent tower, overlooking the town from a steep hill, was the home, until he died recently, of Jean Lurçat, the great tapestry and ceramic artist. Many of his works are displayed permanently in St Céré 'casino', around a big pleasant bar.

Montal
continued

delightful rooms (with breakfast) 150–250F. Shut January, February.

Parc Hôtel, (65)38.17.29: pretty gardens; bedrooms improved; friendly; but since change of ownership many readers give no praise for cooking; menu 45–160F; rooms 66–165F. Shut December.

Château Montal is a 'phoenix' castle. Jeanne de Balsac built it in 1534 for a son who was away at the wars, hiring the greatest artists and builders. Only his body returned, and his grief-stricken mother had her window blocked up. In 1879 an asset stripper auctioned its treasures and sold much of its stone for building in Paris. In 1908 a new owner had it repaired and bought back the treasures from museums and collections at ransom prices. One stone doorway was missing, so Rodin, the great sculptor, made a new one. Little roads; across Bavé river to river Dordogne, then Cère (all meet here).

D30, D14 Castelnau, Bretenoux (10 km)

Hôtel Bureau, Biars-sur-Cère, Bretenoux station, (65)38.43.54: pleasant Relais in same family 50 years. Menu at 38F good value; lovely trout in wine. Don't expect wonders at these prices – a few readers do! Most love it. House wine 11–13F; Sunday lunch 5 courses 60F excellent; rooms 50–65F. Shut December.

Castelnau castle is 11th century, extended in the 100 Years War, it was restored from 1896 to 1932. Once it had a garrison of 1500 men and 100 horses. Its rent was then one egg per year, carried in pomp by four oxen to the Viscount of Turenne. (Guided tours – closed Tuesdays.)

D703 Vayrac, Martel, Souillac (38 km)

Martel – Hôtel Le Turenne, Restaurant La Quercy, (65)37.30.30: modern, in stone and old-style; good bedrooms; try truffle soufflé

Martel: in AD 732, the Saracens (followers of Mahomet – in this case mostly Moors) were stopped at Poitiers by Charles Martel.

(lovely); menu 40–130F; house wine 13F; rooms 57–130F. Nice terrace, attractive restaurant. Shut Dec., Jan., Feb.

Lion d'Or, (65)37.30.16: simple, cheap, needs some decorating; menu at 50F good value; menu 32–90F; rooms 53–63F.

At Gluges (by Dordogne river, D23 from Martel, D43 left – 5 km) – Les Falaises, (65)37.33.59: fine old turreted house; five menus from 38F (3-course, roast guinea-fowl) to rich Quercynois gastronomic at 140F (foie gras; truffled omelette; confit of goose with truffle salad; cabecou – local soft goats' milk cheese; dessert). Very good place to eat. Rooms 70–140F. Shut 1 Jan.–15 Feb.

Souillac – La Vieille Auberge, pl Minoterie, (65)32.79.43: nationally famous; doesn't look old from outside; also annexe with swimming pool; period décor; chef-patron Robert Veril is a member of National Committee of Gastronomy; called 'the Absolute Master' by one of world's greatest gastronomes. Menu 65, 110, 150F; rooms 80–120F. Shut February.

Auberge du Puits, pl du Puits,(65)37.80.32: pleasant inn with good value meals in attractive restaurant; used by locals; traditional cooking; menu 35–115F; rooms 50–100F. Shut Sunday evening, Monday (low season); 1 Nov.–1 Jan.

Otherwise Europe might be Muslim today! Later Martel struck again, won decisively, and built a church on the spot. It grew into a town.

In 12th century, Henry II of England, a Plantagenet, and his wife, Eleanor of Aquitaine, fell out; he accused her of sleeping with a troubadour; shut her in a tower. Their four sons rose against Henry. To pay his soldiers, the eldest, called the Young King Henry, pillaged abbeys, took precious stones from St Adour's body at Rocamadour and stole Sword of Roland. He returned to Martel with a fever, was found by Henry II's messenger lying in agony on a bed of cinders in penitence. Maison Fabri, old mansion with round tower, said to be where he died. 18th-century covered market. Attractive medieval streets and buildings.

Souillac: attractive market town; lively, sometimes crowded midsummer; Dordogne river meets Borrèze here; lovely, lonely country to north.

Grew round abbey in 13th century; abbey disappeared during Revolution. Lovely 12th-century abbey church with Byzantine look. Belfry from other parish church now attached to town hall.

Our way, you enter under huge viaduct.

Ambassadeur, av Gen. de
Gaulle, (65)32.78.36: true
Périgourdine cooking with
cèpes, foie gras, truffles,
confit; duck; tripe; gained
Poêle d'Or (Golden Pan) in
four years (up to '79);
cooking almost faultless;
dining room very formal;
bedrooms neat; five menus
36–145F; rooms 72–155F.

La Roseraie, ave Toulouse,
(65)37.82.69: good old dishes
like estouffade de boeuf
(joint of beef stewed in
tightly closed pot with wine,
herbs, veg); also turkey
Royale (in cream sauce with
truffles); good foie gras in
gastronomic menu; menu 35,
52, 110F; rooms 66–100F;
garden; near river. Shut 1
Oct.–4 April.

D15 left fork at Bourzoies on to D165 becomes D62 after 1 km; through Borrèze, right on D60 Paulin, left on D62 to La Cassagne, La Chapelle-Mouret, Le Lardin-St Lazare (38 km)

Le Lardin – Hôtel Sautet, (53)50.07.22: friendly; cooking highly recommended to me locally and I agree; traditional Périgordine dishes. Simple 40F menu; then progressively gastronomic; try fillet of goose and duck; nice duck in tomato sauce; superb foie gras. Old inn with modern rooms; restaurant over-looks garden. Menu 40–125F; rooms 80–175F. Shut 20 Dec.–20 Jan.

Little roads go deep into countryside of tiny hamlets, farms, orchards, hills, valleys, woods and small streams. You see few people except in distant fields; can get lost on little roads, ending in a farmyard.

Borrèze is sleepy village with a bar-restaurant. D62 starts climbing. At D60 junction, Salignac – Eyvignes château can be seen (entrance 2 km to left – open in season except Tuesday). Medieval fortress, from 12th century, ramparts around it. Still belongs to family from which came the great Fénélon, 17th-century writer, soldier, archbishop. Covered market in Salignac square.

12th-century church in La Cassagne, and Maurice Delpech's distillery producing fruit and walnut liqueurs and famous walnut apéritif.

Le Lardin: rather dull town in lovely valley of Vézèré; paper mills sometimes smell like cauliflower cooking! Deals in walnuts from nearby farms and truffles.

Over N89 on to D62 to Beauregard-de-Terrasson, Badefols-d'Ans, Hautefort (19 km)

Badefols – Les Tilleuls, (53)51.50.08: pretty, real old village inn opposite castle; nice bar and restaurant used by locals; attractive garden with vine, trees, table and chairs. Six-course dinner

Beauregard looks down on charming little town of Terrasson on bank of Vézèré river, with slate-roofed houses down hill to river banks.

Hautefort
continued

with entrecôte steak cost 32F; menu 32–50F; house wine 10F; Bergerac 20F; rooms 53F, 68F (bath). Shut Christmas–15 Jan.

Commerce, (53)51.50.07: attractive; regional specialities; simple 35F menu; menus 35–60F; wines from 10F; rooms 55–75F. Shut part August.

Road rises overlooking valleys of vines and poplars, passing Peyraux Château (lived in; cannot enter; but lovely views from entrance court).

Badefols-d'Ans: pretty; good views; 12th-century domed church; 14th–15th-century château, burned 1945; restored.

Hautefort: 17th-century château, more like a 'love' château of Loire than 'fighting' château of Périgord. Original castle of 12th century belonged to Born family; Bertrand de Born, troubadour, wrote songs of love and war. His brother, helped by Richard Lionheart, tried to take castle, so he enlisted Richard's brother 'Young King Henry', heir to English throne, to defend it. In 1186 his brother destroyed it when he was away. Bertrand became a monk. New 17th-century château. Restored; burned out 1968; restored again by Baroness de Bastard who lives there. Queen Mother stayed there in '78. (Open to public.) Lovely views.

D62, D5
Tourtoirac, D67
Excideuil,
D705, N21
Perigueux
(50 km)

Tourtoirac – Des Voyageurs, (53)50.42.29: shaded, quiet garden by river Auvezère: old-style hotel; all Périgourdine specialities; also 3-course 36.50F menu with choice of steak, pork chop, stuffed tomato; menu 36.50–80F; rooms 64–138F.

Excideuil: interesting medieval town with old buildings and ramparts; ruins of historic castle which changed hands frequently between warring lords, English and French; then Protestants and Catholics. Talleyrand family let it deteriorate, moved furniture, even chimneys to their house in Chalais.

Poste, (53)50.42.05: beside river; remarkable 45F menu (soup; hors d'oeuvres; ham; omelette or fish; meat course with veg.; cheese and dessert); also 35F menu; rooms available.

At Eulalie-d'Ans (4 km on D5 from Tourtoirac), Mme Bony has one of best bargain meals in Périgord. We had soup, tomato salad and pork brawn, chicken, two veg.; salad; cheese and ice cream – 28F including self-help litre of wine.

At junction of D705, N21, 9 km to right on N21 at Sorges – just opened – museum of the truffle, culinary fungi called Black Diamond; press-button film on how they hunt for them with pigs and dogs; how they grow beneath oak trees under earth. Open afternoons except Tuesday. Guided 'truffle trail' walk – 3 km; 1 hr. Shop selling them – smallest cost us 28F; but what a souvenir of Périgord to slice into your omelette!

Index

Names of hotels and restaurants appear in *italics*.

Adour, river 41, 42, 43
Aigrefuille-d'Aunis 36
A La Bonne Foi 95
Alençon 58
Allier, river 74
Alliés 101
Altair 22
Alzenay 31
Ambassadeur 212
Amboise 61, 177, 178
Amiens 117
Andelle, river 88
Anduze 76
Angers 168, 193
Angleterre (Chalôns Sur
  Marne) 122
Angleterre (Lamballe)
  139
Angleterre (Laon) 121
Angoulême 196
Annecy 129, 130
Appeville-Annebault 81,
  82
Argent-sur-Sauldre 188
Ariège, river 48
Armoric 152
Armorique (Fouesnant)
  153
Armorique (Locqueric)
  143
Artuby, river 106
Aubance, river 169
*Aub-des-Etangs du
  Buissonnet* 120
*Auberge Alphonse
  Mellot* 93
Auberge Bon Laboureur
  190
Auberge Bretonne 159
*Auberge Chappelle sur
  Vire* 55
*Auberge de Deux
  Magots* 158

Auberge de Kervéoch
  148
Auberge de la Fôret 114
Auberge de la Ramberge
  63
Auberge de la Sagne
  206
*Auberge de l'Etang
  Ronsard* 191
Auberge de Pen-Mur 158
Auberge des Voyageurs
  179
Auberge de Toulfoën
  155
Auberge du Haut-Clos
  173
Auberge du Mail 62
*Auberge du Manoir des
  Ports* 138
*Auberge du Moulin-
  Bureau* 67
*Auberge du Pont
  Calleck* 155
Auberge du Puits 211
Auberge du Rosmeur
  148
Auberge du Soir 196
Auberge du Sombral 206
*Auberge du Vieux
  Moulin* 116
Auberge du Vieux Puits
  81
Auberge la Poste 128
Auberge Lyonnais 130
Auberge Madelaine 60
Auberge Normande
  (Carentan) 54
Auberge Normande
  (Dreux) 84
Auberge Paysanne 61
*Auberge Petite
  Fadette* 66
Auberge Pontoise 38

*Auberge Porte du
  Crous* 96
Auberge St Jean 173
Auberge St Laurent 153
Aubigny-sur-Nère 188
Aubinges 187
Au Bon Accueil 162
Auch 46
Au Chapeau Rouge 161
Audierne 148, 149
Au Faison Doré 130
Au Fer à Cheval 147
Au Gâteau Breton 63
Au Grand Cerf 181
Aulne, river 145
Au Marais 34
Au Petit Vatel 58
Au Progrès 127
*Au Rendezvous des
  Chauffeurs* 81
Au Rocher de Cancale 99
Au Trou Normande 87
Auvergne 52, 74
*Aux Armes de
  Champagne* 122
Aux Bons Enfants 116
*Aux Vendanges de
  Bourgogne* 126
Aven, river 154
Azay-le-Rideau 175
Azincourt 115

Badefols-d'Ans 213
Badefols-sur-
  Dordogne 203
Bagnoles-de-L'Orne 58
Bain-les-Bains 124
Baise, river 46
Balcons de la
  Mescla 106
Bannière de France 121
Bar de la Criée 148
Bardouillière 177

Bar-le-Duc 122
Barrage du Sautet 103
Barrier 177
Barrois 123
Baugé 192
Baugy 187
Bayonne 20, 42, 43
Bazas 44
Beaufort-en-Vallée 193
Beaugency 182, 189
Beauregard-de-
  Terrasson 213
Beau Rivage 33
Beausejour 81
Beau-Site 125
Beautfran 40
Beg Meil 152
Belhade 40
Belle Epoque 129
Belle Etoile 201
Bellegarde 92
Bellegarde-sur-
  Valserine 129
Bellencombre 88
Belle Rive 208
Bellevue (Ambois) 63
Bellevue (Mimizan) 40
Bellevue (Montrichard)
  64
Benet 34
Bénodet 150, 152
Besançon 126
Bestrée 149
Beynac 201
Biarritz 43
Bias 41
Blérancourt 120
Blériot Plage 112
Blois 180
Bocamps 116
Bois-Tireau 176
Bonaventure 191
Bonne Auberge 154
Bonnet 202
Bonningues-les-Ardres
  115
Borrèze 213
Boule d'Or 192
Boulogne 10, 113
Bourg-des-Comptes 28
Bourg en Bresse 100
Bourg-Lastic 71
Bourzoies 213
Bouziès 206
Boves 118
Boyer 121
Bracieux 181

Branne 40
Brantôme 196
Brasserie Alfred 113
Brasserie Louis 37
Brëme, river 127
Brenne, river 61
Brerville 90
Bretagne (Lesconil) 151
Bretagne (Pontorson)
  159
Bretenoux 210
Bretesche Castle 28
Brinon-sur-Sauldre 188
Brion 193
Brionne 83
Brioude 73
Brissac-Quincé 169
Brittany 27
Bruz 28
Bubry 156
Buchy 88
Budan 172

Caberets 206
Cagnes 108
Cahors 205
Cajarc 207
Calais 10, 111
Camaret-sur-Mer 145,
  146
Cancale 163
Candé-sur-Beuvron 180
Capbreton 42
Carbonne 47
Cardaillac 209
Carentan 54
Castel 68
Casteljaloux 44
Castellane 105, 106
Castelnau 210
Cavan 141
Célé, river 207, 208
Central (Digne) 105
Central (Léon) 41
Central (Pougues-les-
  Eaux) 96
Central (St Malo) 21
Chabrol 196
Chalet de la Source 74
Chalet-Suisse 30
Chalôns Sur Marne 122
Chalo-St-Mars 90
Chalou 90
Chalouette, river 90
Chambord 181
Chargé 61
Charolles 97, 98

Chasselas 99
Château Beauregard 181
Château Chambord 181
Château Davayet 70
Château de Beaumesnil
  83
Château de Bellingese
  119
Château de Cazeneuve
  44
Château de Chaumont
  179
Château de Chazeron 69
Château de
  Chenonceaux 63
Château de Cheverny
  181
Château de Courances
  91
Château de Kernuz 151
Château de la Grange
  186
Château de Maleffre 59
Château de Marcy 174
Château de Maupas 187
Château de Parentignat
  73
Château de Talcy 189
Château de Talmont 33
Château de Villandry
  176
Château de Gué
  Péan 178
Château-du-Loir 192
Château du Pray 61
Château d'Usson 38
*Château Haute-
  Borde* 179
Château-la-Vallière 192
Châteaumeillant 68
Château Montal 210
Château Montgeoffroy
  193
Châteauneuf-les-Bains
  68
Châteauneuf-sur-
  Loire 185
Château Renault 61
Châteauroux 66
Château Tonquédec
  141
Château Tournoël 70
Châtelguyon 69
Châtillon 186
Chaumière-Savoyarde
  103
Chaumont-sur-Loire 179

Chavignol 94
Chênehutte-les-Tuffeaux
171
Chenonceaux 11, 63,
178
Cher, river 65, 68, 178
Cherbourg 53
Cheval Blanc (Magny-en-
Vexin) 89
Cheval Blanc
(Mouliherne) 192
Cheval Blanc (Vire) 55
Cheval Rouge (Montoire)
61
Cheval Rouge (Villandry)
176
Chevenon 96
Chez Annette 60
Chez Fanchu 148
Chez Jules 113
Chez Marcel 209
Chez Zizine 113
Chiens du Guet 21
Chinon 173
Choisy au Bac 120
Ciron, river 44
Clairière de l'Armistice
120
Claix 103
Clermont-Ferrand 70
Cléry-St Andre 182, 183
Cléty 115
Climat de France 121
Club 114
Cluny 98
Col des Leques 105
Col de St Pierre 75
Combourg 25, 159
Commerce (Badefols)
214
Commerce (La Ferté)
182
Commerce (Oucques)
189
Commerce (Villefranche-
du-Périgord) 205
Compiègne 119
Comps-sur-Artuby 106
Concarneau 152, 154
Conches-en-Ouches 83
Condom 45
Continental
(Cancale) 163
Continental
(Châteauroux) 66
Continental
(Condom) 45

Contrexeville 123
Coq d'Or 111
Cordeliers 44
Cormatin 98
Corneville-sur-Risle 81
Corniche des Cévennes
75
Corniche L'Armorique
142
Corps 103
Corsaire 27
Côte d'Argent 41
Coulon 34
Cour-Cheverny 181
Cours-les-Barnes 187
Couttet 131
Couture-sur-le-Loir 191
Couze, river 73, 203
Couze-et-St-Front 203
Couziers 173
Créon 40
Crevon, river 88
Croas-ar-Go 145
Crozon 146
Cunault 171

Damville 84
Darney 124
De Bretagne 162
Decize 96
De France (Angers) 168
De France (Auch) 46
De France (Bourg en
Bresse) 100
De France (Branne) 40
De France (Combourg)
26
De France (Domfront) 57
De France (La Chartre)
191
De France (Les Eyzies)
200
De France (Monpazier)
203
De France (Ornans) 127
*De France et
d'Angleterre* 35
De la Paix 23
De la Plage 114
De La Source 137
Des Carmes 208
Des Dunes (Blériot
Plage) 112
Des Dunes (Dinard) 22
Des Flandres 116
Des Grottes 207
Des Remparts 36

Des Voyageurs 214
Dieppe 86
Digne 105
Dinan 24, 136
Dinard 22–3, 137
Dol-de-Bretagne 162
Domaine à Dumas 87
Domfront 57
Domino 199
Domme 201
*Domrémy-la-
Pucelle* 123
Dordogne 9
Dordogne, river 39, 52
et seq
Douarnenez 148
Doullens 116, 117
Dourdan 85, 90
Dreux 84
Dronne, river 196
Druye 176
*Du Bon Laboureur et du
Château* 64
Du Centenaire 200
Du Centre 42
Du Chalet 160
Du Château
(Châteauneuf) 68
Du Château (Combourg)
25
Du Château (Josselin)
156
Du Château (Nerac) 45
Du Guesclin 160
Du Lac (Combourg) 26
Du Lac (Huelgoat) 144
Du Lac (Soustons) 41
Du Mouton Blanc 160
Du Parc (Chateauroux)
66
Du Parc (Florac) 75
Du Parc (Mimizan) 40
Du Parc (Murol) 72
Du Périgord 199
Du Perron 189
Du Pont 208
Du Port (Dieppe) 87
Du Port (L'Aiguillon) 34
Du Port (Loqueric) 143
Du Sorgia 129

Ecu de Bretagne 189
Elbeuf-sur-Andelle 88
Elincourt-Ste-Marguerite
119
Ellé, river 155
Epernon 84

Epte, river 88
Espagnols Point 145
Esplanade 201
Etampes 90
Etoile d'Or 185
Etrépagny 88
Eulalie-d'Ans 215
Europe 144
Excideul 214

Family Hôtel 141
Ferries 16–17
Fiennes 112
Figeac 207
Fillièvres 116
Flandre 119
Florac 75
Flumet 130
Foix 47, 48
Fontainebleau 79, 91
Fontevraud-l'Abbaye 173
Fouesnant 152, 153
France (Camaret) 146
France (Vire) 56
Frévent 116
Frontenac 207
Fronton Hôtel 43
Fruges 115

Gai Soleil 127
Gambetta 171
Gap 104
Garonne, river 40
Gault, river 61
Gazeran 84
Génève 99
Gennes 169
Gien 93, 186
Gisors 88
Gluges 211
Goyen, river 149
Grand Café 90
Grand Cèdre 104
Grand Hôtel (Chinon)
  174
Grand Hôtel
  (Concarneau) 154
Grand Hôtel (St Aignan)
  65
Grand Hôtel du Metz et
  Commerce 122
Grand Hôtel du
  Vendôme 59
Grand Monarque 59
Grand Vatel 178
Grasse 106
Grenoble 102

Griffons 197
Grousse d'Ail 31
Guérande 29
Guînes 112
Guingcamp 140
Guîtres 38

Harcourt 83
Hardinghen 111, 112,
  113, 115
Hautefort 213
Hédé 26, 159
Hendaye 43
Hermelingen 115
Hesdin 116
Hossegor 42
Hostellerie Beau Rivage
  206
Hostellerie de la Caillère
  180
Hostellerie de la Cloche
  188
Hostellerie de Loire 169
Hostellerie de Plaisance
  39
Hostellerie des Trois 89
Hostellerie du Château
  179
Hostellerie du Moulin et
  du Chateau de Rognac
  199
Hostellerie du Vieux 26
Hostellerie Gargantua
  173
Hostellerie La Folie 96
Hostellerie Lanterne 178
Hostellerie Le Griffon
  120
Hostellerie Ourida 31
Hostellerie St Martin 192
Hostens 41, 44
Hôtel Audoye-Lons 48
Hôtel Bains 106
Hôtel Bretagne 141
Hôtel Bureau 210
Hôtel Christiana 130
Hôtel d'Avaugour 24
Hôtel de Dijon 118
Hôtel de France 139
Hôtel de France et
  Rotisserie du Chat qui
  Tourne 119
Hôtel de la Gare 171
Hôtel de la Levée 26
Hôtel de la Mère
  Poulard 161
Hôtel de la Place 68

Hôtel de l'Oise 72
Hôtel de Paris et du Coq
  Artequin 209
Hôtel des Cascades 56
Hôtel des Cédres 176
Hôtel des Châlets 206
Hôtel des Grottes de
  Trabuc 76
Hôtel des Meritis 69
Hôtel des Sources 125
Hôtel du Château 60
Hôtel du Col 102
Hôtel du Commerce 140
Hôtel du Lac 41
Hôtel du Morvan (Luzy)
  97
Hôtel du Morvan (St
  Honoré-les-Bains) 97
Hôtel du Nord 88
Hôtel du Parc de la
  Grande 33
Hôtel du Port 153
Hôtel du Rampart 94
Hôtel du Val d'Allier 74
Hôtel Elysée 66
Hôtel France 37
Hôtel France et
  Fuchsias 53
Hôtel Golf de la
  Bretesche 28
Hôtel la Paix 121
Hôtel la Palmeraie 30
Hôtel La Pointe du
  Grouin 164
Hôtel le Béarnais 42
Hôtel Le Cygne 57
Hôtel l'Eléphant 124
Hôtel le Théâtre 32
Hôtel le Turenne 210
Hôtel l'Océan 43
Hôtel Loubat 38
Hôtel Loustan 43
Hôtel Marebaudière 157
Hôtel Marguérite 24
Hôtel Notre Dame 183
Hôtel Porte St Pierre 21
Hôtel Prieuré 132
Hôtel-Restaurant Henri
  Robert 96
Hôtel-Restaurant Paul
  Fôret 184
Hôtel Roche 23
Hôtel St Christophe 123
Hôtel St Michel 181
Hôtel St Roch 117
Hôtel Sautet 213
Hôtel Ti Al Lannec 142

Houdan 89
Huelgoat 144
Huismes 174
Huisne, river 59

Ile de France 90
Ile St Martin 174
Indre, river 174
Inguiniel 156
Isle, river 38
Isole, river 155
Issoire 72

Jard-Sur-Mer 33
Jargeau 185
Jeanne d'Arc 75
Jeanne de Laval 170
Jonzac 38
Joséphine 118
Josnes 189
Josselin 156
Jouy 189
Julien 73

Keran Nod 142
Kernascléden 155
Kersicot 152

La Bai 153
La Balme 102
La Balme de Sillingy 129
La Baule 29, 159
L'Abbaye (Cluny) 98
L'Abbaye (St
    Cyprien) 203
La Bel Air 72
Labenne 42
La Bon Bonnière 42
La Bonne Etape 63
La Borne 187
Labouiche, river 48
La Bourboule 72
La Brèche 62
La Bresche-Arthur 162
La Bretesche 159
L'Abris des Flots 136
La Bruyère 58
La Bûcherie 65
La Camusière 193
La Capelle 114
Lacapelle-Marival 209
La Capitainerie 185
La Cappeville 88
La Cassagne 213
Lac Chambon 72
La Chapelle-des-
    Marais 29, 159

La Chapelle-Mouret 213
La Chapelotte 187
La Charité-sur-Loire 95,
    187
La Charlotte 113
La Charrette 25
La Chartre-sur-le-Loir 191
La Châtre 66
La Chaumette 80
La Chaumière 187
La Chauvinière 105
La Chope 116
La Closerie de Genets
    107
La Clusaz 130
La Croix-en-Touraine 63
La Croix-Madame 28
La Devinière 173
La Digue 161
La Douane 154
La Faisanderie 117
La Farigoule 108
Lafayette 47
La Ferté-Bernard 59
La Ferté-St Aubin 189
La Ferté-St Cyr 182
La Feuillandine 111
La Forêt-Fouesnant 152,
    153
La Fregate 81
La Gavotte 141
La Grand'mare 83
La Gravinis 157
L'Agriculture 92
La Grilloute 69
L'Aiglon 105
L'Aiguillon 34
Laillé 28
Laita, river 155
Lalinde 203
La Landrais 137
La Madelaine 208
La Maison Blanche 132
La Marine 86
Lamballe 138
La Ménéstrel 114
La Meuse Gourmande
    123
La Moderne 87
Lamotte-Beuvron 188
La Mure 103
Lancrans 129
Landévennec 145
Langeac 74
Langeais 175
Lanmeur 142
Lannion 141, 142

Lanvallay 136
Lanvéoc 145
Laon 121
La Paix 73
La Parious 73
La Passagère 136
La Pescaline 207
La Petite Auberge (Laon)
    121
La Petite Auberge (Le
    Havre) 81
La Plage (esconil) 151
La Plage (St Michel) 142
La Poissonière 191
La Poste 97
La Poste et Champanne
    73
La Poterie 138
La Promenade 208
Laqueuille 71, 72
La Racaudière 176
La Renaissance 177
La Richardais 137
La Rivage 183
La Roch 94
La Roche Bernard 158
La Rochelle 35
La Roche-sur-Yon 31
La Roche-sur-Yon-
    Gallet 31
Laroque des Arcs 206
La Roseraie 212
Larresingle 46
La Sauve 40
La Sauventet 46
La Strada 65
La Taverne (Cahors) 205
La Taverne (La
    Rochelle) 35
La Tête Noire 64
La Toque Blanche 84
La Tourne-Broche 36
La Tranche 33
L'Aubergade 123
L'Auberge 94
Laverdac 45
Lavardin 61
La Vauban 53
La Vendée 32
La Verrerie 187
La Vicomté 136
La Vieille Auberge
    (Brioude) 73
La Vieille Auberge
    (Casteljaloux) 44
La Vieille Auberge
    (Pouilly-sur-Loire) 186

La Vieille Auberge
  (Souillac) 211
La Vieille Forge 37
La Vieille Renommée
  144
La Ville-ès-Nonais 136
Lay, river 34
Le Baron 27
Le Bec-Hellouin 81
Le Bourg 209
Le Buisson 203
Le Cantalon 69
Le Capucin Gourmand
  150
Le Centre 199
Le Channel 111
Lecoq-Gadby 27
Le Contentin 53
Le Croisic 30
Le Dauphin 90
Le Débarcadère 30
Le Faou 145
Le Fret 145
Le Frikou 148
Le Garden 68
Legé 31
Le Grand Monarque 175
Le Grand St Vincent 191
Le Gué-de-Loir 191
Léguer, river 141
Le Havre 80
Le Landais 38
Le Lardin-St Lazare 213
Le Manderley 185
Le Minaret 152
Le Minihic-sur-Rance 137
Le Monastère 98
Le Mont-Dore 71, 72
Le Mont-St-Michel 160
Lempdes 73
Le Neubourg 83
Léon 41
Léon 198
Le Panorama 72
Le Pavillon 104
Le Petit Coq 81
Le Petit Robinson 137
Le Picotin 119
L'Epine 122
Le Pompidou 75
Le Pouldu 155
Le Prieuré 171
Le Quéré 168
Le Rabelais 102
Léré 93, 186
Lerné 173
Les Acacias 89

Le Saintongeais 38
Les Aix d'Augillon 187
Les Alouettes 90
Les Aromes 107
*Les Cadets du
  Gascogne* 44
Lescale 203
L'Escale du Port-Arthur
  183
Les Chênes 104
Lesconil 151
Les Eyzies 199
Les Falaises 211
Les Fontaines 177
Les Gachetières 182
Les Glycines 89
Les Houches 132
Les Muscadelles 107
Les Navigateurs 32
Les Oiseaux 103
L'Espadon 29
L'Espérance 153
Les Peyrascas 105
Les Pins 33
L'Esplanade 92
Les Ponts-de-Cé 169
Les Quatres Chemins 35
*Les Rochers et la
  Chrissandière* 129
Les Roches-l'Eveque 191
Les Rosiers 169
Les Rousses 128
Les Sables-d'Olonne 32
Les Salstices 183
Lestangue 46
Les Tilleuls 213
Les Tritons 150
Les 3 Lys 175
Le Sully 117
Les Vire-Court 150
Les Voyageurs 118
L'Etoile (Les Sables-
  d'Olonn) 32
L'Etoile (St Thibault-
  St Satur) 94
Le Tourne 40
L'Europe 90
Le Valmarin 22
Le Vast 53
Le Vendôme 180
Le Wast 115
Le Yaudet 141
L'Hermitage-Lorge 140
Libourne 38
Licques 115
Lignyen 123
Ligny-le-Ribault 182

Limoges 196
Linières-Bouton 192
Lion d'Argent 67
Lion d'Or (Candé) 180
Lion d'Or (Château
  Renault) 61
Lion d'Or (Guînes) 112
Lion d'Or (Martel) 211
Lion d'Or (Valençay) 66
Locquirec 142
Locronan 146, 147
Logis de Brionne 83
Logis de la Cadenne 39
Lohéac 28
Loir, river 59
Loire, river 52, 79, 94,
  95, 167 *et seq.*
Lombez 47
Longvilliers 85, 90
L'Oreidu Bois 124
L'Oronge 75
Lot, river 206
Loue, river 127
Luçon 34
Lumres 115
L'Univers 86
L'Universe 55
Luxeuil-les-Bains 125
Luzy 97
Lyons 79
Lyons-la-Fôret 88

Mâcon 79, 98, 99
Magny-en-Vexin 89
Mail 100
Maintenon 84
Maître Boscq 106
Malbuisson 128
Mançay 189
Manche Océan 157
Mandres-Sur-Vair 124
Manoir de Kerroch 155
Manoir de Moëllien
Manoir du Stany 154
Manoir du Vaumadeuc
  137
Manoir Fleuri 70
Mantes-la-Jolie 89
Manzat 69
Marchenoir 189
Marcilly-sur-Maulne 192
Marçon 192
Marée Bleue 157
Marmite Dieppoise 87
Marseilles-les-Aubigny
  187
Martel 210

Mas de Cariteau 207
Mas Pommier 101
Mauves, river 182
Mauvoy 189
Mazé 193
Megève 131
Mende 75
Ménestreau 189
Ménez Hom 146
Mercuès 205
Mérens-les-Vals 46
Meung-sur-Loire 182
Mialet 76
Milly 91
Missillac 159
Moderne (Cluny) 98
Moderne (Gisors) 88
Monaco 80
Mon Auberge 80
Monçay 182
Monchel-sur-Canche 116
Moncontour 139
Mondoubleau 59
Monistrol-d'Allier 74
Monpazier 203
Montagne-St-Michel 144
Montal 209
Montbrun 207
Montdidier 118
Montendre 38
Montesquieu 47
Montfort-sur-Risle 81, 82
Montgeoffroy 193
Montguyon 38
Monthou-sur-Cher 178
Montlieu 38
Montluçon 68
Montmirail 59
Montmuran castle 26
Montoire 61, 191
Montpellier 73, 76
Montrichard 64, 178
Morateur 108
Morbier 128
Moreuil 118
Morez 128
Morgat 146
Morlaix 143
Morogues 187
Mortain 56
Mouliherne 192
Moulin à Poivre 112
Moulin de Coët Diquel
  155
Moulin de l'Abbaye 196
Moulin de Mombreux
  115

Moulin de Rosmadec
  154
Moulinex 90
Moustey 40
Moustiers Ste Marie 106
Mouthe 128
Mouthier-Haute-Pierre
  127
Mozac 69, 70
Muret 47
Murol 72
Muzillac 158

Nacqueville 53
National Fort 22
Nazelles 177
Négron 177
Nemours 92
Nérac 45
Néris les Bains 68
Nérondes 187
Neufchâteau 123, 124
Nevers 79, 96, 187
Nièvre, river 96
Nice 108
Nogent 192
Nogent-le-Roi 84
Nohant 66
Noizay 177
Nonancourt 84
Normandy (Dieppe) 87
Normandy (St Brevin) 30
Norroy 124
Nouvelle Cuisine 13
Noyant 192

Odet, river 150, 152
Old Richmond 87
Olivet 182, 183
Orléans 182, 183, 184
Ornain, river 122
Ornans 127
Ostellerie du Vieux 101
Oucques 189, 190

Pailhés 47
Palluau 31
Parc Floral 182
Parc Hôtel 210
Parentis 40
Paulin 213
Pelican 24
Périgord 9
Perigueux 197, 214
Pérouges 101
Perpignan 44, 49
Phoebus 48

Pierre 99
Pissos 40
Plancoët 137
Pléchâtel 28
Plêslin 24
Pleudihen 136
Pleurtuit 24
Plèven 137
Pleyber-Christ 144
Ploërmel 157
Ploeuc 140
Ploéven 147
Plouay 155
Ploubalay 137
Plouhinec 148
Pointe de Chemoulin 30
Point du Grouin 163
Pointe du Raz 148
Pommera 117
Pommiers-la-Placette
  102
Pons 38
Pontarlier 127
Pont-Audemer 81
Pont-Aven 154
Pont Calleck 155
Pont Canal 187
Pont-Croix 148, 149
Pont d'Aiguines 106
Pont d'Ain 101
Pont-de-le-Trave 44
Pont de Sologne 93
Pont Farcy 55
Pontivy 156
Pont-l'Abbé 150
Pontorson 159, 160, 162
Pornic 31
Pornichet 30
Portlets 40
Post 38
Poste (Bénodet) 152
Poste (Domfront) 57
Poste (La Châtre) 67
Poste (Morez) 128
Poste (Tourtoirac) 215
Pouges-les-Eaux 96
Pouilly 99
Pouilly-sur-Loire 186
Poulas 66
Pourville 87
Prades 74
Prieuré 147
Puy de Dôme 71
Puys 87

Quélen 140
Quercy 9

Quettehou 53
Quimper 148, 150
Quimperlé 154, 155
Quintin 140
Quissac 76

Rambouillet 84, 90
Rance, river 22, 23, 24, 25, 136
Ravenoville 54
Redon 28, 159
Reilhac 74
Reims 121
Réjaumont 46
Relais de Bacchus 180
Relais de Fompeyne 44
Relais de la Poste 188
Relais des Chasseurs 45
Relais des Gentians 128
Relais des Maîtres Poste 59
Relais des Templiers 189
Relais du Roch 155
Relais du Roy 140
Relais Fleurie et Restaurant Le Coq Hardi 186
Relais St Gilles 31
Rennes 26, 159
Restaurant Au Fer à Cheval 148
Restaurant Boule d'Or 174
Restaurant des Cèdres 176
Restaurant des Terrasses 25
Restaurant Diane de Meridor 173
Restaurant Euzkalduna 42
Restaurant Jean Bardet 66
Restaurant Jeanne 185
Restaurant La Baita 132
Restaurant La Coquille 23
Restaurant La Petite Marmite 176
Restaurant La Quercy 210
Restaurant La Ruche 177
Restaurant Le Drouet 121
Restaurant Le Fénéton 205

Restaurant Le Richelieu 35
Restaurant Les Plantagenets 168
Restaurant Le Vieux Port 35
Restaurant Noë 180
Restaurant Perdrix 49
Restaurant Poker d'As 126
Restaurant Relais St Jean 49
Revermont 100
Revigny 122
Rientort-de-Randon 75
Rieux 47
Rigny 174
Rilly-sur-Loire 179
Riom 68, 69, 70
Robin de Bois 182
Rochebonne 21
Rochecorbon 177
Rochefort 36
Rochfort-Montagne 71
Roc Trévezel 144
Romarche, river 103
Rome 176
Romphaire 55
Rossignol 201
Rostassac 205
Rothéneuf 163
Ruisseauville 115
Rumengol 145

Saché 176
St Aignan 65
Saint Albert 200
St Amans 75
St André-des-Eaux 159
St Antoine 142
St Arcons-d'Allier 74
St Aubin 192
St Benoît-sur-Loire 185
St Brévin-les-Pins 30
St Briac 137
St Céré 209
St Chély-d'Apcher 75
St Cirq-La-Popie 206
St Colombier 158
St Cyprien 201
Saint Cyr Hôtel 182
St Cyr-sous-Dourdan 85, 90
St Efflam 142
St Eloy-les-Mines 68
St Emilion 39
St Fiacre 145

St Gervais-d'Auvergne 68
St Gervais-les-Bains 131
St Gildas-des-Bois 28
St Gobain 121
St Guerche-sur-l'Aubois 187
St Hilaire-du-Harcouet 57
St Hilaire-St Mesmin 182, 183
St Honoré-les-Bains 97
St Hubert 181
Saint-Jacques (Angers) 168
St Jacques (Terminus) 208
St Jacques-des-Guérets 191
St Jacut 137
St Jean du Gard 75
St Lary 46
St Laurent-de-Trèves 142
St Laurent-en-Grandvaux 128
St Léger-en-Yvelines 90
St Lô 53
St Loup-sur-Semouse 125
St Lyphard 29, 159
St Lys 47
St Malo 20, 21, 136, 163
St Malo-de-Phily 28
St March 30
St Marie 147
St Mathurin 193
St Michel-des-Andaines 58
St Michel-en-Grève 142
St Nazaire 30
St Nectaire 72
St Nic 146
St Paul de Vence 108
St Pierre-Eglise 53
St Porchaire 37
St Privat-d'Allier 74
St Rémy-La-Varenne 169, 170
St Rivoal 144
St Saens 88
St Samson-sur-Rance 137
St Sauves d'Auvergne 71, 72
St Servan 22, 136
St Suliac 136
St Thibault-St Satur 94
St Thibault-sur-Loire 94

St Vaast-La-Hougue 53
Ste Mere-Eglise 54
Saintes 37
Saire, river 53
Salamandre 201
Salignac 104
Sancerre 79, 93, 94, 186
Sans Celma 49
Saramon 47
Sardon, river 69
Sarlet 200
Sarthe, river 58
Saugues 74
Sauliac 207
Saumur 171
Savigny 59
Savoie 100
Savonniéres 176
Scholly 203
Seignosse 42
Seugne, river 38
Siorac-en-Périgord 203
Sioule, river 69
Sisteron 104
Soleil d'Or 83
Sole Meunière 111
Souillac 210
Soustons 41
Splendid Hôtel 103
Steir, river 150
Ster Laita 155
Sully 79
Sully-sur-Loire 92, 186
Symphorien 44

Table des Cordeliers 45
Tal-ar-Groas 145
Talcy 189
Talmont 33
Tauves 71

Taverne Berrichonne 181
Térenez 145
Terminus 208
Terminus 55
Terrass 126
Terrasse 209
Tessy 55
Thalamot 152
Théville 53
Thiviers 196
Thones 130
Torcy 88
Toul Broch 157
Toulon 97
Tour d'Argent 138
Tour d'Auvergne (Pont-
l'Abbé) 150
Tour d'Auvergne
(Quimper) 150
Tours 176
Tourtoirac 214
Trans 160
Trebeurden 141
Tréboule 148
Trianon et Plage 35
Troisgots 55
Trou 191
Trous Normand 115
Ty Douz 144

Union de la Marine 114
Ussé 174
Uzeste 44

Val de Loire 169
Valençay 66
Val Joli 178
Vallières-les-Grandes
179

Vannes 157
Varangeville 86
Vascoeuil 88
Vauban 22
Vayrac 210
Vée, river 58
Vence 107
Vendôme 59, 190
Verdon, river 106
Vernou 177
Vers 206
Vesouls 125, 126
Vianne 45
Vieil-Hesdin 116
Vieille Auberge 74
Vieille Brioude 74
Vienne, river 173
Vieux-Boucau 41
Vieux Donjon 83
Vilaine, river 28, 158
Villaine-les-Rochers 176
Villa Marinette 84
Villandraut 44
Villandry 176
Villefranche-du-
Périgord 205
Villegenon 187
Vire 55
Viry 98
Vittel 124
Vizille 103
Voiron 102
Volvic 70
Voreppe 102
Vouvray 177
Vouzon 189
Vuillafans, river 128

Wamin 116
Windsor 86